EASTER RISING
THE TRIAL

CW00552840

EASTER RISING 1916
THE TRIALS

Seán Enright

MERRION

First published in 2014 by Merrion

an imprint of Irish Academic Press
8 Chapel Lane
Sallins
Co. Kildare

British Library Cataloguing in Publication Data
An entry can be found on request

978-1-908928-36-8 (cloth)
978-1-908928-37-5 (paper)
978-1-908928-38-2 (e-book)

Library of Congress Cataloging in Publication Data.
An entry can be found on request

Printed in Ireland by SPRINT-print Ltd

This book is for Jack

Contents

Acknowledgements

I owe a special debt to Aideen Carroll who has given unstinting support and I am grateful for that. I express my gratitude to the Irish Military Archives and in particular to Hugh Beckett, whose knowledge of the archives has been of great help. I acknowledge the permission of that organisation to quote extracts from the Bureau of Military History (BMH) witness statements and to reproduce the evidence in certain trials.

I acknowledge the kind assistance of Robin Jenkins and the staff of the Leicestershire County Archive for their help in respect of the records of the Leicestershire Regiment and for permission to reproduce the photograph of General Blackader. I am also grateful to Adrian Wilkinson, curator of Lincolnshire Regimental Archive and Captain Holt, curator of the Lancer's Archive at Grantham. I acknowledge the generous and knowledgeable help of Cliff Housley, Trustee of the Regimental Museum of the Sherwood Foresters, Chilwell, Nottingham. My thanks also to Michael Ball, National Army Museum, Chelsea. Permission for the use of the photograph of Asquith leaving Richmond Barracks was kindly granted by Pádraig Óg Ó Ruairc. The photograph of Colonel Sapte is by kind permission of the Fusiliers Museum of Northumberland. I acknowledge permission of the Kilmainham Gaol Museum to use the photograph of Eamon de Valera, Sackville Street and prisoners en route to Kilmainham. Extracts from the Wylie memoir are reproduced with the permission of The National Archives, Kew (TNA) Public Record Office (PRO) 30/89/2.

I am indebted to the staff of the National Library of Ireland, the Public Record Office at Kew, London, and the Bodleian Library in respect of *A Short History of rebels*.

I also thank my wife Lorna, and Moya Enright, Ben Haseldine, Matt Dempsey, Davide Corbino, David Purcell and Owen Griffin, D.J. Enright, Jack Enright and Will Enright.

SEÁN ENRIGHT

Abbreviations, Explanations and Biographies

DMP   Dublin Metropolitan Police. This force was unarmed and mainly uniformed and exercised a policing jurisdiction within an eight-mile radius of Dublin Castle. The force numbered 1,203 in 1916.[1]

DORA   Defence of the Realm Act 1914 and 1915.

DORR   Defence of the Realm Regulations.

FGCM   Field General Court Martial – Staffed by three officers. At the Easter 1916 trials there was no Judge Advocate. This was a simplified form of court martial intended for use against soldiers on active service. There were few protections for an accused.

GCM   General Court Martial – in which there were between five and 13 officers staffing the court. A Judge Advocate appointed by the office of the Judge Advocate General provided legal advice. This method of trial secured significant legal protections for the accused.

G Men   G Division of the Dublin Metropolitan Police was dedicated to combating politically motivated crime. They were known as 'G Men' and that is how they are referred to in this work.

JAG   Judge Advocate General. The Judge Advocate General had responsibility and oversight of all trials carried out by the Army. In 1916 the JAG was Sir Thomas Milvain, KC. Sir Thomas was 72 and in very poor health. At the time of the Rebellion, the office was effectively being run by his deputies.

ICA   Irish Citizen Army.

IRB   Irish Republican Brotherhood. A secret society dedicated to the overthrow of British rule in Ireland. This organisation had infiltrated the Irish Volunteers.

IWM   Imperial War Museum.

RAMC   Royal Army Medical Corps.

RIC   Royal Irish Constabulary. A uniformed and heavily armed constabulary, policing all parts of Ireland, except Dublin. In 1916 the force had been depleted by recruitment to the Army but still numbered 9,491.

THE SOLDIERS

Major General Friend, General Officer Commanding the troops in Ireland in Easter 1916. When Casement's arms shipment was intercepted on Good Friday, General Friend took the view that the threat of a rebellion was over. General Friend immediately took home leave in England. He returned to Dublin after the Rebellion broke out, arriving back on the morning of Tuesday 25 April. He took little active part in the suppression of the Rebellion pending an investigation into his absence.

Brigadier General William Lowe had retired before the Great War. His last posting before retirement was Colonel in charge of the Cavalry Records and Inspector of Cavalry. He was one of many retired officers who were 'dug out' of retirement to assist in the war effort. In 1916, he held command at the Curragh, in County Kildare. Lowe assumed command in the absence of Major General Friend. He made the first decisive counter attack early on Tuesday morning, forcing a bridgehead from Kingsbridge railway station in the west of the city to Dublin Castle in the city centre and setting up cordons around rebel positions.

General Sir John Grenfell Maxwell, General Officer Commanding the Forces in Ireland. He was an able and pugnacious general known to his troops as 'Conky'. He commanded the Second Brigade at the battle of Omdurman. After the battle he led the march on the Khalifa's palace. He served as governor in Nubia and Omdurman, before going to South Africa to suppress the Boers. In the Great War he served on the Western Front and in Egypt. He was appointed Commander in Chief Ireland after the Rebellion broke out. At the time of his appointment, his wife was getting ready to undergo a serious operation. He caught the night train to Holyhead and then went by destroyer to Dublin, arriving at 2am on Friday 28 April.

Brigadier General Blackader DSO (1869–1921). This officer served as President of a standing court martial. Blackader was Commanding Officer of the 176 Brigade, part of the newly-formed 59 Division. Blackader was born into a family of modest means, without influence. He married at 19 to avoid fathering a child out of wedlock. He remained married throughout his life. Most of his career was spent in Africa. He was mentioned in despatches twice and awarded a DSO at Ladysmith. He later ran a concentration camp during the Boer War. He served on the Western Front from 1914 until 1915. He was a well-regarded officer, known to his men as 'Old Black'. He was preparing his new brigade for service in France when news of the Rebellion came through. Blackader would have had courts martial experience in the army but he had no legal qualifications.

Brigadier General Byrne (1874–1942). He was Deputy Adjutant General and has been described (erroneously) in many histories as Maxwell's 'legal chief'. Byrne was not a lawyer, his post being administrative rather than legal. He arrived in Ireland after the Rebellion had broken out. Byrne was an Irish Catholic from Derry. He joined the Inniskilling Fusiliers in 1893 and later served at Ladysmith, where he was wounded. In August 1916, Byrne was appointed Inspector General of the RIC. He was suspended in January 1920 for reasons which remain unclear. The rank and file objected strenuously to his dismissal. *Hansard* 4 March 1920, vol 126, col 605. In 1921, he was called to the Bar at Lincoln's Inn. He was later Governor General of the Seychelles (1922–1927), Sierra Leone (1927–1931) and Kenya (1931–1937). KCMG. CB.

Brigadier Ernest Maconchy CMG, DSO (1860–1945). Born in Devon, this officer was President of a standing court martial (replaced at his own request on 4 May by Colonel Sapte). Maconchy was commissioned in 1880 with the Royal South Downs. He spent his entire career in India. He was awarded the Distinguished Service Order for his part in repelling a night attack by a large body of Indian rebels at Ghazirat. At the height of the attack, the young Maconchy led a counter charge with fixed bayonets. He was wounded but his action proved decisive. He retired in 1914. He was brought out of retirement to command the 178 Brigade, part of the newly-formed 59 Division. His troops included the Foresters who suffered heavy casualties at Mount Street Bridge Dublin, where many young Foresters were killed by rebel attacks as they made their way into the city. Maconchy would have had courts martial experience but he was not a lawyer.

Lieutenant Colonel Douglas Sapte (1869–1942). Sapte was from a Huguenot family that settled in the north of England. He followed his father into the Northumberland Fusiliers. Sapte enlisted in 1885 and spent most of his long career serving in India and Africa. He retired in early 1914 but was recalled on the outbreak of hostilities. He was posted to the Irish 10 Division and served at Gallipoli and France as a staff officer. Colonel Sapte arrived in Dublin on 4 May and took over courts martial duty from Brigadier Maconchy, who related that Sapte had been sent over by the Judge Advocate General's department. This was incorrect. Sapte was not a barrister or a solicitor. He had no legal training and his experience of capital courts martial was probably negligible. He was President of the Court that tried, amongst others, Harry Boland, Seán MacDiarmada and James Connolly.

2nd Lieutenant William Wylie, Kings Counsel, was a member of the Officer Training Corps based at Trinity College Dublin. He prosecuted many of the prisoners and later wrote a compelling memoir.

2nd Lieutenant Ernest Victor Longworth. A member of the Irish Bar and one of the Officer Training Corps based at Trinity College. He prosecuted a number of the trials following the general surrender.

2nd Lieutenant Alfred Bucknill, an admiralty barrister. He was sent to Ireland with General Maxwell to provide legal advice. He was commissioned in the autumn of 1915 and posted to Egypt, under General Maxwell. After the Rebellion broke out, he arrived in Dublin as part of Maxwell's retinue. Bucknill was not in the best of health; he was suffering from severe sciatica. More cogently, he was not attached to the office of the Judge Advocate General and had no independent powers. It has previously been thought that he was Deputy Judge Advocate General in Dublin in 1916. He did not assume this post until June 1917.

THE IRISH EXECUTIVE

Baron Wimborne, Lord Lieutenant and Governor General -- Head of the Irish Executive, the representative of the Sovereign. He enjoyed no executive powers save for the exercise of the royal prerogative of mercy.

Sir Augustine Birrell, Chief Secretary of the Irish Executive, answerable in theory to the Lord Lieutenant but this practice had fallen away. Birrell was a member of the Cabinet at Westminster, based almost entirely in London. He was accountable to the Cabinet.

Sir Mathew Nathan, Permanent Under Secretary, based at Dublin Castle. He was answerable to Birrell, the Chief Secretary but was the effective day-to-day head of the Irish Executive. His main political agenda concerned effective recruiting to the Army. This may explain his reluctance to avoid antagonising nationalists and in particular, his failure to take action against the Volunteers/Citizen Army in the weeks leading up to the Rebellion.

THE POLITICIANS

John Redmond MP – Leader of the Irish Party, which favoured Home Rule.

John Dillon MP – A constitutional nationalist. Deputy Leader of the Irish Party. Dillon was at his home in Dublin during the Rising. While the executions were in progress, he crossed over to London, where he delivered a memorable but ill-judged speech to the House of Commons on 11 May.

H. H. Asquith – Prime Minister from 1908 to 1916.

THE REBELS

Thomas J. Clarke: Served 15 years in prison for his part in a bombing campaign in England. He later became a member of the Supreme Council of the IRB and a member of the Military Committee of the IRB. He ran a tobacconist shop in Parnell Street, which was used as cover for covert meetings. He was a signatory to the proclamation. He was executed.

James Connolly: Commandant General of the rebel forces in Dublin. A signatory to the proclamation of independence. He was executed.

Patrick H. Pearse: Commander in Chief of the Army of the Irish Republic. Pearse was trained as a barrister. He founded and ran St Enda's School at his residence in Rathfarnham, Dublin. That institution turned out many young men who took part in the Rebellion. He joined the Volunteers in 1913. He became a member of the IRB Military Committee. Pearse wrote the proclamation of independence and later gave the order for surrender. He was later executed.

Seán MacDiarmada: A member of the IRB, a signatory of the proclamation and one of the key planners of the Rebellion. He was executed.

Éamonn Ceannt: Commanded the garrison at the South Dublin Union. Also a signatory to the proclamation. He was executed.

Joseph Plunkett: A member of the IRB. He had no military experience or training but he became one of the planners for the Rising. He was a signatory to the proclamation. He was extremely ill at Easter 1916 and his condition was probably terminal. He was executed.

Thomas MacDonagh: A teacher and playwright. A signatory to the proclamation. He commanded the garrison at Jacob's Biscuit Factory. He was executed.

John MacBride: Fought against Britain in the Boer War with the Irish Brigade. Later married Maude Gonne but was quickly divorced. He lived in penury in Dublin for some years before acquiring a job with the Dublin Corporation as a water bailiff. He held a position of command at Jacob's Biscuit Factory. He was executed.

Eoin MacNeill: A professor of early Irish. Also Chief of Staff of the Irish Volunteers. MacNeill learned at a very late stage that a rebellion was afoot. He issued the countermand order which hugely reduced the turnout on Easter Monday. Some weeks after the Rebellion he was tried by General Court Martial and sentenced to life imprisonment.

THE ARMIES

The British Army: HQ at the Royal Hospital Kilmainham for old soldiers. On Easter Monday there were about 2,000 officers and men stationed in Dublin. There were also a significant number of officers on leave in Dublin. There were additional units at the Curragh, Templemore and Belfast. There was also a small unit of artillery at Athlone which was soon brought up to Dublin.

Georgius Rex: Veteran reservists, better known to Dubliners as the Gorgeous Wrecks. Some of these veterans were in their 50s and 60s. They were loyal to the Crown. They were ambushed by Volunteers on Easter Monday and suffered five fatalities. Most of the survivors took refuge in Beggars Bush Barracks which was close by. These men helped garrison the Barracks for the rest of Easter Week.

Officer Training Corps: Known as the OTC, a small reservist training unit based at Trinity College Dublin.

Ulster Volunteers: Formed by Sir Edward Carson to resist Home Rule.

The National Volunteers: The Volunteers were formed in 1913 to ensure that Home Rule came about. In 1914 this force split. The Redmondites became the National Volunteers, who were committed to achieving Home Rule by supporting Britain in the Great War. As the war dragged on the National Volunteers dwindled in size and influence.

The Irish Volunteers: after the split with the Redmondites, the splinter group became the Irish Volunteers who were dedicated to ensuring the government did not renege on the promise to grant Home Rule. They offered a counter threat to the Ulster Volunteers. In 1916 the Irish Volunteers numbered about 10,000 active members nationwide. Many of the Volunteers were armed with Lee Enfields and/or Howth Mausers (a single shot rifle). Some were armed with shotguns and/or handguns and many were still unarmed. The Irish Volunteers were infiltrated by the Irish Republican Brotherhood and manoeuvred towards rebellion.

About 1,300 Volunteers and Cumann na mban turned out during the Rebellion.

Irish Citizen Army: formed in 1913 by trade unionists to protect workers against organised strike breakers and the excesses of the DMP. By 1914 the ICA numbered several thousand but shrank rapidly. The Irish Citizen Army coalesced into a small military force bent on the overthrow of capitalism. By Easter 1916, the ICA numbered just a few hundred. The Army was headed by James Connolly with Michael Mallin as Chief of Staff. Approximately 220 ICA men and women turned out at Easter.[2]

The Hibernian Rifles: In a country not short of private armies, the Hibernian Rifles was the smallest, numbering about 150. In Easter 1916, a total of about 30 men turned out and served at the GPO.

List of Plates

recuperating at the Royal Hospital Kilmainham. He was awarded the Order of St Michael and St George for his part in the supression of the Rebellion.

12. Major C.H. Heathcote of the Sherwood Foresters, who supervised all the executions barring Pearse, MacDonagh and Clarke. Courtesy of the Foresters Museum.

13. Captain (later Lieutenant-Colonel) Martyn M.C. of the Sherwood Foresters, who led the assault on the South Dublin Union. Courtesy of the Foresters Museum.

14. Brigadier General Blackader (front row seated on left with peaked cap and dark moustache). Blackader tried Pearse, MacDonagh, Clarke, Ceannt and many other prisoners. Courtesy of the Leicestershire County Archive.

15. Colonel Douglas Sapte (front row, third from left, seated with monocle and pith helmet). Sapte tried Connolly, MacDiarmada, Harry Boland and Joseph Plunkett amongst others. Courtesy of the Fusiliers Museum of Northumberland, taken Rawalpindi, 1908.

16. Liam Cosgrave speaking after his by-election win in Kilkenny in the summer of 1917. After the Rebellion he narrowly escaped execution. A few years later, during the Civil War, he was President of the Executive Council of the Irish Free State. In this period 77 men were executed by Military Tribunals authorized by his government. Courtesy of the Irish Military Archives.

CHAPTER ONE

Buried in the Archives

During the course of the Rebellion a large part of Dublin city centre was laid waste.[1] The human cost was greater: not less than 450 lives were lost and just over 2,600 wounded.[2] Most of the dead were Irish, being civilians shot down in the confusion of street fighting, sometimes dying in the fires, felled by flying masonry or crushed by stampeding crowds. Many wandered into the combat zone and were shot down. In some instances, bystanders were murdered in cold blood. The shooting of Sheehy-Skeffington and two other journalists is an infamous example, and the North King Street Massacre is another. Some of the casualties were women, a handful were children – the youngest was just a toddler – and the oldest was 82.[3]

Historians rarely recall the victims of the Rebellion. It is the fate of the rebel leaders that is remembered best. As to the prime movers in the Rebellion, a few, like Pearse welcomed execution. But others hoped for prisoner-of-war status under the Hague Convention. They believed the Great War was on the brink and they might secure a place at a peace conference.[4] Perhaps they might have done so but for the fateful events of that Easter weekend, notably Casement's lost arms shipment and the countermand by MacNeill that brought about the collapse of the Rebellion in circumstances that could only end in trial and execution. Even a brief glance at colonial history showed that Westminster's response to rebellion was to invoke criminal law. Attaining belligerent status is the most difficult aspiration of every revolutionary movement and for the leaders of the 1916 Rebellion it was beyond their grasp.

It was in these circumstances that the leaders and many others were tried. There has never been any doubt about the involvement of those executed nor of the prisoners who were part of the general surrender in Dublin – although the same can hardly be said of the prisoners from the provinces who were rounded up merely on suspicion of taking part. In any event, an evaluation of whether the prisoners were afforded due process does not depend on assertions of guilt or culpability.

What actually happened in the trials that followed the surrender is still emerging. Between 1 May and 3 July over 3,226 men and women were arrested and filtered through Richmond Barracks in Dublin. Of these, 1,867 were deported[5] and 171 prisoners were tried. Whether the prisoners were tried by martial law or due process was then an issue of some immediate political importance. It affected the government military recruiting campaign in Ireland and public opinion abroad, particularly America, which had yet to enter the war. After the Rebellion, Asquith argued that the prisoners had been tried by due process:

> `'These sentences which have been passed by these`
> `courts martial are not passed under martial law at`
> `all. Martial law has really nothing to do with it.`
> `They are passed under the authority of the Defence`
> `of the Realm Act by tribunals which have statutory`
> `jurisdiction.'`[6]

There is no doubt that Asquith believed this was factually correct.[7] Although few of the Home Rulers accepted this and neither did the Judge Advocate General (JAG).[8]

During the three weeks following the surrender, all the trials were held in camera, that is to say, the public and press were excluded. The only witnesses to what had taken place were the officers who tried and prosecuted the prisoners. The secrecy surrounding the trials fuelled suspicion. Pressure for disclosure of the trial records was brought to bear in Parliament and in the press. There was even a legal challenge to the 'in camera' order being prepared. To meet public concern Asquith agreed to make the trial records public.[9] There were, however, other vested interests at work: behind the scenes, the Army Council at Horse Guards prevaricated and delayed.

It was not just about Ireland. There were wider concerns about the trial and executions of soldiers on the Western Front. These soldiers were being tried under the same Field General Court Martial system used in Dublin. The fact that soldiers had been executed on the Western Front was public knowledge but the scale of the executions was not known. In the House of Commons, ministers declined to reveal the number of executions – *'not in the public interest'*.[10] More disquietingly, government ministers colluded to prevent the grim circumstances of those trials becoming known.[11] This issue had begun to simmer during the course of the war and there were a trickle of increasingly pointed questions in Parliament about the courts martial of soldiers.[12]

The secrecy surrounding the courts martial process was jealously protected by the Army Council. The public spokesman for the Army Council was Sir Reginald Brade, Permanent Under-Secretary of State for War.[13] Sir Reginald, a subtle career civil servant, resisted inquiries by journalists and backbenchers into courts martial on the Western Front. The Army Act permitted a prisoner to obtain a copy of his trial record but not anyone else. Prisoners rarely bothered to get a trial transcript after the event and of course the trials that gave rise to most concern were those where the prisoner had been executed. Whenever journalists or parliamentarians asked to see trial records, the answer was always the same: 'If the man is dead, unfortunately, consent cannot be given.'[14] There was nothing unfortunate about it as far as the Army was concerned. This was their trump card.

In respect of the Easter Week trials, the Army Council recognised that the imminent release of trial records was capable of causing acute political embarrassment in its own right.[15] By a side wind it also threatened to unravel the policy of avoiding public scrutiny of the courts martial system on the Western Front.

Sir Reginald and the Army Council campaigned to reverse Asquith's promise to make public the Easter Week trial records. Sir Reginald argued that disclosure of the Dublin trial records might impugn General Maxwell's decision to hold the trials in camera or put in danger witnesses who had given evidence. The uncertain nature of the evidence in a few cases was cited.[16] He played on fears that disclosure might lead to a resurgence of nationalist opinion or simply damage the recruitment campaign in Ireland.

In February 1917, the legal challenge to Maxwell's 'in camera' order was heard in the High Court. The action failed.[17] A few weeks later the new government under Lloyd George announced that it would not publish the Easter trial records on the ground that this would be *'most detrimental to the public interest'*.[18]

In the corridors of power, Sir Reginald continued to fight and win the argument not to disclose the trial records of men executed on the Western Front. In this way, the Easter Week trials became bound up with concealing the truth about courts martial and the execution of soldiers on the Western Front.[19] What took place on the Western Front and in Dublin was consigned to the archives for decades. Something of the truth leaked out to the public but rumours about the trials on the Western Front were usually disbelieved as too shocking to contemplate. In Ireland, accounts of the Dublin trials were passed by word of mouth from prisoners to a suspicious public. A letter written by Irish prisoners was smuggled out of Lewes Prison. The letter, which received wide publicity helped fan the flames of suspicion and anger[20] which lasted for generations.

It was not until the turn of the century that the Public Record Office released the trial records relating to the executed prisoners. The rest of the trial records had apparently been destroyed as part of a routine cull – that may or may not be true but it was not quite the end of the matter because a number of other trials records have now emerged, casting new light on these extraordinary events.[21]

It was not just access to trial records that has obscured this aspect of history. The complex nature of the justice system then in place has caused some historians to misunderstand or overlook the subject. Others have accepted or at least not disputed Asquith's assertion that the prisoners were tried by due process.[22] That is one of the issues that this work examines.

By mid-May, nearly all the Dublin prisoners accused of taking part in the Rebellion had been tried. The round-ups in the provinces were complete and nearly all of the prisoners brought up to Dublin had been tried. The first death sentence was passed on 2 May and the last was imposed on 17 May.[23] At this point we see a shift in events. Not a return to normality by any means but for the few remaining trials, the process of summary trial by Field General Court Martial (FGCM) was replaced by General Court Martial (GCM), a step that carried some protections for the accused.

The area of critical importance runs from the general surrender on 30 April until 17 May. During this period 160 prisoners were tried by FGCM. The trials were held in camera. The prisoners were not represented and not permitted to give sworn evidence in their own defence. Ninety death sentences were passed and of these 15 were carried out.[24] It is now possible to identify trial records for a significant number of prisoners. Every year more secondary sources continue to open up and there is now sufficient new material to change our understanding of these trials and their place in legal history.

There have been so many books written on the Rebellion and at least two distinguished studies of the executed prisoners.[25] The emphasis of this study is more about the trial process. This crucial moment of history raises difficult questions about the operation of the rule of law in times of crisis. Any inquiry into the circumstances of these trials must start with events in Easter Week itself.

CHAPTER TWO

Rebellion and Surrender

The Rising was the worst kept secret. The German High Command knew about it, as they had supplied the arms shipment. The British Admiralty knew and informed the Army that the arms ship 'was due to arrive on 21 April, and that a rising was timed for Easter Eve'. Dublin Castle was informed. The information could hardly have been more specific but nothing was done.[1]

At Dublin Castle, Lord Lieutenant Wimborne already had a strong intuition about what was in the wind, the Volunteers had been practising night attacks on Dublin Castle. His warnings to the Chief Secretary were ignored, despite other information from a reliable police informant. To Wimborne, the threat was still imminent, even after Casement's capture, the failed arms landing and MacNeill's countermand. Wimborne's instinct was confirmed by the theft of 250 pounds of gelignite from a local quarry. Intelligence, which later proved reliable, suggested the gelignite was moved to the Citizen Army Headquarters at Liberty Hall on Easter Saturday.[2] Dublin Castle continued to dither.

All members of the Citizen Army knew. In the weeks before Easter, the Kimmage garrison at Count Plunkett's estate was swelled by returning émigrés. Most of these men knew what was in the wind and those who did not know soon learned. There were others who had come over from Britain to take part in the Rising. Margaret Skinnider, who fought at Saint Stephen's Green, took annual leave from her teaching job in Glasgow and caught the ferry over for the coming rebellion.[3]

Most IRB members had been informed. Elements of this secret oath-bound organisation had steered the Volunteers towards rebellion over many months.

After the Rebellion, the leaders encouraged the rank and file to say at their trials that they had not known of the Rebellion in advance.[4] It also suited the Army and Westminster to promote the idea that the actual rebels were few and the rank and file were essentially loyal but misguided. There is no doubt that many Volunteers knew the Rebellion was on. Days before, men openly stocked up with ammunition and one young Volunteer joked about being the next Chancellor of the Exchequer.[5] There were, even so, a surprising number who had no inkling that the planned manoeuvres were anything more than a route march,[6]some shooting for prizes and a parade.

MacNeill's discovery of what was afoot and his cancellation of the 'manoeuvres' planned for the Sunday was a major body blow for the planners. But over the following 24 hours, a small group of men and women worked to mobilise as many as could be contacted.

The Army had undoubtedly let its guard down. General Friend, Commander in Chief of the forces in Ireland, returned to London on home leave as soon as news that the arms landing had been foiled.[7] On Easter Monday, the crowd at Fairyhouse Races was swelled by army officers and by Volunteers.[8]

Like any city, Dublin had problems arising from poverty and deprivation. Most Dubliners, however, were reasonably content with their lot and the spring sunshine brought people out walking, picnicking or pursuing the modern craze for cycling.

Monday 24 April

One of the men mobilising on Easter Monday was Éamonn Ceannt, making his goodbyes to his wife and son and pulling his equipment on. His wife Áine later remembered: 'He had a lot to carry – a large bag full of ammunition, an overcoat and a bicycle. I helped him to put on his Sam Browne belt and then adjusted his knapsack.'[9] It was the last time this family would be together. It was a scene being played out in many homes in Dublin as men and women abandoned work or family and set off to muster points in different parts of the city. Mrs Francis Fahy stopped 'to park her cat and her canary' before going on to the Four Courts.[10] She was one of hundreds of women who mobilised.

Many Volunteers who missed the callout made their way in twos or threes to the city centre. Some were able to catch up with their company and others attached themselves to whatever unit lay in their path. One of those who missed the muster point was James Burke, an NCO in the Volunteers. Burke had suffered a bayonet wound in the affray at Bachelor's Walk after the Howth arms landing. He had made a full recovery and on Easter Monday, Burke and two other Volunteers walked the streets searching for their battalion. They were stopped by a policeman asking where they were going. Burke later recalled 'I took a small .32 (revolver) out... and told him that was our business. He quietly moved back...'[11]

At Kimmage, the émigré Volunteers assembled, armed with a 'shot gun and pike to each man'. Armed and laden with equipment, they marched to Harold's Cross Road where they boarded a tram.[12] Their captain bought 56 one-way tickets to the city centre.

The GPO was overrun and the staff and customers were turned out into the street. The small group of soldiers guarding the building had no ammunition for their guns and barricaded themselves in the 'instrument' room. Their NCO was shot in the face and his detachment quickly surrendered. The GPO was fortified:

```
'Every window on the ground floor was smashed
and barricaded with furniture, and a big placard
announced:  "Headquarters  of  the  Provisional
Government of the Irish Republic." At every window
were  two  men  with  rifles  and  on  the  roof  the
parapet was lined with men.'13
```

It was a day of iconic images: the flags over the GPO; the arrival of the O'Rahilly in an open-topped De Dion Bouton. As he laconically observed: 'I helped wind the clock, I've come to hear it strike.'[14]

At Dublin Castle, an attempt was made to storm the gate at the Upper Castle Yard. Here, DMP Constable James O'Brien was shot dead but the attackers hesitated, unsure of the level of resistance. They broke off the attack and took over the Evening Mail offices overlooking the Castle. The City Hall was also seized and barricaded.

Many buildings were occupied without violence, including the South Dublin Union, the Jameson Distillery at Marrowbone Lane, the Mendicity Institute and the Four Courts. At Saint Stephen's Green, Constable Michael Lahiff was shot dead. The Green was occupied and barricades were put up. Here, an old man who would not part with his lorry was shot and killed.[15] Jacob's Factory was also occupied and fortified. In the chaos that followed a local man was killed.

At the GPO, Pearse emerged into the street and read the proclamation to a puzzled crowd. The first significant engagement took place soon after at Nelson's Pillar where a squadron of 100–150 British Army Lancers appeared from the Rotunda hospital riding up in single file.[16] A ragged volley was fired from the GPO and the column of Lancers broke up, some wounded troopers being held up in the saddle by their comrades as they wheeled and cantered away. A large bank holiday crowd looked on in disbelief.

As the afternoon wore on the street filled with onlookers. Three British soldiers sniped at the GPO while 'The crowds grew more and more reckless, passing under the line of fire.' A drunken Australian soldier stood under the Volunteer position, eating a sandwich. He was left undisturbed. A large party of Dublin Metropolitan Police hovered around Nelson's Pillar, while firing continued. They were left undisturbed and eventually they were marched off by their inspector. The DMP were withdrawn from the streets and did not appear until after the Rebellion was over.[17]

Unsuccessful efforts were made to block the street by overturning a tram.[18] Eventually a bomb was put on the tram and fired on until it exploded and blocked the street to the satisfaction of the Volunteers. The explosion shattered the glass display at Noblett's sweetshop and some of the crowd began to help themselves from the window. The looters were women and they were joined by children, their arms heaped with sweets and chocolate. Their numbers were swelled by the arrival of young men. Other shop windows were broken and the looting became 'systematic and general'.

Before the Rising began the Volunteers had acquired a quantity of police batons, anticipating that the Rebellion might bring about public disorder. Nothing could have prepared them for the sight in Sackville Street where hundreds of people milled around rubber necking as the looters ran wild. A crowd of army wives – 'separation women' – also gathered and began to scream insults and throw shards of broken glass at Volunteers. James Connolly could not spare men to deal with the disorder[19] and the street descended into chaos.

A great many Volunteers marched out that morning with no real understanding of the scale of the enterprise. By late afternoon they were in a life-or-death struggle, some running low on ammunition and food and all cut off from family. Female Volunteer couriers could still move round the city with relative freedom. As Helena Molony left City Hall bearing a message, she was stopped by a slightly built man, Halpin, who had intimations of his own mortality. He had left home that morning leaving his wife in her sick bed. He scribbled out a few words and handed the note to Molony: 'a note for the ould mott'. [20]

There were other engagements that day, including an attempt to capture the Magazine Fort in Phoenix Park. The guard were held up and a quantity of rifles seized, but the magazine could not be breached. Five bags of gelignite were laid, the fuse was lit and the attackers and the prisoners scattered. A young man who ran to raise the alarm was shot down and killed moments before the explosion reverberated all over the city.

British troops were ambushed at the Four Courts. There was also heavy fighting on the outskirts of the South Dublin Union. In the south east of the city a column of reservists, the Georgius Rex, were ambushed at Northumberland Road as they returned from a route march. They suffered five fatalities. These reservists, known as the 'Gorgeous Wrecks' or sometimes more unkindly 'Gods Rejected' scrambled into Beggars Bush Barracks which was defended by a handful of officers and men. The barracks had very little ammunition and no food. The senior officer was Lieutenant General Sir Frederick Shaw, who had seen service against the Fenians at Tallaght in 1867.[21]

MacNeill's countermand reduced the Rebellion to a shadow of what it might have been and the deployment of men reflected the reduced turnout and the Volunteer's lack of military experience. This lack of tactical experience was particularly marked at Saint Stephen's Green where the rebels dug slit trenches but failed to occupy the Shelbourne Hotel and other buildings dominating the Green. There were other serious problems for the insurgents. The lack of men meant that the plan to take Trinity College had to be abandoned. Trinity dominated approaches to the centre of the city and this constituted another serious setback. There was also the aborted attack on Dublin Castle, which became the focal point of the Army fight back on Monday evening.

Another battleground was the telephone and telegraph system. In the first few hours of the Rebellion there were more than a few Post Office employees engaged in cutting wires and cables[22] but there were many loyal Post Office employees who were equally adept at splicing and mending.

The failure to take the telephone exchange at Crown Alley, off Dame Street was a big reverse. A party of Volunteers were only yards from the exchange when they were turned back by an old lady who shouted a warning 'the place is crammed with military'.[23] In fact the military only arrived some minutes later. These soldiers were able to fortify the building and this allowed Dublin Castle to coordinate a telling response.

There were worse setbacks for the rebels. Apart from Oranmore, Enniscorthy and north County Dublin, the country had failed to rise in support. In many parts of the country the Volunteers had mobilised. In Cork, over 1,000 men turned out and in places as far apart as Limerick and Donegal,[24] men mobilised and then dispersed for lack of leadership. There was a spate of shootings but these quickly stopped.[25]

On Monday evening, Dublin Castle was reinforced by a full battalion. The troops had forced a passage across Dublin, losing seven men en route. Once established at the Castle, they launched a series of attacks on City Hall which were successfully repulsed but by the end of the day, City Hall was all but overrun, with just a small number of Citizen Army clinging on in the upper floors. Even by Monday evening it was plain that the Rebellion had stalled.

Tuesday 25 April

Reinforcements under Brigadier General Lowe arrived at Kingsbridge station on the western outskirts of Dublin in the early hours of the morning. Lowe's strategy was dictated by the need to reinforce Dublin Castle in the centre of the city. This was to be achieved by driving a wedge between the rebels on the north and south of the Liffey and to close off and isolate rebel positions.

Elsewhere the Army were already taking the initiative. Overnight a detachment of soldiers had left Dublin Castle. Carrying heavy machine guns, they crept through the back streets and slipped into a side entrance of the Shelbourne Hotel and the United Services Club overlooking the rebel positions on Saint Stephen's Green. Just after dawn the machine guns opened up. After clinging on a while, the Citizen Army were forced to run for safety to the Royal College of Surgeons on the edge of the Green.

Later that morning *The Irish Times* published a short, dramatic edition that carried a proclamation of martial law on the city and county of Dublin.[26] The proclamation, signed by the Lord Lieutenant and Governor General Wimborne, threatened unstated but serious sanctions against those found carrying arms. Wimborne's proclamation and the proclamation of the Irish Republic could be found nailed up here and there around Dublin.

The only other newspaper to publish was the new *Irish War News*. Priced at one penny, the paper announced the establishment of the Republic. But for the countermand, the Rebellion would have been widespread and a newspaper was a logical step to secure public support. But on the Tuesday, Dublin was divided between rebel outposts and army positions. Snipers operated on both sides. Looters and sightseers wandered the streets. Volunteers selling *The Irish War News* was just another sight that caused people to rub their eyes with disbelief. [27]

At the South Dublin Union, the skirmishing continued throughout the day. At Dublin Castle the fifth Battalion of the Royal Dublin Fusiliers emerged. This unit, under Lieutenant Frank O'Neill, carried out a series of bayonet charges on the rebel position in the newspaper offices:

> 'plaster and powdered brick were flying in showers from its facade. The fire was to cover the advance of our soldiers. But in spite of this we saw more than once, one of the running figures pitch forward and fall. Late in the day the position was carried by the Fusiliers.'[28]

At the GPO the garrison waited for an infantry assault and watched as looters made free. A sports shop was set on fire. A crowd of children ran in and carried out the stock of fireworks, piled them in a heap and set them off. Many of the GPO garrison peered from the roof as the fireworks exploded, with Catherine Wheels going up and down the street.[29]

Despite intermittent firing, the city centre was still thronged with people but it was not the firing that cleared the streets that evening but a heavy shower of rain.[30]

Wednesday 26 April

On Wednesday just after dawn, escorted by torpedo boats, the *SS Patriotic* was the first of a number of improvised troop ships to dock at Kingstown. The Staffs, Sherwood Foresters and Leicestershire regiment began to disembark scouts. A battalion major of the Leicestershire Regiment was appointed town commander of Kingstown. The streets were barricaded and curfew notices posted, announcing the imposition of martial law. Intelligence was sparse; an officer sent to reconnoitre the area by his commanding officer was told: 'I have no map to give you... do the best you can.'

The Sherwood Foresters also deployed. The night before, the Foresters had been compelled by an officious embarkation officer at Liverpool to leave their heavy equipment at the quayside, including their Lewis guns and grenades.[31] Most of these young men were raw recruits from Nottingham, Newark and Mansfield, the tight-knit communities that made their living coal mining or lace making. Arriving at the quayside at Kingstown, the men were lined up with their rifles facing out to sea. These men needed to learn how to use their rifles quickly and this was judged to be the safest way to do so.

One battalion of the Staffords marched south to garrison the munitions factory at Arklow. Two battalions of the Foresters, heavily laden with equipment, marched on Dublin via Stillorgan and came through weary but unscathed later that day.

Two more battalions of the Foresters marched directly to Dublin via Ballsbridge. On their route they passed the Elm Park bombing school where they were joined by a group of training instructors. The Foresters found their route was lined with welcoming faces. Captain Dietrichsen, battalion adjutant of 2/7 Foresters had some time previously sent his wife and children to Dublin to live out the war. They were part of the welcoming crowds. Dietrichsen, his wife and two young children, Fred and Beatrice were briefly reunited at the roadside. It was the last time they would be together.

In the city centre, a fresh proclamation was posted by Dublin Castle.[32] This proclamation revoked the right of a citizen to be tried by a jury for offences contrary to the Defence of the Realm Regulations. Under this regime civilians would be tried by courts martial.[33]

While this was taking place *HMS Helga* and *HMS Sea Lark* steamed up the Liffey and berthed by the Customs House. Their guns were trained on

Liberty Hall, which was thought to be a rebel stronghold. Fire was opened. The bombardment was supported by artillery from Tara Street. After an hour the shelling ceased, and the Royal Dublin Fusiliers rushed Liberty Hall and found it deserted. The Fusiliers used Liberty Hall as a base to seal off the area and close in on the GPO. Shelling was then opened on a rebel strong point at the junction of Bachelor's Walk and Sackville Street. The Army had begun to tighten its grip.

Elsewhere in the city, other dramas were unfolding. In the south of the city, at Portobello Barracks, Captain Bowen-Colthurst was about to take a course of action with momentous consequences. Colthurst was the scion of a landowning family near Cork. He had served in the Royal Irish Rifles during the retreat from Mons and while the entire British Expeditionary Force was falling back, Bowen-Colthurst insisted on advancing. He was sent home because his manic, intemperate streak made him dangerous to his troops. At the outbreak of the Rising he was suddenly thrust back into the front line at Portobello Barracks.

The night before, Colthurst had clubbed and then shot and killed a youth by the name of James Coade. He had also taken three unlikely prisoners. One was Francis Sheehy-Skeffington. In a city that was not short of eccentrics, Skeffington outdid most, being a small, bearded figure in cape and knickerbockers, a well-known advocate of pacifism, vegetarianism and women's rights. The second prisoner was James MacIntyre who had edited *The Toiler,* a government-funded propaganda sheet.[34] The third was Thomas Dickson, also a journalist. He was later described by the Royal Commission as a 'Scotchman and deformed'[35] in a way which intimated that these were both heavy afflictions. A contemporary described him as 'about four-foot-six, a grotesque figure in a black coat with curious eyes'.[36] Life had been cruel to Dickson and it had made him hard. He edited *The Eye-Opener,* exposing the private lives of Dubliners, goading and taunting his victims with singular cruelty. His paper was also a cover for blackmail: people paid Dickson handsomely not to print stories.[37]

By Wednesday morning, Colthurst had been up most of the night praying for guidance. He then went down to the guardhouse and assembled a squad of seven men. The prisoners were brought out and asked to walk to the end of the yard, which they did. They had no idea what was to follow. As they reached the end of the yard and turned, the soldiers opened fire and the three men fell. As the bodies were being stretchered away, Skeffington showed signs of life and was shot again.[38] The bodies were buried in the barracks that same morning. Mrs Hannah Skeffington and her redoubtable sisters arrived soon after, looking for news of 'Skeffy'. They were briefly arrested and then ushered out of the barracks having been told nothing of Skeffington's fate.

The barrack wall was quickly repaired. The news of these events would trickle out slowly with far-reaching implications. But Colthurst remained on duty. A fellow officer later recalled this very tall, stooping, heavily armed figure 'raging along the perimeter of the walls . . . shouting and yelling'.[39]

Meanwhile on the west side of Dublin, the garrison in the Mendicity Institute faced a mass assault. One of the defenders, Richard Balfe, described the final minutes:

> 'Our ammunition and supplies were now exhausted.
> We came then under severe grenade and machine gun
> fire. During this attack Willie Staines and myself
> were wounded by a bomb. Heuston bandaged Staines who
> was wounded in the head. I had lost complete use of
> my arms and legs but was fully conscious. Heuston
> ordered the surrender and put out a white sheet.'[40]

At Lisburn Street in the north of the city centre, Denis O'Callaghan gathered up a group of Volunteers and attacked Linen Hall Barracks, forcing a breach in the wall and securing the surrender of 24 soldiers. The Volunteers had too few men to hold Linen Hall and a decision was taken to deny the Army the chance to use Linen Hall as a base. Oil drums were tipped over and the barracks were set on fire[41] and blazed for days.

Back on the southern outskirts of Dublin the Sherwood Foresters were approaching Northumberland Road, a long straight tree-lined road that led to the Grand Canal crossing at Mount Street and on to the city centre.

What happened next was dictated by an order issued to all troops disembarking from England:

> 'the head of the columns will in no case advance
> beyond any house from which fire has been opened,
> until the inhabitants of such house have been
> destroyed or captured.'[42]

The Army had information that these roads were defended and that the Georgius Rex had suffered casualties at Mount Street Bridge. Close by there were other undefended bridges that gave direct access to the city centre. The Foresters arrived at Northumberland Road and, marching in a line of four, made for Mount Street Bridge, determined to carry out orders come what may. They were fired on from the front and the flanks.

The heart of the defence was Clanwilliam House on the north bank of the canal on the corner of Mount Street. This large Victorian townhouse dominated the crossing. On the south side of the canal, the School Hall was occupied by five Volunteers and a smaller number of men occupied positions in Northumberland Road, notably Michael Malone and Tom Grace.

Here began the battle of Mount Street Bridge. The troops, led by officers with drawn swords, tried to rush the bridge but were beaten back. Captain Dietrichsen was one of the first officers to be killed. The battle of Mount Street Bridge raged all day. Every so often a whistle would sound. An officer would rise, sword in hand and the men charged with bayonets fixed. These men did not lack courage and the bridge and the surrounding streets became littered with dead and dying soldiers, mostly teenagers it should be said.

Brigadier Maconchy, leading the Sherwood Foresters, found himself saddled with direct orders from GHQ 'not to attempt anything on the flank'. This order came too late to stop a small group of Foresters setting off to outflank Clanwilliam House. They had gone only a few hundred yards when they were commandeered by Lieutenant General Shaw at Beggars Bush Barracks. Shaw appointed Lieutenant Gerrard to command this small group of Foresters and despatched them to deal with snipers who had been plaguing the barracks. Lieutenant Gerrard had been home on leave from the Dardanelles campaign. With Lieutenant Gerrard was Sergeant Gamble who had been invalided home from the Western Front and was probably looking forward to a quiet posting. The encounter was described by Lieutenant Gerrard:[43]

> 'I was over the wall first, followed by QM Sergeant Gamble. As soon as I got over the wall, at a range of about 200 yards, about eight Sinn Feiners advanced from the direction of the city. I saw them coming towards us, firing. There was what they call a fairly sharp fire fight. These men were standing up, not lying down. They came out of their trenches to meet us. They were very brave, I remember. They did not know how many of us there might be. The first casualty was Q.M. Gamble. He was shot dead, under the right eye. I was the next casualty.'

Brigadier General Lowe's final instructions to the Foresters were delivered from the safety of the Royal Hospital. His orders were explicit: 'come through at all costs'. [44] The result was further unnecessary carnage. An officer later wrote that 'B Company as a fighting unit had practically ceased to exist, all its Officers, its Sergeant Major and all the sergeants being either killed or wounded.'[45]

At 25 Northumberland Road, the defenders were finally overwhelmed by sheer weight of numbers. Michael Malone was shot dead at the top of the stairs and his companion Tom Grace took refuge in the cellar. Grenades were thrown in after him but he was able to shelter behind an old cooker. The house became a blazing furnace and Grace was able to escape as smoke and fire billowed out. While this scene was being played out Volunteers on the other side of the road were running from the School Hall, which had come under sustained attack.

Soon after, the final assault on Clanwilliam House took place at Mount Street Bridge. Assisted by officers from the Bombing School, another charge across the bridge was made. A party of soldiers hurled grenades through the windows and the Foresters followed with fixed bayonets. None of the defenders survived.[46]

In the course of this encounter the Sherwood Foresters suffered shocking casualties: 30 killed and 130 wounded.[47] Colonel Fane, who was wounded, was later decorated for his leadership, although it might be said the Army had been careless with the lives of the men.

A few hundred yards away was another redoubt at Boland's Mills. Here tragedy was followed by farce. Eamon de Valera, patrolling the outskirts of Boland's Mills, encountered confusion over the password. The sentry, Seán Byrne, later wrote:

> `'we would not let him in although we knew who he was.'`[48]

On the other side of the city, the Lord Lieutenant struggled to exert control over his own forces. Confined to the Vice-Regal Lodge in Phoenix Park, Lord Lieutenant Baron Wimborne 'swilled brandy' and drawled orders over the telephone in bad French to confuse eavesdroppers.[49] His efforts to stop looting in the city were laudable but increasingly hopeless. A proclamation issued that evening confined pub opening hours from 2pm to 5pm. Another proclamation issued in Wimborne's name was posted announcing a curfew from 7.30pm – 5.30am. This had little effect on a volatile city and the streets were crowded.[50] In Sackville Street looters still swarmed through the shops. In a boot shop ragged women and children sat in the windows 'trying on boots and shoes'.[51]

Thursday 27 April

Snipers operated on both sides. Volunteers had put a dummy sniper on the roof of a nursing home near Mountjoy Square. The dummy drew fire all week, while Volunteers took advantage of the diversion. A sniper operating from Fitzroy Avenue made things 'hum' throughout the Rebellion. This man continued to operate after the surrender. The houses at Fitzroy Avenue were searched several times 'but he ran about from roof to roof' and continued to avoid capture.[52] Another sniper operated on the roofs opposite the Royal Hibernian Hotel: 'a man might hide for weeks on the roofs of these houses among the chimney stacks and never be found'.[53]

Combating the snipers was difficult and dangerous work and grenades were not always available. In the city centre the Army became increasingly ruthless. Civilians on the streets were presumed to be hostile. Householders who twitched curtains or opened doors risked being shot and indeed some were.

On Thursday afternoon, on the southern outskirts of the city, the 2/7 and 2/8 Sherwood Foresters attempted to enter the city along the South Circular Road and over the Rialto Bridge. In order to do so, they needed to bypass the South Dublin Union workhouse which was occupied by Volunteers. The South Dublin Union overlooked the bridge and the Volunteers directed 'a perfect shower of bullets' on the unfortunate Foresters.[54]

The Foresters attempted to clear the South Dublin Union by a series of frontal assaults but were beaten back after fighting at close quarters. The fighting that day ended in a stalemate but under cover of failing light the Foresters were able to cross the bridge and arrived at the Royal Hospital Army HQ after dark.

In the city centre, little traffic stirred in the streets, apart from a handful of army vehicles and an occasional ambulance. Improvised armoured cars also appeared. Boilers taken from the Guinness breweries were fashioned into turtle-shaped shells, bolted to flat bed lorries and used to ferry troops and provisions around the city.[55] Each armoured car carried 22 men 'packed like herrings'. The armoured cars were backed up to a house allowing the men inside to rush the building and set up a strong point to command the street.[56] The improvised armoured cars had limitations. At O'Connell Street, two Volunteers concentrated their fire on the driver's aperture, bringing the armoured car to an abrupt halt. Late that night, the Army towed it away under cover of darkness.[57]

During interludes in the fighting, the mob appeared and the looting continued. A high-class fruiterer in Grafton Street was stripped bare:

> 'They swarmed in and out of the side door bearing
> huge consignments of bananas, the great bunches
> on the stalk, to which the children attached a
> cord and ran away dragging it along. Other boys
> had big orange boxes which they filled with tinned

and bottled fruit. Women with their skirts held up
received a shower of apples and oranges and all
kind of fruit which were thrown from the upper
windows.'[58]

Later that day, close to the GPO, James Connolly was wounded in the
arm. He was wounded again while supervising the erection of a barricade
at Abbey Street. A small party under the command of Major Morrogh
of the Royal Irish Regiment had clambered up on an adjoining roof and
fired down on the barricade.[59] Connolly suffered a compound fracture of
the tibia and fibia.[60] In considerable pain he made his way back towards
the GPO. He was found in Princes Street and brought into the GPO
on a stretcher. Connolly provided much of the energy and direction at
the GPO. His wound could not have come at a worse moment for the
insurgents.

Artillery was deployed to fire into Sackville Street. Shells soon landed
on *The Irish Times* warehouse setting fire to rolls of paper. The fire brigade
were confined to barracks on account of the shooting and as the day wore
on the fires gathered pace and spread to adjoining buildings and to some of
the street barricades, which were made up with paper and furniture. This
was the scene described by a Volunteer:

'The whole area was one mass of flames but the
GPO had not as yet caught fire but it was only a
matter of time until this would also be on fire.
Shells were constantly bursting on the roof and
many of the Rathfarnham Company who occupied the
roof had received facial wounds.'[61]

By late evening the fire had spread to Hoyte's chemist, where chemicals
exploded. With the fires now unchecked, the flames spread from building
to building and to the upper storeys of the GPO. The GPO garrison
were withdrawn to the lower floors where they built new barricades in
anticipation of a frontal assault. Frank De Burca, watching from a window
of the GPO, saw 'A huge wall of flame towering to the sky and great billows
of smoke. The noise of bursting shells and tumbling walls and roofs was
indescribable.'[62] Linen Hall Barracks, only a few hundred yards away also
blazed so brightly it impeded movement on both sides.

The Army struggled to enforce the curfew order given the night before.
It was an all but hopeless task and occasionally the Army drove the crowds
indoors by firing rifle shots over their heads.

In most streets there was no street lighting[63] and this also contributed
to the death toll. Sentries were nervous and perhaps a little trigger-happy.
At Amiens Street, an army sentry shot dead a naval officer and seriously
wounded a hotelier. The shooting resonated of murder.[64] On the other
side, a Volunteer shot dead Thomas Joze who was returning home from his
chemist shop at Dame Street. Joze was deaf and it is likely he did not hear
the challenge by the sentry.[65]

There was far worse to come. In the city centre, North King Street became
the scene of the most intense fighting. Here the Staffords tried to dislodge
the defenders who were clinging on tenaciously to their perimeter. In this
densely populated street, people were trapped in their homes as the Staffords
and the rebels fought it out, house by house. The Staffords, maddened by
heavy casualties, began to shoot non-combatants. The massacre of North
King Street had begun.

Friday 28 April

In the early hours, Lieutenant-General Maxwell arrived in Dublin to take
command. Known as 'Conky' to the troops, he was a pugnacious and
confident general. As a much younger officer, Maxwell had commanded a
Brigade at Omdurman, Sudan in 1898. He had served as governor in Nubia
and Omdurman, before going to South Africa to suppress the Boers. In the
Great War he served on the Western Front and in Egypt his handling of the
Sennusi unrest showed a subtle mind[66] although his readiness to dispense
with due process was well documented.[67]

Maxwell had been in London where his wife was about to undergo a
serious operation. When called upon, he did not hesitate and went up on
the night train to Holyhead with a small retinue of officers.

The letter from the War Office detailing Maxwell's instructions set out
his powers:

> `'to take all such measures as may be in his opinion necessary for the prompt suppression of the rebellion in Ireland'.`

The letter of instruction also permitted him to try civilians by courts martial
under the Defence of the Realm Act.[68] None of these instructions amounted
to the granting of martial law but that too was changing.

The Cabinet had met while Maxwell was still bound for Holyhead and
decided that martial law should be proclaimed over all Ireland. Maxwell's
first sight of Dublin may also have affected his view of the task ahead:

'From the sea it looked as though the entire city of Dublin was in flames.' [69]

The destroyer carrying General Maxwell

'...steamed up to the North Wall, silent and dark. The Custom House stood out against a background of fire. There were at least four distinct fires burning, and great flames were leaping up in different places as if the whole city north of the Liffey was doomed. Occasionally one heard the crack of a rifle and the knocking of machine gun fire.'[70]

Arriving at the North Wall, Maxwell and his party climbed aboard two cars and set off skirting the ruins of Liberty Hall and avoiding the GPO and the Four Courts. They found army piquets were placed almost every 50 yards. At one checkpoint Maxwell's car was slow to stop and was almost fired on before arriving at GHQ, the Royal Hospital in the west of the city.[71]

Here, Maxwell learned that the Cabinet had ordered nationwide martial law to be imposed and it is likely that he took the view that his powers had been dramatically increased.[72]

This, perhaps, was the moment when those charged with the suppression of the Rebellion took a wrong course. The law permitted the Army to assist the civil authority to suppress rebellion and recognised that there might be extreme circumstances in which martial law might exist but that it could not prevail longer that the crisis permitted. At that moment martial law was necessary in Dublin. That necessity would pass within 72 hours but martial law remained in force countrywide for many months. The reasons why the Executive permitted this were pragmatic: 'it spreads terror among the disaffected'. A more powerful reason can be gleaned from the advice given by the government law officers: martial law allowed the Army to take steps 'where there may be no appropriate regulation under DOR'.[73] In other words, General Maxwell could do whatever he thought necessary without needing to consider what the law permitted. For these reasons, all that followed the proclamation of martial law inevitably came to be tainted with illegality. The rule of law was the first casualty of the new administration.

Some insight may also be gleaned from Maxwell's command structure. Maxwell's second in command in Dublin was Brigadier General Byrne. In Professor Townshend's outstanding history, he refers to Byrne as Maxwell's 'legal chief'.[74] In fact, Byrne was not a lawyer.[75] Nor was he attached to the office of the Judge Advocate General. Other distinguished historians have repeated the error.[76] Byrne was Deputy Adjutant General – an administrative post, not a legal post. Maxwell had no 'legal chief'. Once this key fact is recognised a great deal of what followed can be more readily understood. The only lawyer on Maxwell's staff was Second Lieutenant Alfred Bucknill, an admiralty barrister, who was sent over to ensure that the Army kept within the law.[77] Bucknill was an officer of the most junior rank, commissioned only months before. He had served under Maxwell in Egypt and arrived in Dublin as part of General Maxwell's retinue. Bucknill was in poor health, as he was suffering from sciatica. He lacked the rank or any authority to influence this famously strong-willed general. Unfettered by either law or lawyers, Maxwell was guided by pragmatism.

Maxwell's first step was to place the Irish executive under his control. At the apex of the Irish Executive was Baron Wimborne, who was the Lord Lieutenant[78] and head of the civil administration. Executive power lay with his Chief Secretary, Sir Augustine Birrell. They protested to Maxwell that nationwide martial law was 'most inadvisable'[79] but it had already been decided. Maxwell recalled the meeting rather differently: 'I saw the Lord Lieutenant and Mr Birrell today, they did not altogether appreciate being under my orders.' [80]

It was certain that some urgent action was necessary. While Maxwell asserted his grip on power, the infrastructure of the city was grinding to a halt. The police had been off the streets for some days. The Four Courts were occupied by the insurgents and courts of summary jurisdiction had ceased to sit. There were no newspapers, no news, just proclamation and counter proclamation nailed up here and there on walls and doors. The trams and trains had stopped on the first day of the Rising. Gas supplies had been cut off and coal ran short. People did not work and were not paid. The banks were shut, the post interrupted, pensions were not paid and the wives of soldiers serving overseas did not receive their weekly allowances. For many, lack of money was no longer the driving factor. In the inner city, food was running desperately short. Supplies of milk, meat and butter were exhausted. By Friday, only the bakeries stayed in business and these were running short of flour.[81] Outside Army HQ in front of an army guard 'bread carts were looted by hungry mobs'. [82] In the suburbs, the hoarding of food began. Shops were besieged with customers as food stocks began to run low.[83]

Maxwell issued a proclamation announcing his intention to shell buildings occupied by rebels. Proclamation No. 1[84] invited non-combatants to leave their homes and pass through the military cordon to safety. The sad reality was that many civilians never saw the proclamation because they were already trapped in their homes.[85] The inner-city slums and tenements were the worst affected. These people were without money or connections. They had nowhere to go and many who stayed were driven out of their homes when the crisis was reached.

The cordon around insurgent positions continued to tighten. The shelling intensified and as the hours passed, fires on the roof of the GPO threatened to overwhelm the building. For some there was a route of escape. The Volunteers had dug their way from building to building until they reached the Coliseum Theatre. The women, Red Cross personnel and the wounded were smuggled out. The prisoners were taken out of the burning building and invited to run to the Army lines.

The rest of the garrison readied to evacuate the building and relocate elsewhere. Michael O'Rahilly led a breakout but his patrol was all but wiped out and he was badly wounded. He raised himself to his feet to run and was shot again. Mortally wounded, he crawled into a doorway where he wrote a letter to his wife and children:

> 'Darling Nancy I was shot leading a rush up Moore Street and took refuge in a doorway. While I was there I heard the men pointing out where I was and made a bolt for the laneway I am in now. I got [more] than one bullet I think. Tons and tons of love dearie to you and the boys and Nell and Anna it was a good fight anyhow. Please deliver this to Nannie O'Rahilly, 40 Herbert Park, Dublin. Goodbye Darling.'

In the smoke and confusion the remnants of the garrison evacuated as the GPO burned. James Connolly was brought out on a stretcher. His wound was turning gangrenous and the slightest movement caused him to shout in agony.[86] The garrison fragmented in the confusion. Many were able to get as far as Moore Street. The men were now exhausted from thirst, lack of food and sleep:

> 'As soon as one sat down, one's head began to nod over one's rifle.'[87]

Saturday 29 April

The position at Moore Street was no longer tenable. Artillery units had been brought up. Close by the Sherwood Foresters and the Royal Irish Regiment could be seen massing for an attack.[88]

At a little after 12.45pm Pearse agreed to negotiate terms of surrender. At 2.30pm Pearse met with General Lowe at the barricade in Moore Street. He was taken to army GHQ where he met briefly with General Maxwell and signed the surrender.

The note written by Pearse indicated an unconditional surrender. Although as part of those discussions, Pearse was told that the prisoners would be dealt with under the Defence of the Realm Regulations.[89] It may be that this was intended as a statement of fact rather than an inducement but it also contained an implicit promise that the prisoners would be dealt with by what was then, due process. This may have offered some comfort to Pearse although it is unlikely that this factor would have swayed his decision; the die was cast and his mind was fixed on surrender.

The news of the surrender came as a surprise to many Volunteers. The remnants of the GPO garrison were called out into the road where they were spoken to by one of their officers:

> 'We were told we would have to pile our arms in O'Connell Street. Then we were given a "Right Turn" and marched into O'Connell Street. At this time we were guided by British soldiers stationed along the route at intervals. We threw the arms in a heap at O'Connell Street and then formed up in single or double lines.' [90]

Names were taken down. The available evidence suggests that most prisoners gave their full names and addresses. A few, like the McGallogly brothers from Scotland, gave false names – they were wanted in Glasgow for stealing gelignite.[91] One officer moved down the line taking names. He stopped in front of a prisoner. Neither man spoke but the officer jotted down a name and moved on. 'It's his brother' a voice said. [92]

A few prisoners who were not part of the general surrender narrowly escaped summary execution at the point of capture. Some army officers had fostered the idea that rebels deserved none of the protections of the laws of war. But apart from events at North King Street, common sense and humanity prevailed.[93] Not all those surrendering were held. Some of the youngsters were sent on their way. Martin Walton, aged 14, was one of those surrendering at O'Connell Street. An officer stopped in front of him: 'he gives me a clip on the ear and tells me to get the hell home'.[94] A number of youths were sent off in this way.

James Connolly was moved by stretcher to the hospital at Dublin Castle. One of the Foresters recalled him 'haggard and pale' on the makeshift stretcher.[95] The GPO garrison were marched to the Green outside the Rotunda Hospital, where they were joined by the prisoners from the Four Courts. One officer, 'a very decent type' quietly advised the prisoners that if they had any incriminating items on them they should 'drop it on the ground'.[96] Another officer, Captain Percival Lea Wilson was a malignant presence. A few of the prisoners were physically maltreated. No toilet facilities were made available and the men were prevented from standing to relieve themselves. No water or food was provided overnight and the prisoners lay heaped one on top of another.[97] Late the following morning the prisoners were marched to Richmond Barracks where they were lined up for searching, with some fainting with thirst.[98]

Sunday 30 April

Word of the surrender had reached Enniscorthy and North County Dublin where the Rebellion had flourished. The Army granted two Volunteer officers from Wexford safe conduct to Dublin where they saw Pearse at Arbour Hill prison.[99] Richard Mulcahy, then an unknown Volunteer officer, also came up from Ashbourne. The order to surrender was confirmed.

The remains of the North King Street garrison surrendered that morning, followed by the Citizen Army at Saint Stephen's Green.

There is direct and compelling evidence that the leaders expected to face the death penalty and hoped to secure the lives of their men.[100] And so rebel garrisons surrendered in disciplined units, led by their officers and carrying their arms. This method of surrender was civilised and honourable but it was hardly prudent to allow the Provost Marshals the opportunity of identifying junior Volunteer officers. This decision allowed the Army to build an evidential case against many and for a few, this would mean execution.

But there was one last military engagement that would have a significant bearing on the trial process that followed. It took place at Patrick's Park, beside Saint Patrick's Cathedral. The Army anticipated taking the surrender of the remaining garrisons at Jacob's biscuit factory and the South Dublin Union that afternoon. Not all the rebel outposts were aware of the plans for surrender and of those who did, many wanted to fight on. It was in these circumstances that the South Staffords were fired on from Jacob's and casualties were inflicted.

Among the onlookers were two men who would play a crucial role in the trials that followed. One was Major James Armstrong. The other was a member of the Officer Training Corps at Trinity College, Second Lieutenant William Wylie, Kings Counsel. A few days before the Rebellion, Wylie and his wife had left their baby with the maid and taken a weekend break by the lakes near Killarney. When the news of the Rebellion broke, they had borrowed 'an ancient T. Ford' and rattled anxiously back to Dublin, where they found the maid sitting on the steps of their house in Merrion Square watching the shooting. The baby, as it turned out was safe and Wylie joined his unit.

The man with Wylie was Major James Armstrong, the Assistant Provost Marshal. Armstrong was Irish, a regular officer, on leave from the front. Armstrong would be the main witness in many trials. The shooting at Jacob's on that Sunday afternoon formed the basis of all of his evidence.

The news of the surrender signed by Pearse and Connolly was brought to Jacob's. After some discussions MacDonagh was allowed under a flag of truce to move back and forth between Jacob's factory and the South Dublin Union, organising the surrender. Éamonn Ceannt also visited his outpost at Marrowbone Lane. Here, the garrison was well provisioned and well armed.[101] The upbeat mood was abruptly punctured by the news of the surrender.

Later at Jacob's biscuit factory the garrison assembled in the basement ready to surrender. Among those surrendering were 'several girls – some armed'.[102] Soon after, the garrison marched out to Patrick's Park. As they marched, more than a few just slipped away.

The surrender of the garrison at Jacob's biscuit factory was taken by Lieutenant Wylie who recalled the scene at Patrick's Park: 'MacDonagh was in full uniform with brown field boots and McBride was in an ordinary lounge suit.' Writing 20 years later, Wylie recalled the moment vividly: 'the two leaders standing laughing and talking in front of their men'.

The mechanics of the surrender were civilised but bizarre: 'MacDonagh and McBride led the Jacob's biscuit factory garrison, about 130 in all, down the street. They were lined up and their names and rank taken, also it was noted if they were armed, and with what weapons'.[103]

Soon after, the South Dublin Union garrison marched to the surrender point, although here again, a few men slipped away into the crowd.

The South Dublin Union garrison formed up behind the Jacob's factory men. Their arms were surrendered and the names of the men were taken. Both columns were marched to Richmond Barracks. This precise sequence of events led army officers to lose track of who had surrendered from which garrison and this would have consequences for the trials that followed.[104]

At Boland's Mills the pattern was much the same, although here, army officers declined to take women prisoners.[105] De Valera's garrison marched into the street where the order to ground arms was given. Many of the men broke their guns on the road.[106] The prisoners were searched and relieved of any remaining equipment and were marched away from the city centre to the Royal Dublin Showground in Ballsbridge.

The Rebellion was over, although sporadic sniping continued. It seems likely that a few of the snipers who had dogged Beggars Bush Barracks all week, took refuge in Irishtown where they continued to fire for some days. They were pursued by the Leicestershire regiment utilising 'a contracting cordon'.[107] Dublin was otherwise quiet. The fires in Sackville Street still blazed but the fire brigade were now free to tackle the fires.

Later that day Lord Wimborne issued a communiqué from the Vice-Regal Lodge:

```
'Yesterday, Pearse, the rebel leader, surrendered,
and the great bulk of his supporters in the city
and throughout the country have done likewise.'[108]
```

CHAPTER THREE

Trial and Punishment

'Rebels considered suitable for trial are being tried
by Field General Courts martial under the Defence of
the Realm Act in Dublin. As soon as the sentences
have been confirmed the public will be informed as
to the result of the trial. Those prisoners whose
cases could not be immediately dealt with are being
sent to places of confinement in England. Their
cases will receive consideration later.GHQ Dublin
press communiqué - Sunday 30 April).'

This was General Maxwell's plan to deal with the aftermath of the Rising.
The temptation to apply the wisdom of hindsight might be tempered by
recognising the situation faced by Maxwell. The death toll was heavy. Bodies
lay in the streets and the hospitals were filled with the dying and wounded.
The GPO, lower O'Connell Street and the adjoining area were charred and
blackened ruins. Many fires were still smouldering and the fire brigade
were out pulling down buildings on the point of collapse. There were food
shortages and there were still snipers operating on the outskirts of the city.
No doubt the Army Council expected a decisive response and in the days
that followed the press urged Maxwell on to a draconian response.

But underlying Maxwell's decisions, there were legal difficulties that
would soon come home to roost.[1] Once the prisoners were shipped out of
the martial law area, there was no legal power to hold them. When they
reached England there was no power to require them to be tried by courts
martial under DORA[2] and although they might be tried by jury there, the
logistical and evidential difficulties would be considerable.[3] Nor was there
any legal power to bring them back into the martial law area. Some weeks
later, ex-post facto internment orders were obtained but even these were of
questionable legality.[4] Although DMP men later crossed over to mainland
Britain and combed the internment camps at Stafford and Frongoch, only
one prisoner was ever brought back for trial.[5]

It would have been entirely feasible and logistically simpler if the
prisoners had been moved to the Curragh and held pending trial for

common law offences of treason and riot to which there could be no defence.

The rush to trial or deportation was remarkable. In Dublin, the Rebellion was over and this fact was confirmed by Dublin HQ to the Army Council at Horse Guards:

```
'the rebellion is practically crushed.'⁶
```

The same was true in the country. There had been scattered incidents but order had been quickly restored and a surrender of guns was well underway even before the Rebellion collapsed. Army reinforcements were being turned back at Liverpool docks and two cavalry regiments were returned to barracks. The crisis was over.[7]

Sir Edward Carson offered the Army the services of the Ulster Volunteers and Redmond had offered the National Volunteers.[8] Maxwell declined both offers and this is a good indicator of his confidence. Some historians have suggested that Maxwell may have been spurred on by the menace of a German invasion.[9] But the internal army memos do not suggest any fears of a German landing or a revival of the Rebellion.[10]

Maxwell was set on acting quickly; trying as many as he deemed necessary and deporting the rest. It remains a mystery, however, why Maxwell resorted to deportations, as it served no discernible purpose except to radicalise young men and alienate entire communities. But once Maxwell had decided on this course of action, he had to act swiftly. By 30 April there were well over 1,000 prisoners and the figure was rising by the hour.

The centre of events in Dublin was at Richmond Barracks in Inchicore, to the west of the city. Here a solid granite gateway opened onto a vast marching square, flanked on all sides by substantial walls. Richmond Barracks was capable of billeting over 1,500 soldiers, and although there were cells for barely 200 prisoners, it was still the largest barracks in Dublin and it was close to army HQ at the Royal Hospital in Kilmainham. The Army began to move all the prisoners to Richmond Barracks where they were packed into cells and other makeshift holding areas.

At this point Maxwell's officers suddenly realised that they might have difficulty proving the identity of those who were senior or who played an active role in the Rebellion. The task should have been easy. None of the leaders tried to conceal their rank. They surrendered at the head of their troops. Most were in uniform and carried weapons to the point of surrender where their details were given to waiting army officers. In general terms the same is true of the rank and file. Many but not all were in uniform and quite a number carried arms to the point of surrender. Most gave their real names when asked.

At this point the British army was overwhelmed by the sheer number of prisoners. And it seems that there was a growing realisation among the prisoners that they were at risk of trial and execution. Active co-operation began to evaporate. The difficulties faced by the Army were compounded by other factors. Most of the prisoners had some days' growth, they were 'dirty and unkempt' and some were bandaged and hardly recognisable.[11] Many of the GPO garrison were covered in a white dust that made it impossible to distinguish the dark green uniforms of the Citizen Army and the grey-green worn by the Volunteers. Quite a number were not in uniform, MacBride wore a lounge suit, while Halpin, a slightly-built Citizen Army man was covered in soot, having tried to hide up a chimney in City Hall.[12] One prisoner was a van driver for Easons booksellers, who being 'fairly drunk' had joined the South Dublin Union garrison as it marched to the surrender point. He was unable to extricate himself and was detained.[13] A Polish sailor was also caught up in the arrests and he too, was shipped off to England in captivity.[14] One of the prisoners from the South Dublin Union had become mildly deranged[15]and quite a number were wounded and were laid up at Dublin Castle Red Cross Hospital or in half a dozen other hospitals around the city. With more prisoners en route from the provinces it was a scene of near chaos.

The officers from G Division of the DMP were sifting through the prisoners as they arrived. The Army, somewhat belatedly, had started to carry out identification parades and examine seized documents in an attempt to put together a legal case against specific prisoners.

In order to make way for more prisoners, the deportations began at once. Those marked for deportation were marched from Richmond Barracks across the city to the docks at the North Wall. On 30 April, 489 men were deported.[16] One prisoner, Brennan Whitmore, recalled the march:

> `'As we went we were pelted with garbage and filthy epithets by the scum of the city.'`[17]

Arriving at the North Wall, the prisoners were given life belts and herded into cattle boats.[18] The cattle holds were 'packed' with prisoners. For these men there was no food, water or toilets. Many of the prisoners were exhausted and slept but others vomited over themselves or others. The stench became 'overwhelming'.[19] The first batch of prisoners were seen arriving at Holyhead by a *Times* journalist who watched the lines of men: dejected, most hatless and without coats, shivering on the quay.[20]

Back at Richmond Barracks, General Maxwell started to identify officers who would prosecute the trials and officers who would act as judges. There were difficulties in finding officers suitable to try the prisoners and Maxwell sent an urgent request to Horse Guards for officers with experience of courts martial work although in fact none were sent. In the interim, Maxwell selected two Brigade commanders who had come over from England leading territorial units. Brigadier General Blackader would chair one standing court and Brigadier Maconchy, the other. Both of these brigade commanders had courts martial experience but no legal training. Maconchy had retired from the Indian army in 1914. He was what the Army termed 'a dug out'– an officer eased out of retirement as the need for experienced commanders became acute. He commanded the 178 Brigade. Maconchy, protested against courts martial duty on the ground that he had Irish relations, some living in Dublin. He was persuaded to serve. He was replaced a few days later by Colonel Sapte, another colonial soldier 'dug out' of retirement.

Brigadier General Blackader commanded the 176 Brigade. As a young officer he had married 'in a hurry' to avoid scandal but he had stayed with his wife. He made his reputation in Africa where he was decorated after the siege of Ladysmith and later commanded a concentration camp in the Natal hinterland. In the Great War he had a distinguished record on the Western Front.[21] A big man, with a dark heavy moustache, he was known to his men as 'Old Black'.

Finding officers with suitable experience to prosecute the prisoners was also a difficulty. The officer who prosecuted most of the trials that resulted in executions was Lieutenant William Wylie, Kings Counsel. Just before the surrender, Wylie was detailed to guide two battalions of troops across Dublin. Leading the way and passing Dublin Castle; he caught the eye of the Attorney General and the Solicitor-General who were standing at the gate. They recognised Kings Counsel, despite his uniform and 'laughed'. [22] It was as a result of this chance encounter that the Attorney General put his name forward to conduct the prosecutions. On the night of 30 April, at a little after midnight, Wylie was summoned to GHQ to see Deputy Adjutant General Byrne. He was given orders to conduct the prosecution of the rebels. The next morning Wylie made his way to Richmond Barracks where Brigadier General Blackader and Colonels German and Kent were waiting.[23]

The officer who prosecuted in Brigadier Maconchy's court was Ernest Longworth, a member of the Irish Bar. Longworth was a confirmed bachelor and a man with literary leanings.[24]

Longworth and Wylie were contemporaries at the Irish Bar. They were both commissioned in 1914 at the Officer Training Corps at Trinity College Dublin. Both specialised in civil law and neither had experience of courts martial work.

In later years, Longworth would act as Judge Advocate in many trials by military courts.[25] Wylie became a High Court Judge who was known to slip away to go fox hunting during court hours. His lean figure and hook nose would become a familiar sight on the hunting field for decades.

Monday 1 May

The trials were due to start that Monday but there were 'legal difficulties' Maxwell later wrote, without elaborating.[26]

The central problem for the Army was that the Proclamation of 25 April[27] revoked the right to trial by jury for offences contrary to the regulations made under DORA and required trial by court martial under the Defence of the Realm Act. But the proviso to section 1 of the Act[28] prevented a court martial from imposing a death penalty, save where the breach of the regulations was carried out with the intention of assisting the enemy: Germany.

Most army officers firmly believed that German soldiers had actually taken part in the Rebellion. There was much talk about German snipers[29] and German gold but none was found. The Aud, pursued by British warships, had been scuttled with her cargo of guns and there was no admissible evidence that could be called at short notice that the foremost prisoner, Pearse, had acted 'with the intention of assisting the enemy'.

By 1 May the whole court martial process had stalled. Internal army memos give the merest hint of this crisis.[30] Pearse's determination to sacrifice his life has been well documented and what emerged was a unique and disturbing moment in history. Pearse wished to be shot by the Army and there is no doubt the Army wished to shoot Pearse. All that stood between them was some proof that he had acted 'with the intention to assist the enemy'.

At this point, Maxwell was inclined to disregard the terms of his appointment and press on and try the prisoners under martial law.[31] His DAG, General Byrne, argued that the courts martial scheme sanctioned by Parliament under the Defence of the Realm Act would avoid political repercussions later.[32]

It was at this crucial moment while Maxwell hesitated, that Pearse wrote a letter to his mother. After finishing the letter, he added a postscript which he placed at the head of the first page where it could hardly be overlooked by his captors: 'I have reason to believe that the German expedition on which I counted actually set sail but was defeated by the British fleet.'

The letter was seized and handed to Lieutenant Bucknill. The charge, alleging rebellion, 'for the purpose and with the intention of assisting the enemy' was drafted the same day. Pearse was moved to Richmond Barracks for trial. The letter would form the cornerstone of the prosecution case.

Inside Richmond Barracks there was intense activity. Outside, Dubliners walked freely through the ruins of the city. Bread was rationed for a few days and Dublin Corporation and the charitable organisation St Vincent de Paul organised food relief.[33] The Dublin Metropolitan Police were back on the streets[34] and *The Irish Times* published, again. The issue, famously dated 28–29 April and 1 May sounded a return to normality in Dublin. Although the curfew remained in force there were still snipers operating in the south of the city at Irishtown, which was cordoned off by the Leicestershire regiment, drawing in street by street and house by house.[35] A single suspected gunmen was captured but for the most part, the snipers simply melted away. Elsewhere in Dublin, raids by mixed parties of Army and Police were rounding up suspects in large numbers.

The Chief Secretary, Birrell, offered to resign and Asquith accepted.[36] Sir Mathew Nathan, the Under Secretary followed two days later. The only member of the Irish Executive left was Wimborne, the Lord Lieutenant, who held a ceremonial post. It has been said that the civil administration in Ireland was 'defunct' during the period in which executions took place. That perhaps misses the point, as the functions of the Irish executive had been taken over by the Military. Wimborne, isolated in the Vice-Regal Lodge on the edge of Dublin penned a series of letters to General Maxwell offering dinner, fellowship and advice in what was ultimately an attempt to re-assert the authority of his office. [37]

Tuesday 2 May

At Westminster, the Home Rule leader Redmond received a letter from his deputy Dillon, who had spent most of the Rebellion trapped in his home in Dublin. Dillon's message was stark: 'urge strongly on the government the extreme unwisdom of wholesale shooting of prisoners'.[38]

Dillon had correctly anticipated Maxwell's next step. The same day, General Maxwell telegraphed the War Office at Horse Guards: 'I hope the politicians will not interfere until I report normal conditions prevail . . . there is still work to be done.'[39] Maxwell set about the task straight away. Pearse, Clarke and MacDonagh were tried and sentenced to death that morning. Three others were tried and convicted but sentence of death was commuted to penal servitude.[40]

The deportations continued apace: 308 internees were embarked on cattle boats from the North Wall.[41] Maxwell also issued a proclamation which offered a 72-hour amnesty to allow the surrender of all arms and ammunition or 'be severely dealt with'. [42]

Outside Army HQ, Dublin city centre was heavy with traffic, There were carts carrying dead horses, twisted metal, rubble and 'a trail of Red Cross nurses on bicycles, in their print dresses and white overalls'. [43]

For several days after the surrender, free movement was almost impossible. 'Any person who ventured away from his front door was held up, questioned and searched, almost every few hundred yards.'[44] On a boundary that broadly corresponded to the north circular and the south circular roads around the city, the Military maintained a cordon. Within this area, civilians might move but passes were required to move from one checkpoint to another.[45] Embarkation abroad was limited to a few named ports. The police vetted would-be passengers.

Although the courts were still closed,[46] the Dublin Metropolitan Police were active and the round-up of looters had already begun. Some 431 arrests were made for looting and no matter how crowded the prisons were there was still room for more. 134 looters went to gaol.[47] The Provost Marshal was also rounding up looters in the ranks of the Army. Many soldiers had been unable to resist helping themselves from smashed shop fronts or stealing money or watches from prisoners.[48] Where there was evidence, the Army prosecuted.[49]

Wednesday 3 May

The first of the executions, of Clarke, Pearse and MacDonagh, took place at 3.45am. Alfred Bucknill recalled that when MacDonagh was brought to the yard at Kilmainham, 'he came down the stairs whistling'.[50] Bucknill recalled that each of the prisoners died 'bravely'.

The bodies of Pearse, MacDonagh and Clarke were taken by horse-drawn wagon to Arbour Hill Barracks.[51] The bodies made a lasting impression on the prison chaplain: 'in pools of blood, still warm and limp, eyes bandaged, mouths open'.[52] The dead men were laid side by side in a grave that stretched 60 feet across.

In Dublin city centre the task of clearing up was well underway. There were burnt-out trams and many more lorries and cars gutted by fire or turned on their side to form barricades. Dead bodies were still turning up, a few at North King Street were found in shallow graves and many others were found in gardens and in the rubble.

Back in Richmond Barracks, 19 prisoners were tried and sentenced to death. Maxwell confirmed death sentences in respect of Edward Daly, William Pearse, Joseph Plunkett and Michael O'Hanrahan. All other death sentences were commuted to prison terms.

At Westminster, Birrell arrived back from Ireland and met Asquith privately; they had been long-standing cabinet allies. Asquith had been Prime Minster for eight years, 'the unquestioned master' of the political landscape. His reputation was that of an administrator and an orator but there were many aspects to his character. He was known as 'Squiffy' to his friends as he sometimes drank when discussing affairs of state, although the consensus was that this did not affect his judgment.[53] He had become jaded in what were the dying months of his premiership and his determination to prosecute the war was questioned by a hostile press. It had been a difficult month for the government, which had almost fallen over the Conscription Bill. Now, the Rebellion in Ireland had forced the resignation of his friend, Birrell, one of a dwindling number of allies. Asquith stared out of the window and wept.[54]

When the news of the first executions came through that day, Asquith had required Lord French, the Commander in Chief of the British Home Forces, to explain the hasty executions. Asquith was reassured by Lord French that Maxwell had acted 'in strict accordance with military and martial law'.[55] Charles Townshend has pointed out that these men were tried under DORA, not martial law. That is certainly what Asquith intended but it is probable that Lord French had bluntly stated his understanding and he may have been far closer to the truth than might first appear.

French was a soldier of the old school.[56] As far as he was concerned, martial law existed in Ireland and his memo reflected his understanding. In the spring of 1916, the Army executed five men for treason in Macedonia and three death sentences were imposed in Egypt for offences contrary to martial law.[57] In May alone six soldiers were executed on the Western Front. Although the Rebellion in Ireland was closer to home, as far as Lord French was concerned, it was business as usual and he telegrammed Maxwell to reassure him that he enjoyed the full confidence of the government. Maxwell, no doubt reassured, pressed on with his work.

In order to understand why Asquith did not intervene, it is necessary to appreciate his attitude to government. Some insight can be gleaned from a cabinet meeting convened to discuss the upcoming Somme offensive: the Generals feared heavy casualties and were incensed when Asquith arrived 'dressed for golf and evidently anxious to get away for his weekend'.[58] The point is not that Asquith was incompetent or neglectful, it is that he delegated. His understanding of military law and martial law was probably no better than any educated man of his time. Quelling the Rebellion was new territory for him and he found himself overtaken by events in Dublin.

That day Asquith announced to the House the executions of Pearse, Clarke and MacDonagh. No voices of dissent were raised, although a few argued for caution. Redmond, with considerable foresight warned:

> 'that out of the ashes of this miserable tragedy
> there may spring up something that may re-bound.'[59]

Thursday 4 May

At Westminster a curious backbencher questioned Asquith about the trial of captured rebels. He asked: 'how he proposes that justice shall be meted out to the rebels taken in arms; whether they will be tried by court martial or by a civil tribunal . . .'

The Prime Minster:

> 'It is not desirable to say more at the moment than
> that all appropriate measures are being taken, and
> have been taken, to deal with the rebellion and
> those responsible for it.'[60]

In fact, early that morning, Edward Daly, Michael O'Hanrahan, William Pearse and Joseph Plunkett were executed at Kilmainham. News of the executions reached London that afternoon and Asquith recalled Maxwell to London. Asquith's concerns were twofold. The first concern was the apparent haste and number of executions. Secondly, there was also the position of Constance Markievicz. Maxwell had wired London indicating that he would execute Markievicz if she was convicted.[61] Later that night Lord French wired Maxwell in case he took any further steps before leaving Dublin for London:

> 'the prime minister has told me to impress upon
> you the necessity of avoiding anything which might
> give rise to a charge of hasty procedure ... '

The trial process at Richmond Barracks continued that day where 36 prisoners were tried and of these 31 were sentenced to death, including Heuston, Colbert, Ceannt and Markievicz. In Cork, Thomas Kent[62] was tried and sentenced to death.

The process of confirmation and execution was interrupted, as Maxwell noted irritably the next day:

'I was, owing to my sudden departure to England,
only able to deal with the following: William
Cosgrave, John McBride, Thomas Hunter. These are all
important leaders and in the case of Cosgrave and
Hunter thought fit to commute the death sentence.'[63]

In Dublin, parties of soldiers and police continued to carry out wholesale arrests. The sense of apprehension was palpable:

'Everybody is afraid to express his views. Martial
Law is supreme.'[64]

The curfew was reinforced by a blackout in some areas.[65]

Friday 5 May

At dawn, John MacBride was executed.[66] Later that day, the deportations recommenced, with another 376 prisoners being embarked from the North Wall.[67] Eleven other prisoners were tried and sentenced to death.

In Dublin the trams began to run again. Military passes were no longer required but the curfew remained in place.[68]

Back in London, the Cabinet sat and heard from General Maxwell. The Cabinet extracted a promise from Maxwell that no woman would be executed, as the political fallout would be too great. Maxwell was also strongly encouraged to execute only where strictly necessary and bring the process to a swift conclusion.[69] Maxwell set off for Dublin again later that day.

Saturday 6 May

Maxwell returned by morning to another letter from Lord Lieutenant Wimborne trying to re-establish the authority of his office: 'I am for the present head of the Irish Executive. I should be glad therefore if you would communicate directly with me . . . '[70]

Maxwell pressed on with the process of confirmation. Sentence of death on Countess Markievicz was commuted but confirmed in respect of Mallin, her commanding officer at Saint Stephen's Green.

Sentence of death was confirmed in respect of Ceannt (one of the signatories to the proclamation) and Colbert, one of his junior officers. Sentence of death was also confirmed on Thomas Kent in Cork and J.J. Heuston who had been in command at the Mendicity.   Many other death sentences were commuted that day, including the rest of the Mendicity prisoners.

Sunday 7 May

The process of searching the homes of known Volunteers continued. Connections were made with other Volunteers and the net widened. Seán MacDiarmada's home was searched by Captain Orchard of the Leicestershire regiment. On the dining room sideboard he found a large number of sealed envelopes. One was opened and turned out to be a mobilisation order. The entire bundle of letters was seized and Captain Orchard set out with a party of soldiers to deliver the mobilisation orders:

```
'I delivered the rest personally with an escort
of men and I had some fun doing it too as they
all swore they knew nothing about it when asked
"How long they had been in the Irish Volunteers?"
I would then produce the notice ... I arrested my
man in every case.'
```

Rumours that there would be further executions swirled around Dublin. Feelings had become 'extremely bitter'[71] and extended to those who had no sympathy for the rebels. John Dillon asked Wimborne to intervene but he said he had 'no authority'.[72] Wimborne was due to dine with Maxwell that night and promised to raise the issue with General Maxwell and he did so. Although it seems that Maxwell did not tell the Lord Lieutenant that four more men were to be executed that night.[73]

Monday 8 May

At 3.45am the next round of executions began. Michael Mallin, Éamonn Ceannt, J.J. Heuston and Con Colbert were shot at Kilmainham.

The firing parties were assembled at Army HQ at the Royal Hospital and marched down to Kilmainham and issued with ammunition.

The prisoners at Kilmainham were brought down to a central passageway. Each prisoner was blindfolded – on one account three of the prisoners declined to have their eyes bandaged.[74] These requests were refused. The prisoner's wrists were tied. A small white card was tied to mark the prisoner's heart. He was then walked to the yard.

Each soldier carried a Lee Enfield rifle. The firing party included a Lieutenant, an NCO and 12 men. The firing squad was lined up at ten paces from the prisoner. From that distance a volley of rifle fire inflicted devastating damage.

After the executions, the bodies were brought immediately to Arbour Hill military prison. The bodies were buried 'un-coffined, in a trench'. A short funeral service was carried out by the prison chaplain.

Later that day 203 prisoners were deported to England.[75]

In Dublin, the revulsion against the executions was beginning to become evident. In Maxwell's judgment, executions had to take place – it was just a question of how many. He later appeared perplexed that Dubliners who had opposed the Rebellion should also be concerned about executions.

Part of the answer may be that the executed men were so well known in Dublin. The Pearse brothers, MacDonagh, Plunkett and O'Hanrahan were part of Dublin literary and artistic society. MacBride's exploits in the Boer War were the stuff of legend and he too, was a familiar figure on the Liffey Quays where he worked as a water bailiff. Heuston was a railway clerk, Ceannt was a civil servant and Colbert was an office worker.

Similar considerations may apply to whose sentences were still unknown; men like Connolly and William Partridge who had strong trade union connections in Dublin or Cosgrave who had worked for the relief of poverty in the city. This was the context of another round of executions.

It also seems likely that many Dubliners and country people did not distinguish between executions following trial and the other killings carried out by soldiers; Skeffington, Dickson, McIntyre, James Coade, Rice, Dockery and others. The list was becoming longer by the day. This, perhaps, was a moment when ancient hatreds began to stir.

The press, notably *The Irish Times* and *The Irish Independent* had called for draconian action against the prisoners. In the days that followed, *The Irish Independent* urged Maxwell to execute Connolly and MacDiarmada, the remaining two signatories. *The Irish Independent* was owned by the industrialist, William Martin Murphy. He and Connolly had been central protagonists in the bitter strike of 1913. Some perceived a final ugly blow in an old vendetta.

At the Vice-Regal Lodge Wimborne could already sense the direction events were taking and his anger spilled over. In the months before the Rebellion his warnings had been ignored. Now after the event, he had been sidelined by General Maxwell, whom he judged to be following an equally disastrous policy.

Wimborne understood the impact the executions might have on recruitment to the British army. It is likely that he also sensed much more had been lost. He resigned later that day but before doing so penned a cold letter to Maxwell protesting the latest round of executions.

```
'No one in Ireland besides a few experts will
believe that I am without influence in settling
the cases of capital sentences or admit that I had
no responsibilities in the matter. I am therefore
bound to express my opinion and to take all means
at my disposal to ensure them being considered.'[76]
```

Tuesday 9 May

In the early hours of the morning, at the Detention Barracks in Cork, Thomas Kent was executed for the killing of Head Constable Rowe.

Back in Dublin, the deportations continued. Another 197 men were embarked on cattle boats from the North Wall.

Later that morning, MacDiarmada was tried and convicted. Connolly was tried, propped up in his bed in the Red Cross hospital at Dublin Castle. He was also convicted.

Wednesday 10 May

Maxwell confirmed the death sentences on Connolly and MacDiarmada and wired the Cabinet setting out plans to execute the men the following morning.[77]

That morning Dillon raised the executions at Westminster and invoked a formal debate:[78] The House having signified assent the motion stood adjourned overnight.

Another crucial development followed within hours. Major Sir Francis Vane had arrived at Horse Guards. His protests about the murder of Sheehy Skeffington had not been acted upon and he had come over to London and demanded to see Lord Kitchener, the Chief of the Imperial General Staff. Sir Francis related the whole wretched story[79] and Kitchener, who was always jealous of the reputation of the Army, despatched a furious telegram to Maxwell: 'Is this true?'[80]

At 4.35pm that afternoon Asquith gave instructions:

```
'no more executions until further orders'.
```

A flurry of telegrams followed, including one reflecting concern that events in Dublin were out of control: 'please wire receipt of my two telegrams'.[81] In fact the 'wires' show that Maxwell was in constant touch with London and did not plan any unauthorised step. Maxwell's last wire timed at 10.45pm requested instructions and showed the first signs of uncertainty:

```
'Shall I commute the sentences?'
```
[32]

At 11.45pm came the reply from Westminster:

```
'Do not commute the sentences ... but suspend
execution until further orders.'
```

MacDiarmada was held at Kilmainham Gaol where he was visited by Father Patrick Browne in his cell. The cell was lit with a weak gas lamp. Supper was brought and the prisoner ate. As the hours wore on Browne sat on the single stool in the cell while the prisoner limped back and forth and talked.[83] In the early hours an officer appeared at the cell door and announced the execution had been put off. The prisoner was philosophical: 'It's only going to be postponed. But you never know.' Father Browne departed but looked back to take in the cell:

```
'He slept on the floor of the cell and when I was
going away, he was arranging his coat on his boots
to make a pillow for his head.'
```
[34]

Thursday 11 May

General Maxwell was up for most of the night. He knew the House of Commons would be debating his actions the following day and he needed to respond effectively. The memo that was prepared is remarkable for the clarity and precision of its drafting and is very different from Maxwell's florid style. It is a fair inference that it was drafted by Lieutenant Bucknill.[85] The memo[86] was sent under cipher and was timed at 3.20am and set out the categories of men who had been executed. Category A included those who were leaders and who had signed the proclamation. In this group there were Pearse, Clarke, Plunkett, MacDonagh and Ceannt – to which group, General Maxwell suggested that Connolly and MacDiarmada also belonged.

Category B included 'those in command of rebels actually shooting down troops, police and others'. This group included Daly, O'Hanrahan, MacBride, Colbert, Mallin, Heuston and William Pearse. Category C included those found guilty of murder, namely Thomas Kent, in Fermoy.

It appears that even before the House sat to debate the motion raised by Dillon, Asquith resolved to defend Maxwell's decisions and to rescind the order suspending the execution of Connolly and MacDiarmada.

Here, context is everything. For Asquith, events in Ireland were an unwelcome distraction from the Great War, which threatened the very fabric of the Empire, which was the source of so much wealth and prestige. This factor came into sharp focus in the spring of 1916. The Somme offensive had been planned to strike a decisive blow in the war. It had been intended as a joint Anglo-French venture. But French losses at Verdun made it necessary for the British army to carry the burden of the offensive. What had been planned as an action that might strike a decisive blow became an offensive to relieve the pressure on the French at Verdun. But the British Expeditionary Force was undermanned, insufficiently trained and the offensive was deferred from the spring to the summer. As the months passed, the momentum was shifting in favour of Germany. The swift suppression of the Rebellion would release troops for the Western Front. Asquith could hardly do anything other than support General Maxwell. At 14.45pm, even before the House convened, Asquith directed that the executions should go ahead.[87]

In the hospital wing of Dublin Castle, Connolly was recovering from his operation. He spent some time with Father Aloysius and made his confession. He was courteous but 'feverish'. His wound troubled him and he had been unable to sleep.[88]

Back at Westminster, Asquith gave a commanding performance. He defended Maxwell, who had shown 'discretion, depth of mind and humanity'. He told the House that the two remaining signatories were awaiting execution and he did not intend to intervene. Asquith finished with an announcement that he was travelling to Ireland that night.[89]

Dillon addressed the House again about 'the horrible rumours which are current in Dublin, and which are doing untold mischief'. Dillon's speech was emotionally charged and invited sympathy for the rebels. It showed very poor judgment and the journalists in the strangers gallery noted the other Home Rulers were gripped by 'embarrassment and chagrin'.

A letter to *The Times* the next morning captured the mood of the nation: 'Why this tender solicitude for the just fate of rebels?'[90]

But in Dublin there were rumours of the wildest kind: that 50 men had been shot in Royal Barracks,[91] and summary executions at Eden Quay and North King Street. Other rumours were fostered by the troops for their amusement: a mass grave at Arbour Hill[92] and Richmond Barracks.[93] Privately Lord Kitchener and Asquith were becoming aware that there was substance to some of the rumours. Another of Bowen Colthurst's victims had come to light: James Coade, an unarmed teenager who had played no part in the Rebellion. And there was confirmation of other killings at North King Street,[94] Eden Quay, the Guinness Brewery[95] and at Amiens Street.[96] As the weeks wore on there were a steady trickle of parliamentary questions laid down about shootings of civilians by the Army.[97] Dublin was a small city and the impact was considerable.

Back in Dublin, Father Aloysius, the priest ministering to Connolly was called at home and told his 'services would be needed at 2am'.

At 11pm Connolly was woken from a deep sleep and told he was to be shot in a few hours.

Friday 12 May

At 3.15am MacDiarmada was shot in the yard at Kilmainham Gaol. As the execution was underway, Connolly was removed from the Red Cross Hospital at Dublin Castle and brought to Kilmainham in a horse-drawn wagon. What took place was later related by Father Aloysius in a way that was both factually correct but misleading:

> `'He was put sitting on a chair. And the order was`
> `given. They fired.'`[98]

In fact Connolly, blindfolded, dressed only in pyjamas was slumped backwards, semiconscious in a chair, oblivious of the firing squad.[99] It was an undignified and grotesque death. Although for him, at least, death came swiftly.

Later that morning hundreds more prisoners were deported to England. A little while after they embarked, the destroyer carrying Asquith to Dublin docked at the North Wall. Asquith met with General Maxwell and later visited Richmond Barracks. Some prisoners later recalled that breakfast was dramatically better: there were no more hard tack biscuits and weak tea – bacon, eggs and jam were the fare. Asquith went down to meet the prisoners. His attempt to shake hands with the prisoners was accepted by some and rebuffed by many. It was an early and not too subtle variant of 'good cop–bad cop' but most of the prisoners were not impressed.[100] Nor were the soldiers who Asquith had sent to quell the Rebellion. Now hungry soldiers begged bacon from the prisoners.[101]

In the course of the next 24 hours Asquith wrote a series of hurried notes to Maxwell, one written at Dublin Castle and others from the Vice-Regal Lodge. These notes are unique, being orders from a serving prime minister to a general in a martial law area dictating how the trials of insurgents should be conducted. Asquith's main concerns were that trials for murder should take place in public. It is entirely unclear why Asquith thought that other trials should have been treated differently.[102] Nor did Asquith raise any concerns about the trials that were still in progress. And it should be kept in mind that the power to stop these trials lay with Asquith not Maxwell.

These events raise so many questions. Perhaps the most important one is why the prisoners were tried by courts martial even after the crisis had abated. There is no direct evidence on this issue. Some insight can be gained from evidence to the Royal Commission that year. The executive in Ireland believed that juries and sometimes lay magistrates were partial in cases with a political dimension. It was very difficult, almost impossible, to get a conviction. Only the Resident Magistrates, who sat in the cities and large provincial towns, could be relied upon but their powers were limited to summary offences.[103] Therefore trials by the Military provided a reliable and swift tribunal.

The proclamation suspending jury trial was not revoked and as the suppression of the Rebellion continued, few voices of protest were raised. *The Times* observed that the executions were 'absolutely necessary to teach the traitors who take German money that they cannot cover Dublin with blood and ashes without forfeiting their lives'. [104]

Derogations from due process are always easiest where there is an identifiable class of defendants who have struck at the foundations of society. Although it is then that the rule of law is most needed.

CHAPTER FOUR

The Trial Regime

Questions were raised afterwards about the legality of the trials. Asquith and General Maxwell insisted the trials had not taken place under martial law, where all turned on the power of the Army. They maintained that the trials took place under the Defence of the Realm Act. If that contention was correct, then trials were defensible, lawful and could not be impeached by public opinion, propaganda or before the courts. In order to evaluate the arguments it is necessary to explain the distinction between a trial under martial law and a court martial under the Defence of the Realm Act.

Martial Law

Martial law had been routinely invoked in the colonies as the last line of defence against insurrection or disorder that could not be suppressed by troops acting under the direction of the civil administration.[1]

It was recognised that where martial law was invoked, a governor might take all steps reasonably necessary to put down a rebellion.[2] However, once rebellion was suppressed, martial law simply evaporated and civil law had to prevail. The reality was that the precise point at which martial law might be invoked and was finally extinguished was always uncertain. The area of greatest controversy related to the practice of the military trying and executing captured insurgents during a rebellion. The law recognised that such a power existed.[3] But the shooting of prisoners after a rebellion was not permitted by law.[4]

The reality, however, was that in times of crisis the Army enforced martial law in the Empire to whatever extent that it thought necessary. This usually involved setting up military courts to try, and where expedient, to execute prisoners. This occurred in 1798 in Ireland, in India (1857), Jamaica (1865) and against the Boers (1901) to name but a few instances.

The exercise of this power by the Army was limited by the judgment of senior officers and the knowledge that acts done under martial law were justiciable by the courts after the emergency was over. If an officer was sued for acts done during martial law, the only defence was that of necessity or an Act of Indemnity passed by Parliament. These strictures, whilst discouraging excesses, did not prevent them from happening. Military Courts convened under martial law tended to act with despatch and it was not unusual for prisoners to be tried and executed within days of capture. Prisoners were usually unrepresented and had little or no opportunity to call witnesses or make out their case. In the aftermath of the Jamaica Rebellion, 354 men and women were executed following summary trial by military courts.[5] In the Boer conflict 48 prisoners were executed.[6] In 1915, 47 sepoy soldiers were shot after the Singapore Mutiny and a few years later, another martial law episode resulted in the massacre at Amritsar.

The Simon Commission[7] observed that a proclamation of martial law 'does not confer on officers or soldiers any new powers. It operates solely as a warning that the Government, acting through the military, is about to take such forcible and exceptional measures as may be necessary for the purpose of putting down insurrection.'[8] Plainly there were occasions when necessity required an extreme response, although this may have led some to think that the trigger for extreme action was martial law rather than necessity. Most senior officers in the British army had served in the Boer War where the primary strategy involved the application of martial law to Boer commandos and an indifferent and sometimes hostile civilian population. For these officers martial law was a familiar prospect.

In Dublin in 1916, martial law was proclaimed on the second day of the Rising[9] and was soon extended nationwide for many months. It was a reflex action to rebellion but 24 hours later there was another proclamation issued under the Defence of the Realm Act. This proclamation required trial by courts martial for persons believed to have contravened the Defence of the Realm Regulations.

The background to this was simple. The Great War had caused Asquith to consider what might need to be done in the event of invasion of Britain or some other military emergency. Although martial law had been routinely deployed in the colonies, it had not existed in mainland Britain for centuries and it was a deeply unpalatable option. And so Parliament passed the Defence of the Realm Act 1914[10] which permitted courts martial of civilians for offences contrary to the regulations.[11] It was an early experiment in special powers.

It was the first of a series of parliamentary measures to deal with the emergency. It is sufficient for our purposes to know that statute[12] conferred a power to suspend the right to elect jury trial 'in the event of invasion or other special military emergency' and to require trial by courts martial. Under this regime civilians were triable by court martial, as if they were soldiers.[13] This was the trial regime triggered by proclamation on 26 April in Ireland[14] and it was the trial regime that General Maxwell was authorised to implement.

Trial under the Defence of the Realm Act

Under this regime, prisoners tried for capital offences were usually tried by General Court Martial, a method of trial that carried important legal protections for the accused. These included the taking of the Summary of Evidence[15] and a proper opportunity of preparing a defence, 'free communication with witnesses, and with any friend or legal adviser the accused wished to consult'.[16] The rules of procedure also placed an obligation on the convening officer to arrange for witnesses the defence wished to call 'whose attendance can reasonably be procured'.[17] There was also an entitlement to legal representation at trial.[18] These rules might be dispensed with but only rarely and then only when 'absolutely necessary'.[19] Where a General Court Martial was convened it was necessary to appoint a Judge Advocate, who controlled the course of the trial, gave legal rulings and a summing up. The number of officers required to sit on a General Court Martial were no fewer than five. All trials were to take place 'in open court and in the presence of the accused'.[20]

The Manual of Military Law stipulated that where it was not 'practicable' to convene a General Court Martial, the officer commanding could convene a Field General Court Martial (FGCM).[21] The FGCM was a rudimentary form of trial reserved for soldiers on active service. It carried few protections for the accused. The dominant purpose of trial by FGCM was not to administer justice (although that was desirable) but to maintain army discipline on the front. During the Great War 3,000 British soldiers were sentenced to death after trial by FGCM. Over 300 were executed.

From the perspective of General Maxwell, the sifting of prisoners at Richmond Barracks might have required many hundreds of prisoners to be tried. He felt impelled to carry out these trials with speed and believed he had a free hand to do so. With just a few strokes of his pen he ordered that all trials take place by FGCM. It is likely that was a step that Asquith had simply not foreseen[22] and it was one of the key moments in the suppression of the Rebellion. In essence, Maxwell utilised a crude system used by the Army to maintain discipline on active service, to try civilians in Dublin in the aftermath of the Rebellion.

The dramatic impact of Maxwell's order can be seen by a brief examination of the FGCM system, where only three officers sat on the Court. The prisoner had a qualified entitlement to have free communication with his witnesses and any friend or legal adviser he wished to consult. These protections could be removed by the convening officer where 'military exigencies render it impossible or inexpedient'.[23] Additionally, in the Easter Week trials, there was no Judge Advocate.[24]

Trials by FGCM were, as a matter of law, held in public[25] but because these trials were usually convened near the Front, no member of the public ever tested the rule. In relation to Easter 1916, the public and press were not admitted to the trials. Maxwell later asserted that he ordered that the trials should take place in camera for reasons of public safety and the administration of justice. On these issues, Maxwell's observations were vague and there are reasons to doubt that he ever addressed his mind to these considerations.[26] However, the actuality was that these trials were held in camera.

As to defence evidence, a civilian in Ireland was not entitled to give evidence on his own behalf.[27] He could make an unsworn statement and could call other witnesses in support.

If the prisoner was convicted, the case was reviewed by the convening officer who had power to confirm or overturn convictions and vary sentence. There was no appellate process in the modern sense, although in every capital case the conviction was subject to the independent scrutiny of the Judge Advocate General. The royal prerogative of mercy provided a final avenue of redress.

CHAPTER FIVE

Pre-Trial Process

By 1 May, there were over 1,000 prisoners scattered round Dublin. They were held at Richmond Barracks, Kilmainham, Arbour Hill, Royal Dublin Showground in Ballsbridge, Ship Street Barracks and the hospital wing of Dublin Castle. The prisoners in outlying barracks and other holding areas were marched up to Inchicore, where they filed through the massive granite gates of Richmond Barracks and were subjected to the process of sifting prisoners for trial, deportation or release.

The mood among their captors was complex. The prisoners were variously hated, despised, pitied and admired. Some men of the Irish regiments felt the stirrings of nationalism but others in the Royal Irish Regiment and the Dublin Fusiliers were ashamed that fellow countrymen had rebelled against the Empire in its hour of danger. Richmond Barracks seethed with emotions and strong sentiments. It was a toxic and volatile atmosphere that was hardly conducive to fair trials.

Detention Pending Trial

Some of those captured before the general surrender recalled acts of humanity by individual soldiers, providing food and tea to prisoners[1] but there are as many accounts of casual brutality.[2]

The English soldiers were 'mostly decent' remembered one prisoner.[3] This was a view held by many of the insurgents, although the experience of prisoners was often very different. Brennan-Whitmore, a Volunteer officer from Wexford remembered 'kindness and consideration'.[4] Others remembered shouting and bullying. Some were relieved of wallets and watches when they arrived at Richmond Barracks.[5]

The men captured at the Mendicity Institute on the Wednesday were brought to Arbour Hill. They were provided with food and a blanket. Arbour Hill quickly filled up over the next few days. James Crenigan recalled without complaint that there was 'barely space to lie down'.[6] This was the crux of the matter. The Army were unprepared for the huge influx of prisoners.

Liam Cosgrave recalled that

```
'some 60 of us were put in a barracks room in
which there was no furniture or ventilation.'⁷
```

Chronic overcrowding was a common theme in the accounts later written by prisoners.[8] Those who could not be held in secure cells were kept in the gym where the windows were broken and the nights were too cold to allow sleep. None of the prisoners had blankets and most lacked a coat. Many walked around to stay warm and became utterly exhausted.[9]

Lack of food was a pressing issue. One prisoner remembered:

```
'a bucket containing tea and a basket with hard
biscuit rations were brought in. The biscuits were
tumbled out on the floor.'¹⁰
```

This was a shared memory among prisoners although some acknowledged the Army were also short of food.[11]

Lack of sanitation and toilet facilities did not permit the most basic acts of hygiene.[12] Some prisoners were surprisingly upbeat. A Volunteer from Swords watched from his cell window as rain swept down over Dublin: 'Grand thing to be in out of the rain' he observed. [13]

As the days passed hundreds were deported but hundreds more were brought up from Cork, Kerry, Limerick, Galway and Wexford and found overcrowding,[14] lack of toilet facilities and lice. Although it seems that in some cases, complaints were belatedly listened to and acted upon. [15]

The position of the women prisoners was equally difficult. Most of the women were held at Ship Street Barracks with a few vagrants and prostitutes, crammed in with barely space to sit down. After some days the women moved on to Kilmainham, which had not been used as a prison since the turn of the century. Here at Kilmainham there was no furniture or bedding and sanitary conditions amounted to 'a dry closet with no door'. Brigid Martin recalled soldiers around the closet 'jeering'.[16] The decision as to whether the women might be tried hung in the balance for some days but preparations to try the men began at once.

Selection of Prisoners for Trial

There is nothing in army records to show how prisoners were selected for trial. Plainly the Army were most interested in the signatories to the proclamation of independence and those who commanded troops.

The overcrowding and the increasing truculence of many prisoners made this a difficult task. Jack Plunkett, who fought at the GPO, recalled being questioned by an officer about which batch of prisoners he had arrived with:

> 'I said I did not know what batch I had arrived in. He was quite annoyed and spoke as if he thought I was trying to deceive him.'[17]

His experience was common to many prisoners.

The process of selecting prisoners for trial began at once. At the barracks, names and addresses were noted down. As the prisoners arrived they were paraded in the square and searched. Later in the gym, the detectives from G Division[18] walked the lines, picking out those they knew or thought they knew. These police officers had formed the backbone of the police intelligence service; Inspector Love, Constables Buckley and Hoey, Sergeants Gaffney, Bruton and Patrick Smyth. Sergeant John Barton carried an ash walking stick and Constable Daniel Hoey, an umbrella,[19] as they quietly walked the lines of men.

Most of the leaders were singled out in this way; MacDonagh, MacDiarmada, Ceannt, Cosgrave, MacBride and Mallin. These men and many others were all picked out and marched away.[20] Others, like Michael Collins, were not known and were not picked out.[21]

A few prisoners had given false names.[22] Joseph Gleeson, a rank and filer shaved of his moustache and gave a false name. He escaped trial.[23] One, Garry Holohan gave his real name, which was taken down wrongly as Nolan and 'this saved my life'. Holohan had taken part in the attempt to blow up the Magazine Fort. In the course of the raid, a young man by the name of Playfair had tried to raise the alarm and Holohan had chased him and shot him down only seconds before the explosion at the Magazine Fort echoed round Dublin. It was a pointless and shocking killing. Playfair's father was an army officer serving at the Front and the Army were utterly determined not to let the matter go. There was also a younger brother who was available as a witness. The Army had Holohan's name and description but were unable to find him in the press of prisoners.[24]

Some of the prisoners wore the uniform of an officer and were picked out for trial for that reason. Dick McKee was a captain but happened to be wearing a civilian overcoat and he was missed in the sift. The 'G Men' fixed on Willie Pearse because he was in the uniform of a captain. Frank Thornton, one of the Kimmage garrison wore an officer's uniform and his captors assumed, wrongly, that he was the senior officer in his party.[25] He was sent for trial but his senior officer was not.

It was a haphazard and at times capricious process. There had been a perception among many of the rank and file that they might be interned or even released and there was some amusement when Dick Davis, a first aider, was one of the first picked out for trial. This amusement turned to consternation the next day when it was learned that Davis had been sentenced to ten years' imprisonment. Many Volunteer officers were not selected for trial but some of the rank and file were. For example, young men like Liam Tobin from Cork. Tobin held no rank and he was barely out of his teens but he was called out to be tried.

Not all the officers of 'G Division' were hostile. One 'G Man' recognised a prisoner and simply said 'I am sorry to see you here.' [26] And one or two simply looked the other way when they saw a familiar face.[27]

Those not singled out for trial had their names and occupations taken again. Some remembered being fingerprinted.[28] They were then marched to the North Wall for deportation. Their places were taken by other prisoners being brought up from the country to be screened for trial, deportation or release.

Alfred Bucknill recalled that 'the only thing to do was to get the names of officers who could identify prisoners who had taken part in the fighting and having surrendered with arms'.[29] It was not an easy task: 'Some Tommies refused to identify prisoners.'[30] There is evidence that a few officers avoided becoming witnesses. The Four Courts prisoners recalled a tall Major who had been captured with Lord Dunsany and held prisoner. He made no identifications. Liam Tobin formed the view that this officer simply did not want to help.[31]

Lieutenant Chalmers had the misfortune to be in the GPO when the Rebellion began. He had been taken prisoner and spent some hours tied up before joining the other prisoners. During the evacuation of the GPO on the Friday, he and other prisoners were told to run to the safety of army lines. Chalmers was wounded in the leg as he made the dash for safety. After the surrender, Chalmers was taken by DMP Inspector Love to view the prisoners at Richmond Barracks. He was keen to lend his assistance and picked out a number of prisoners.

Sergeant Henry from the Dollymount Training School had been held at the GPO for most of the week. He identified Harry Boland as his captor.

Lieutenant King of the Royal Irish Regiment had been captured near the GPO. He was taken round the cells by the 'G Men' to search for his captor. They came upon the McGallogly brothers from Lanarkshire who were asleep on a floor. Lieutenant King recognised the younger brother, John, aged 17. He was shaken awake and taken off for trial while his brother slept. They would not meet again for many months.[32]

Jack Plunkett recalled that a Tommy held captive at the GPO had been rather too helpful to the rebels while in captivity – washing dishes and working in the kitchen. According to Plunkett this soldier had been put in fear that he might be prosecuted and even shot for assisting the rebels.[33] The soldier, Private James Murray of the Royal Irish Regiment, was only too happy to pick out prisoners. The strategy of recruiting witnesses from the pool of freed captives was not always successful. Five DMP officers held captive at Jacob's factory were presented to their erstwhile captors with a view to identifications being made. DMP constable Patrick Bermingham later recalled: 'We pretended we never saw the men before.'[34] It is not clear whether this was incipient nationalism or the manifestations of a psychiatric condition where captives form a strong bond with their captors.[35]

DMP Constable Heffernan who was held captive at the Four Courts was asked to view his captors but made no identifications. Maurice Collins recalled 'he passed me by although he knew me well'.[36] Collins avoided trial. In fact none of the 23 DMP men held at the Four Courts identified any of their captors.[37]

Jack Plunkett recalled Lieutenant Mahony of the Royal Army Medical Corps, who had been held captive at the GPO. Lieutenant Mahony 'was very indignant' when asked to give evidence. Plunkett later wrote that Mahony 'failed to recognise me when it came to giving evidence against us. I hope the cigar which I had the pleasure of giving him when he was a prisoner was a good one.'[38] Despite his protests, Lieutenant Mahony was required to inspect prisoners with a view to carrying out identifications but insisted that he was 'a Doctor not a policeman' and he made no identifications.[39]

Attempts were also made to rely on officers who took the surrender. One of the officers who took surrenders was Major James Armstrong, who was in Dublin on leave when the Rebellion began. He reported for duty and found himself attached to the 176 Brigade which had just disembarked at Dublin and set up temporary headquarters at Pembroke Town Hall in Ballsbridge. He was recalled as 'a regular officer with a string of ribbons on his tunic. He was sitting with his feet up. He had just been appointed Provost Marshal, a post he did not welcome.'[40] Major James Armstrong proved a willing witness although much of his evidence proved to be factually incorrect.

Captain Rotherham was one of the officers who took the surrender at the South Dublin Union. Eamonn Ceannt and a number of prisoners were brought for a formal identification to take place. In the pre-trial hearing Captain Rotherham deposed that he had 'seen these men yesterday, that he did not know them not having seen them before, that he would not know them again'.[41] The prisoners from Ashbourne were also brought up. Richard Mulcahy, then a junior Volunteer officer, was not picked out by his captors. He avoided trial, was interned briefly and later became Chief of Staff of the Volunteers.[42]

Another route by which prisoners were selected for trial stemmed from seized documents. Senior army officers picked through the ruins of Liberty Hall looking for documents but found nothing of evidential value. A handful of documents were seized from prisoners which gave some insight as to the identity of the senior Volunteers. One was a copy of the Proclamation, which gave the names of the signatories. Another, signed by Connolly referred to MacDonagh, Ceannt, Mallin, de Valera and Daly.[43] These documents helped the Army build on scanty intelligence and to overcome the confusion created during the surrender. When MacBride was searched he handed over a document that showed his rank as commandant at Jacob's biscuit factory. When the Mendicity Institute was overrun a search of the building yielded a notebook that gave Heuston's name and rank. The search party also found an order to Heuston to 'seize the Mendicity at all cost'.[44] And an order signed by MacDiarmada ordering Volunteers 'to report to Liberty Hall on the Monday with arms'.[45] All of these documents were utilised in the trials that followed.

Interrogation

Interrogation was part of the process by which some prisoners were selected for trial. There was no system of interrogation and no rules were in force. No records survive except in the case of Desmond FitzGerald, who made full admissions, the terms of which he partially disputed at his trial. We are therefore reliant, in large part on the accounts given by prisoners, which cannot provide a full picture. It must also be borne in mind that the experience of prisoners could be very different.

There is evidence that prisoners captured in the early days of the Rising were interrogated to secure intelligence, although the questions were often of a basic kind motivated by curiosity as much as anything else. Other questioning by soldiers was occasionally ludicrous 'Who is Sinn Fein?' one prisoner was asked.[46] A few prisoners recalled that brutality was used to secure information about the role of other prisoners[47] although this yielded no information and appeared to tail off quickly.

There were other clumsy attempts to trick information out of prisoners[48] or intimidate them into incriminating others.[49] Occasionally, a soldier in 'mufti' was put in amongst the prisoners to try and get information about the leaders.[50]

Some prisoners were questioned at the point of capture. According to an account by Tom Grace, he readily admitted shooting at troops in

Northumberland Road. Grace did not suggest that any coercion was used by his questioners nor was he brought to trial.[51] William Brennan-Whitmore recalled that even before he was brought to barracks, being closely questioned by an 'austere' colonel who carried out the interrogation with 'meticulous care' but no force or threats were used and nothing came of the questioning.[52]

Once brought to Richmond Barracks, some recalled cursory questioning to establish identity but nothing more.[53] Diarmuid Lynch[54] recalled that there were efforts to question prisoners about where they fought and who their commanding officers were, but these questions were stonewalled by prisoners. Jack Plunkett also recalled interrogation.[55] According to one prisoner, some of the younger detainees were separated from the others and given a grilling.[56] In none of these accounts is it suggested that threats were used.

Eoin MacNeill (Chief of Staff of the Volunteers) recalled that whilst a prisoner at Arbour Hill, the sentries took to firing blanks in his direction. After one such episode he was interviewed by Major Price, the Intelligence Officer at Dublin Castle. He was offered his life in return for a statement implicating the Home Rule MPs Dillon and Devlin.[57] There is no evidence that this technique was used on other prisoners.

The available evidence suggests three conclusions. First, that for the most part, interrogations were not conducted with force or the threat of force. Second, the main purpose of the questioning was to establish the identity of prisoners. In general, evidence obtained by questioning was not relied on at trial although a few exceptions can be identified.[58]

While these investigations were taking place inside the barracks, other lines of inquiry were being chased down elsewhere. Prisoners' homes were being searched and the hospitals checked for wounded.

Search Evidence

Gerald Doyle, a prisoner from Goldenbridge, had the wit to give an old address that was soon searched and 'wrecked' by soldiers.[59] The Ceannt home was also ransacked.[60] The homes of MacDiarmada, O'Hanrahan[61] and MacBride were all subjected to a tidy search. Desmond FitzGerald was arrested at home after escaping from the GPO and trekking home to Bray. There is direct evidence that the homes of each of these prisoners were searched. There is sufficient evidence to infer that prisoners' homes were searched wherever possible. Curiously, evidence gleaned from searches was not used in the trials, although it is clear that in some cases, material seized formed the basis of intelligence reports which went before General Maxwell during the process of confirmation.

The Wounded

The hospitals, especially the Richmond and the Mater, were filled with wounded people, many of them Volunteers. Paddy Morrissey, captured at the South Dublin Union with 'a badly shattered leg' was taken to Richmond Hospital and escaped 'in a milk cart'.[62] Nicholas Laffan, who had held a command role at the Four Courts, sustained a head wound. He was interviewed in hospital and told the DMP officer that he had been wounded while out buying bread. There was nothing to contradict his account and he was left in his hospital bed until he later slipped away.[63] At the Mater Hospital, Patrick McCrea was treated for gunshot injuries while a DMP officer stood guard over him. The nursing staff made a dinner for the DMP man and took this opportunity to usher the wounded Volunteer out of a side door.[64]

The DMP did the rounds of the Dublin hospitals, identifying wounded Volunteers. But they lacked resources and more than a few wounded Volunteers simply chose their moment to slip away. Liam Archer (later Chief of Staff of the Free State Army) was one, and there were many more that were bed-bound but never arrested.[65]

Being wounded might mean that a prisoner was hospitalised and avoided the scrutiny of the 'G Men'. But being wounded was not necessarily a bar to trial. Connolly was tried in his hospital bed and Willie Corrigan was tried despite having facial wounds.[66] Richard Balfe was left for dead at the Mendicity Institute. He was taken prisoner and moved to Richmond Barracks in 'an armed ambulance' but he was too badly wounded to be tried immediately and the delay saved him from trial. William Staines, also wounded at the Mendicity, escaped trial for the same reason.[67]

A number of wounded prisoners were moved to Richmond Barracks but the more badly wounded were moved on to Dublin Castle.

The Red Cross Hospital at Dublin Castle became crowded with wounded Volunteers. Many escaped trial because they were gravely wounded. These included Cathal Brugha, second in command of the South Dublin Union who had sustained a multiplicity of wounds. He was not expected to live. He survived and only a few years later became Minister of Defence in the first Dáil Éireann. Also wounded were Noel Lemass and Harry Colley, later Senator,[68] and Patrick O'Daly who led the raid on the Magazine Fort. Seán O'Keefe, who had been wounded by his own men, was another.[69] A few recovered sufficiently to be deported but for the most part, they were not pursued.[70]

It seems that the DMP understandably took the view that this was the end of the affair rather than the beginning. And so these wounded men were not pursued with vigour. Both the Army and the DMP failed to grasp the obvious fact that these men had been in the thick of the fighting and would later re-emerge as their most determined opponents.

The Young

Some prisoners recalled a staff officer passing through the ranks of prisoners stopping to peer at the youngest prisoners and bark 'Fall Out'. These prisoners were released.[71] Some teenage prisoners were held for over a week but then released.[72] Approximately 121 prisoners aged 18 or under were released in this way.[73] This process weeded out most of the younger prisoners but not all. A small number of teenagers were tried, a few as young as 16.[74]

The Women

The mere fact that a prisoner was a woman was enough to avoid trial, for all but one. Although, contrary to popular histories, women in the insurgent ranks were not confined to cooking, caring for the wounded or messenger duties.[75] Despite the efforts of many senior Volunteers, a small number of women carried arms[76] and, notably within the Citizen Army, fought in the Rebellion.[77] Margaret Skinnider was wounded in the fighting at Saint Stephen's Green[78] and Kathleen Lynn was the senior surviving Citizen Army officer at City Hall. A small number of women were wounded or killed by gunfire.[79] The benign prejudice of the Volunteers who tried to exclude women from taking part in the Rebellion was matched only by the determination of the Army not to try them. When the surrender came, a few of the captured women were simply allowed to walk away. Only one woman was tried.[80] The other 82 captured women were interviewed by Wylie who recommended that a handful be detained and the rest released: 'I chased them off home.'[81] They were, agreed Maxwell, 'silly little girls'. Five were deported and the rest were released.

Wylie later expressed the hope that the women remembered him as 'the gallant Second Lt'. They did not. At least those who wrote about their experiences did not recall Wylie, only the process of interview in which their admissions to taking a full part in the Rebellion were ignored. They emerge as educated, articulate, formidable women. Maire Perolz ran her own newspaper, the *Spark* and acted as a courier in the Rebellion. Helena Molony owned the *Workers' Republic*, which was edited by James Connolly. Winifred Carney was secretary to Connolly in the GPO throughout the fighting and Helena Molony and Dr Kathleen Lynn served at City Hall.

This is how prisoners were selected for trial. Those prisoners who were not sifted out were assigned a number, which was attached to their file. The number does not appear to have borne any relationship to the order in which prisoners were tried or to have any special significance other than provide an insight into the attitude of the Army to the process of trying large numbers of civilians. Prisoners assigned a number were then brought before an Assistant Provost Marshal for the taking of the Summary of Evidence.

The Summary of Evidence

The taking of the Summary of Evidence meant that a potential witness gave evidence before an investigating officer and produced any relevant exhibit. The accused was present at the hearing and was permitted to cross-examine and or make a statement. This practice was laid down in the rules of procedure[82] and was regarded as a protection for the accused. It also fulfilled an important function for the Army in that it was a rudimentary method of establishing if there was a case to go to trial and whether there were gaps in the evidence. We know this procedure took place because there are occasional references in the surviving case papers[83] to prisoners being brought before the Provost Marshal for the Summary of Evidence. Many of the prisoners plainly did not understand what was taking place. Here is one prisoner's recollection:

> 'In Kent's case he enquired if that were a court and if he were bound to answer. Major Armstrong appeared to be amazed at the question and answered "no" to both questions. Kent replying that in that case he would reserve his defence.'[84]

It appears that a Summary of Evidence was taken in respect of most prisoners. The indications are that no Summary of Evidence was taken in the case of Connolly. It is likely that this course was taken because Connolly was recovering from an operation and Maxwell was anxious to move to execution before political pressures intervened.

The officer who took many Summaries of Evidence was Lieutenant Bucknill, who perhaps, was the first officer to appreciate the need to collate evidence in a systematic manner. While the Rebellion was still in progress, Bucknill chanced on Lieutenant Watson of the Royal Irish Regiment. Watson had captured a number of men at the South Dublin Union, the day before. It was Bucknill who took the Summary of Evidence from Lieutenant Watson which identified the men he had captured and the circumstances of the fighting.[85] But as the Army became overwhelmed with prisoners the process became haphazard and chaotic.

The capricious nature of the selection process is illustrated by the fact that those who were captured early in the Rebellion were more likely to face trial and more likely to face a death sentence. All but one of the seven men captured on the first day of the Rebellion at the South Dublin Union[86] were sent for trial. This factor may also explain the courts martial of almost all the garrison at the Mendicity Institute. These prisoners inflicted significant casualties on the Army and surrendered on the Wednesday, three days before the general surrender. Twenty-five prisoners were taken. Two were seriously wounded, while the other 23 were courts martialled.[87] Those captured at later stages of the Rebellion stood a greater chance of avoiding the scrutiny of the 'G Men'. For them, deportation, rather than trial was the more likely outcome.

The Charges

Where the Summary of Evidence disclosed positive evidence of involvement in the Rebellion, a charge sheet was drawn up.

Wylie later asserted that he had framed the charges. This is highly unlikely. The probability is that the charges in the first trials were drafted by Bucknill and perhaps Lord Campbell, the Attorney General.[88]

The first prisoner to be charged was P.H.Pearse. His letter home with its damning postscript (described in Chapter 3) led to the framing of a Regulation 50 charge as follows:

```
'Did take part in an armed rebellion and in the
waging of war against His Majesty the King, such
an act being of such a nature as to be calculated
to be prejudicial to the Defence of the Realm
and being done with the intention and purpose of
assisting the enemy.' 39
```

This became the template for the primary charge laid against every prisoner.

Many prisoners, however, had no intention of assisting Germany. For men like Connolly, the result of the Great War had no relevance, save in so far as it might result in the collapse of capitalism or secure a place at a peace conference. For men like MacBride, his involvement was part of a nationalist struggle. He and many others had no knowledge of the German dimension. Some prisoners set out on manoeuvres on Easter Monday without the slightest idea that there was a rebellion afoot or any notion of assisting Germany.

This one size fits all approach to the charging process may have been entirely apposite to deal with a few of the leaders of the Rebellion but it did not meet the case of most.

A number of prisoners faced a second charge: incitement to cause disaffection. These prisoners included Mallin, Markievicz, Connolly and MacDiarmada. This charge was a direct alternative to the Regulation 50 offence.[90] It was a lesser charge and conviction was not punishable by death. The practice of the court was to consider the Regulation 50 charge first. If the court found that charge proved, there was no reason to consider the second lesser charge because it added nothing to the conviction on the capital charge. The court then routinely entered a formal not guilty verdict on the causing disaffection count. Though not logical, this was almost invariably the approach taken by the courts. In the Dublin trials, nearly all the prisoners were convicted of the Regulation 50 offence and therefore the lesser offence never fell for determination. This was the rule of practice although a single exception can be identified in the 39 cases where trial records can be identified. This relates to James Dempsey, one of the rank and file, who was convicted of both rebellion and incitement to disaffection. No reason is stated on the record but it might be inferred that the court were less than satisfied about the evidence on the primary charge and thought it might not survive post-trial review.

It should not be thought, as some distinguished historians have understandably inferred, that there was anything absurd[91] about acquittal on the lesser charge or to infer that the prisoner 'was found to be innocent'.[92] As to why a second lesser charge was preferred in some cases, there is nothing that distinguished these prisoners from many others. The decision to prefer a second charge must have reflected doubt in the mind of the officer drafting the charge, about the merits of the prosecution case on the Regulation 50 offence.

Following the decision to try a prisoner, he was given a typed copy of the charge. A difficulty for the prisoners awaiting trial at Richmond Barracks is that many were not given a copy of the charge until hours before they were tried. J.J. Heuston, who had been in command at the Mendicity, complained at his trial that he had no notice of the charge against him until a few hours previously. For him and prisoners like him there was no opportunity to consider how the charge might be addressed or rebutted by calling evidence.

Response to Charge

By the end of the second day it had become obvious that belligerent status would not be granted. Pearse denied nothing and as we will see provided the evidence that would convict him. MacDonagh barely spoke. Tom Clarke told one prisoner that the wording of the charge 'with the intention and for the purpose of assisting the enemy' provided him with an honourable basis on which to plead not guilty.[93] Clarke did plead not guilty but when it came to it, offered no defence.

The first executions took place on the morning of 3 May. Ceannt decided to fight his case and encouraged his men to do likewise. Some of the leaders advised the rank and file to say that they had been misled into taking part in the Rebellion[94] and the surviving trial records suggest many of the prisoners followed this lead and made what defence they could.

In these circumstances only one prisoner (Willie Pearse) entered a guilty plea. Some prisoners offered a guilty plea coupled with a denial that they 'assisted the enemy'. Such a plea was deemed to be equivocal and a 'Not Guilty' plea was entered by the court. One prisoner responded to the charge by asking: 'Who are the King's enemies....?' The President of the Court replied 'We'd better put you down "Not Guilty."' [95]

This reflected the practice in capital courts martial in this period – the court often entered a not guilty plea on behalf of the prisoner. Experience showed this was a safer course of action because it required the calling of evidence. This gave the court a fuller opportunity to weigh guilt or innocence or more often, to assess the culpability of the prisoner.

CHAPTER SIX

The Trials

Two standing courts were convened in a wing of Richmond Barracks. For days, the corridor outside was filled with prisoners waiting to be tried. Outside on the barrack square, close to the forge, prisoners stood in small groups or sat on a grass triangle in the sunshine. Every so often prisoners were brought down and a fresh batch of prisoners was marched up the stairs to take their trial. Jack Shouldice later complained that the 'G Men' were present throughout and 'no doubt gave our characters' to the court.[1] His fears were understandable but probably unfounded.

A prisoner described the improvised courtroom in which his trial took place as: 'a very small room with quite a lot of office furniture through which witnesses had to sidle in and out'.[2] Robert Brennan, from Wexford, remembered the three officers conducting his court martial as 'beefy men, resplendent in uniform and decorations'.[3] In one court Brigadier General Blackader sat with Lieutenant Colonel German and Colonel Kent. The President of the other court was Brigadier Maconchy.

'There was an air of righteousness about them which was astonishing' recalled Robert Brennan.[4] Less astonishing, perhaps, if one remembers that the Presidents of the standing courts, Blackader and Maconchy had done most of their soldiering in the colonies. From their perspective, rebellion was the worst crime, far worse than murder or cowardice.

On the day following the taking of the Summary of Evidence, Ceannt, MacBride and the brothers Liam and Phil Cosgrave were ushered into an improvised courtroom. Cosgrave recalled that 'there were four officers, three of whom were seated at a long table – one junior Lieut. Wylie, on left of prisoners'.[5] The preliminaries began:

```
'The officer in the centre informed the prisoners
that they were about to be tried by a Field General
Court Martial and that it was the right of the
prisoner to object to any member of the court.'
```

According to one prisoner the officers introduced themselves by name,[6] which the prisoners thought was old-fashioned courtesy.

The point of the introductions by Blackader was a simple one. The rules of procedure did not permit an officer to sit on a case in which he had personal interest or might reasonably be perceived to have one.[7] The rule was strictly enforced and any breach might result in a conviction being set aside. In this instance, Blackader was commander of the 176 Brigade which had suffered significant casualties at the hands of the men he was about to try. Even by the standards of the day, this was a significant conflict of interest, which required Blackader to step down. The same point might be made about Brigadier Maconchy who was President of the other standing court.[8]

It is clear that the prisoners were not aware of the role the officers played in suppressing the Rebellion. Nor were the prisoners given access to the rules under which the trials were conducted and it is hardly surprising they were unable to formulate an objection on the spot.

One of the prisoners, probably Liam Cosgrave, asked if he could object to the court, as opposed to the individual members. The President replied 'no'.

Legal Representation

At the outset of the trials on 3 May an event took place that the officers staffing the court were not expecting:

> 'The prisoners then inquired if legal assistance were permitted, a question which seemed to puzzle the court not a little and even Lieutenant Wylie.'

Wylie was of course Kings Counsel. Some of the prisoners recalled Wylie because he had helped take the surrender at Patrick's Park and escorted many prisoners to Richmond Barracks. He had frequently 'waved' his pistol around nervously on the long walk to Richmond Barracks:

> 'He did not appear more at ease at the court martial – first declaring that prisoners had the right to have a friend, legal or otherwise, beside him at the trial, who, however would not be allowed to speak save to the prisoner, which he later on amended by allowing the prisoners outside interviews.'[9]

The prisoners were then sent out into the square where they sat on the grass while the Court considered the question.

Wylie's advice to the court, mangled a little in translation, one suspects, was generous to the prisoners. A prisoner was entitled to have a 'Soldier's Friend' at his trial or at least to take legal advice. But there were no unqualified entitlements in a FGCM which was intended to be used for troops on active service,[10] A prisoner, who needed a friend at his trial, had to look to one of the other prisoners and do so quickly.

As a result of Wylie's intervention a barrister was summoned to the barracks to see a handful of prisoners. The barrister, Ronayne, arrived within the hour. Curiously, he too was a Volunteer but he had gone with the Redmondite faction at the time of the Volunteers' split in 1914. He was able to spend a short time with Cosgrave, MacBride and Ceannt.[11] He was not given access to any prosecution papers and was not permitted to represent any of the prisoners at their trial.[12] There is no evidence that any other prisoners were allowed to take legal advice.

There is no doubt that many of the prisoners wanted legal representation and it was badly needed. Eva Gore-Booth instructed Gavan Duffy to go to Dublin and represent her sister, Constance Markievicz. For some days Eva Gore-Booth trailed round Horse Guards in London trying to find someone to issue a pass to Duffy so he could enter the barracks. She was effortlessly batted from one office to another.[13] Other solicitors who made their way to Richmond Barracks were denied access to prisoners.[14] The situation in the provinces was similar.[15]

The prisoners were reliant on the goodwill of Wylie. Sometimes his conduct went further than the call of duty: 'Wylie was appointed for the defence' one prisoner later wrote,[16] with a less than clear grasp of the situation. The reality was that Wylie gave prisoners what assistance he could to elicit evidence, to examine witnesses or set in motion inquiries to trace defence witnesses.[17]

William Wylie's memoir gives a dramatic insight into the question of legal representation. On the evening of the first trials he went to Dublin Castle and raised the matter with James Campbell, the Attorney General:

> 'Campbell would not hear of it. He would give the prisoners no public advertising, he said and would not be satisfied unless forty of them were shot.'[18]

After the trials, the question of legal representation was not pursued with vigour in Parliament. And this is surprising because even by the standards of the time prisoners were routinely represented in criminal trials, if they had the means to pay. Asquith was adept at avoiding questions on the details of the trials. When pressed as to why the trial of Thomas Kent had been held in camera and whether the accused had been represented, Asquith said this:'[19]

> 'In the interest of the public safety it was decided to exclude the public from this Court, at which no counsel appeared for the prisoner.'

Asquith cleverly conjures up an image of a trial where counsel might have attended, if this was desired. The reality was very different. The trials were held in secret and the prisoners were denied counsel. It should be pointed out that four soldiers were tried for murder committed during the Rebellion. Each of these soldiers were provided with legal representation and tried by a General Court Martial with the protection of a Judge Advocate.[20] The contrast could hardly be more striking.

Notes of Proceedings

Wylie later wrote in his memoir that no notes were made but his memory on that issue is not reliable. Trial notes were made by the President of the Court. The notes recorded answers in the narrative form. Some prisoners recalled that not every word or even every sentence that was uttered was written down. The substance of what was said was recorded.[21]Although, Liam Cosgrave later suggested that questions directed by a prisoner to the court were not written down nor were the answers.[22] To take an example, on the second day of his trial Ceannt asked the court that he have the assistance of 'a soldier's friend'. This was refused on the ground that he had not asked for this on the first day of the trial. This exchange is not recorded in the court papers. Plunkett recalled that at the end of his trial the President wrote out a 'final summary'.[23] It is therefore important to remember that the trial records cannot be described as complete. There is one trial (O'Donovan and Shouldice) where the trial record is misleading in important respects.

Legal Experience of Officers Trying Cases

The Presidents of the standing courts were Blackader and Maconchy. Neither had legal qualifications. They would have had experience of courts martial but little or no experience of capital trials. They were both colonial soldiers who had spent most of their careers campaigning in Africa or India in defence of the Empire. As a result of Maxwell's urgent request for officers with courts martial experience, Horse Guards sent over Colonel Douglas

Sapte who had also spent decades soldiering in the colonies. He had retired in 1914 and was recalled by the Army when the Great War broke out. Sapte had no legal qualifications and little or no experience of capital trials.

The recollections of a few prisoners provide some insights into the legal ability of the officers. Jack Plunkett did not dispute his involvement in the Rising but he described the officer presiding over his trial (Colonel Sapte) as a 'buffoon' with no understanding of how to conduct the trial.[24] Jack Plunkett cannot be regarded as an impartial witness: his brother Joe had been shot by firing squad only hours before his trial. Liam Cosgrave, whose recollections were sober and detailed, described the officers' legal skills as 'most elementary'.[25]

Liam Tobin recalled prosecuting counsel opening the case against him and finishing with the words 'and the penalty for this is death'. Tobin recalled the President of the Court disagreed and said the wording of the Act was 'maybe death'.[26] The officers thumbed through the law books and discussed the issue at length. The President was correct as it turned out. Tobin was then 20 years old, from Cork city. A few years later he became Chief of Staff to Michael Collins but in Easter 1916, he was just another 'rank and filer'. Tobin made no complaint about the officers conducting the trial, although he was an articulate prisoner who might have welcomed the opportunity to look at the law books himself. Like most of the prisoners, he felt little more than a spectator at his trial. He recalled at one point the President of the Court becoming angry with an officer who removed his hat without permission; 'I wanted the President to remain calm' he recalled, with massive understatement.

There were many shortcomings in the trial process but Tobin and his co-defendants were certainly given the opportunity to cross-examine witnesses and say what they wished.

Prosecution Evidence

In broad terms the evidence called came from four different categories of witness. First, from officers or policemen held as captives during the Rebellion. Lieutenant Chalmers, held prisoner at the GPO, gave evidence against Diarmuid Lynch who did not dispute being at the GPO but described Chalmers's allegations of maltreatment as 'malicious lies'.[27] Chalmers also gave evidence against Connolly who also refuted the allegations of ill treatment. Lieutenant King of the Royal Inniskilling Fusiliers had been wandering around outside the GPO on the second day of the Rebellion when he was taken prisoner. He gave evidence against both Pearse brothers, Clarke and Connolly. He told the court the prisoners had been well treated. Cadet Mackay held prisoner at Boland's Mills gave evidence against de Valera.

Second, a small group of 'G Men' gave evidence of surveillance carried out prior to the Rebellion, to show association between the leaders.

Third, a number of officers who were involved in taking the surrender gave evidence about the prisoners they took into custody. Into this category fell Henry de Courcy Wheeler who took the surrender at O'Connell Street and Saint Stephen's Green, along with Major Armstrong who took the surrender of the garrisons at Jacob's Factory and the South Dublin Union and Lieutenant Hitzen who took the surrender at Boland's Mill. A few witnesses gave evidence against prisoners who had been seen leading rebel parties before or during the Rebellion. A final category of evidence came from searches of prisoners, which yielded incriminating documents.

In many of the trial records that survive, there was no significant dispute about the evidence given, nor any suggestion of mistake or fabrication. An exception might be Doctor Richard Hayes who fought at the skirmish in Ashbourne, during which the RIC suffered many casualties. Doctor Hayes did not dispute the verdict in his trial but recalled the sergeant who gave evidence against him 'swore the most atrocious lies'.[28]

For the most part witnesses were truthful and restrained. There were cases where the evidence given was at the very least factually inaccurate. An examination of the surviving trial records shows that Major Armstrong routinely identified prisoners captured at the South Dublin Union as having come from Jacob's Factory. Jack Plunkett recalled that a Tommy held captive at the GPO had been put in fear that he might be prosecuted and even shot for assisting the rebels.[29] Plunkett suggests that spurred on in this way he was a compliant and dangerous witness. There may be some truth in Plunkett's remarks. Private Murray gave evidence against a number of prisoners. One trial record is notable – that of Cornelius O'Donovan, a young agricultural student from Cork and his co-accused Jack Shouldice. These two men had spent the week at the Four Courts. Private Murray wrongly identified them as being part of the GPO garrison.

Identification evidence was a source of mistake in a number of cases. Jack Plunkett was mistaken for his brother George, who had held more senior rank. It was a mistake that might easily have resulted in execution. James Dempsey was incorrectly identified as a member of the Mendicity garrison who had threatened to shoot a military prisoner. In fact he had been captured on the Cabra Road.

The Defence Case

Although the scheme of DORA was to treat prisoners as subject to military law, there were differences in trial by FGCM that arose from whether the prisoner was a soldier or a civilian. Most notably a civilian was not entitled to give evidence on his own behalf. He could not be cross-examined by the prosecution or questioned by the court.[30]

The prisoners in the 1916 trials were entitled to make an unsworn statement to the court. An unsworn statement carried less evidential weight than evidence on oath. For those who had a positive case to advance it was a huge disadvantage but most of the prisoners would have been quickly undone if exposed to cross-examination. Curiously, not many of the prisoners would have welcomed the opportunity of giving sworn evidence. Most of the prisoners were devoutly religious and would have baulked at giving perjured evidence with the possibility of execution close at hand.

Mallin, MacDiarmada, Heuston, Markievicz and Ceannt all engaged with the trial process and fought their cases. O'Hanrahan made a short statement acknowledging his involvement in the Rebellion. MacBride gave the Army the documents needed to build a case against him and appears to have deliberately underscored that evidence in his closing address. George Plunkett said little except to deny causing disaffection and added: 'I was in a military organisation and merely carried out my orders.' Cornelius Colbert said nothing and it seems there were other prisoners who took the view that the trial was a formality and said little or nothing.[31]

Many prisoners told the court that they thought they were going on 'manoeuvres' and had no prior warning of the Rebellion. There is little doubt that many genuinely fell into this category. Although there were others who were more heavily involved who were only too happy to adopt this defence. These included J.J. Walsh, later TD for Cork and Harry Boland. Seán McGarry, who was a member of the IRB Executive Council also advanced this explanation and he was recommended for mercy on account that he was misled. A few prisoners like Gerald Doyle and James Morrissey, captured at the South Dublin Union, falsely maintained they were recent recruits and had no idea of what they were getting into.

'I did not fire a shot' was a defence advanced by many of the Mendicity prisoners, which was a highly unlikely scenario.[32] The Mendicity had been the site of a fierce urban battle for 48 hours and significant casualties had been inflicted on the Army. The South Dublin Union had also been the scene of heavy fighting. But here also, some of the men denied taking part in the fighting. Peadar Doyle maintained that he 'never fired a shot' and Philip Cosgrave denied having arms.[33] These accounts are common but stretch credibility. The fact that many prisoners advanced accounts of this nature made it very difficult for the Army to single out men for execution.

A small number of prisoners, like Ned Daly, Michael Mallin, Seán McGarry, Ceannt, James Melinn, Philip and Liam Cosgrave specifically denied any intention to assist the enemy. In the trial records that survive, most prisoners do not address this question and plainly failed to realise it was the cornerstone of the case they had to meet.

Others did not dispute involvement in the Rebellion but denied that they held any rank. Seán McGarry was one of these. James Burke captured at the South Dublin Union removed his sergeant's stripes after capture. When he was brought up for trial, the missing stripes were immediately noticed by the officer who captured him.

A few, like Gerald Doyle, captured at the South Dublin Union denied being armed. James Hughes, who served with the Jacob's garrison, carefully asserted that 'it had not been proved' that he was armed.

Others maintained they had a non-combatant role. J.J. Walsh, told the court that he was in charge of sand and water for use in case of fire. Fred Brooks, captured at the Mendicity said his job was first aid. Michael Scully captured at the Four Courts said he was just a messenger. Desmond FitzGerald (father of Garret) told the court that he had learned of the rising on the Monday 'when my wife told me'. On being told this, he went for dinner at the Globe Hotel and then went to the GPO where he had been in charge of food and caring for the wounded. In his disarmingly full and frank account, he accepted he took a full part and acted out of 'love of country'.[34]

William Partridge surrendered with the Citizen Army at Saint Stephen's Green. He explained his connection with the Citizen Army in terms of being a labour leader and trade unionist (which was true) and that he had been forced into taking part in the Rising against his will (which was untrue).

Few prisoners admitted taking any active part in the Rebellion and, in earshot of the firing squads, clutched at straws. Gerard Crofts said he had a skin disorder that required him to wear gloves and he was unable to hold a weapon.[35] He was, he said, just 'an auxiliary'. Michael Brady asserted that he had resigned from the Volunteers some months before. He had been returning from the races at Fairyhouse when he was forced into the ranks by a Volunteer officer. He named Captain Tom Weafer as the officer responsible. Weafer had been killed in the fighting near the GPO and this defence could hardly be tested. Perhaps that was why the prisoner used Weafer's name.

Cornelius O'Donovan and Jack Shouldice were identified as being members of the GPO garrison. There is no doubt that the allegation was incorrect, as they had spent the week at the Four Courts. But both prisoners were brought up for trial in uniform and neither could advance a credible explanation that would clear them.

Defence Witnesses

On the first day of the trials, the Court made no provision for the accused to call defence witnesses. According to Wylie, on the second day, he took it on himself to ensure that prisoners were able to call witnesses. His account was corroborated by surviving prisoners.

The rules of procedure permitted a prisoner 'to call any available witness for his defence'. Éamonn Ceannt applied to call MacDonagh to give evidence. The trial record shows 'The prisoner calls on Thomas MacDonagh who was not available as he was shot this morning.'[36]

A few of the prisoners called witnesses. Mallin denied being the commanding officer at Saint Stephen's Green. He called Laurence Kettle who had been held as a prisoner at the Royal College of Surgeons. It seems Mallin wanted the witness to confirm that he had been well treated in captivity and Kettle did just that. But when he was cross-examined, he readily agreed that Mallin had been in command. Mallin's case simply unravelled.

A few prisoners like Liam Cosgrave, had important friends in Dublin. For this reason and perhaps Wylie's intervention, he was able to get witnesses before the court.

Most prisoners were not so fortunate in their connections. Gerald Doyle from Goldenbridge called Willie Corrigan as a character witness. Corrigan described the prisoner as 'a very decent fellow'. Farce was never far away, as Corrigan was Doyle's section commander. He was next in the queue to be tried.

What does emerge, is that no prisoners had free access to defence witnesses or any opportunity to prepare their defence, which were protections laid down by the Rules of Procedure.

Duration of Trials

Most of the trials were very short – a matter of minutes. Cosgrave recalled that his entire trial lasted less than 15 minutes.[37] The trial of William Pearse and three others also lasted a similar duration.[38] All four were sentenced to death. Had the officers asked a few pertinent questions they would have discovered that the youngest prisoner, John McGallogly, was only 17.

Verdicts

Of the 160 trials that took place between 2 May and 17 May, one prisoner pleaded guilty and convictions were recorded in 149 cases. In the first week there were three outright acquittals[39] and one on the second week.[40] On 15

May six out of seven Kerry prisoners were acquitted, although this hints of an absence of evidence, rather than a factual dispute.

None of this should be surprising. Most of the prisoners who were part of the general surrender in Dublin were faced with insurmountable evidence and fewer still had an answer to put forward. It might also be remembered that the aim of a FGCM was not to dispense justice, although that was a desirable outcome. The primary purpose of this procedure was the maintenance of army discipline on active service. Under the rules governing these trials, a FGCM was only held where it appeared to the convening officer that the person to be tried had committed the offence in question.[41] Any officer trying the case could hardly dispel that preconception from his mind. Taking a contrary view to General Maxwell was not a step to be taken lightly. In one case, on the Western Front, the President of a court martial was called upon by a senior officer 'to furnish in writing a full explanation of his conduct in allowing an acquittal to take place'.[42]

The position was even more acute for those tried at Easter 1916, where the army occupied the role of prosecutor, witness, judge and victim. The officers who sat on these courts did so despite the prohibition on sitting on cases where an officer might be thought to have a personal interest.

One of the prisoners made this comment about his trial:

'It was interesting to observe the peculiar detached attitude the members displayed not only to persons but to facts also. So long as the maximum amount of evidence against a prisoner was recorded, the truth of this seemed of very minor importance.'[43]

This was a perceptive comment. A close reading of these and other trials of the period show that the Presidents placed a very high priority on ensuring that the confirming officer had the material to justify confirmation.[44]

There were undoubtedly different perspectives on this issue. Brigadier Maconchy who chaired one of the standing courts later wrote that the evidence was such that there was only one verdict possible: 'In many cases I refused to put down what they said as it only made their case worse.'[45] Maconchy's account cannot now be corroborated but there is no reason to doubt it.

One final point on verdict and sentence: the decision of the court was not announced immediately. The findings of the court had no validity until the process of confirmation had been completed. In the final stage of the trial process, the case papers went to General Maxwell to consider confirmation of conviction and sentence.

CHAPTER SEVEN

Post Trial – Confirmation, Promulgation and Execution

Confirmation

Following conviction, the notes of evidence went to General Maxwell. His task was to scrutinise the papers and confirm or overturn the conviction. He also had the power to commute a death sentence or vary a prison sentence.

The Decision-Making Process

Maxwell decided to take into account police intelligence memos. These reports were not produced in court and the prisoners did not see them or know about them. Therefore the prisoners could not test the material by cross-examination. Since they did not know of the reports they could not contradict the material by giving evidence. Nor was it open to the prisoner to put exculpatory material in front of Maxwell although the family of one prisoner was able to do so.[1]

The course taken by Maxwell was comparable to the procedure used by the Army in respect of soldiers convicted of capital crimes. Although the *Manual of Military Law* was silent about the matters that a confirming officer might take into account, the prisoner's disciplinary record and the view of his commanding officer and others in the chain of command would be taken into account.[2] The process usually took at least 14 days.

These prisoners, however, were not soldiers and the timescale was dramatically shorter, being just a day or two.

In an all too respectful biography, Sir George Arthur described the process by which Maxwell confirmed or commuted the sentences: 'the sleepless nights spent sifting evidence and seizing on every scrap of it which might mitigate that guilt'.[3] Between 2 May and 17 May 160 trials by FGCM were completed and 90 prisoners were sentenced to death. The question has to be asked whether there were pressing reasons that required such speed. This is doubtful. As of 30 April reinforcements from England were being turned back at Liverpool docks.[4] In communiqués with London, Maxwell expressed no fears of a threat from the German navy or a resurgence of rebellion in Dublin or elsewhere. This arduous timetable was one of Maxwell's making and it was a recipe for error.

Working very long hours, using incomplete and untested material was hardly a sound basis for making life or death decisions. For some, life or death turned not on what had been proved before the court martial but on police records about the conduct of the prisoner before the Rebellion.

The Decisions

Maxwell's grasp of the origins of the Rebellion was skewed to say the least. He categorised Cosgrave as 'an important leader'[5] although in 1916 Cosgrave was just a Lieutenant.[6] There were a dozen officers in his battalion who outranked him. Hunter was second in command at Jacob's and he was spared but O'Hanrahan, one of his junior officers, was executed.

This process resulted in the execution of Colbert, a junior officer, but not his immediate commanding officer, Murphy or most of the senior officers in his battalion. Willie Pearse, who held the rank of captain, was executed but not de Valera who was commandant of the Third Battalion which had inflicted shocking casualties on the Sherwood Foresters. Thomas Ashe and his men had inflicted heavy losses at Ashbourne but Ashe and his officers were not executed.

There were other anomalies. Quite a number of prisoners were not sentenced to death, but they received long prison terms. Many others were sentenced to death and then had their sentence commuted to short prison terms of three or five-years. At a stroke they suddenly found themselves far better off than those who had never been given a death sentence. [7] By way of example, James Burke an NCO was sentenced to death but his sentence was then commuted to five years' imprisonment. Richard Davis, a non-combatant first aider was sentenced to ten years' imprisonment.

'A Short History of rebels'

When the tide of public opinion began to turn against the executions, Maxwell found it necessary to defend his decisions. On 11 May Parliament was gathering to debate the executions and it was at this point that Maxwell was under most pressure.

Maxwell sent Asquith a resumé of those executed – '*A Short History of rebels*'.[8] There is a strong inference that this document was a distillation of the reports used to confirm or commute sentence. The purpose of the *Short*

History appears to be a justification for Maxwell's actions and perhaps to provide Asquith with ammunition to defend what had been done. It is clear that the *Short History*, drafted by Lieutenant Bucknill, was substantially accurate in respect of most of the prisoners.

In the cases of O'Hanrahan, Colbert and Willie Pearse, the report focuses on their involvement prior to the Rebellion. It is likely that this was why the 'G Men' picked them out for trial in the first place. For these men, the case for execution wore thinnest but Bucknill's analysis was charged with assertion rather than evidence. The report on O'Hanrahan described him as 'one of the most active members' of the Volunteers. This was hardly accurate. He was described as 'an officer in the rebel army' which was correct but he was a junior officer. The resumé against Colbert also smacks of advocacy rather than a recital of fact. There are also some notable errors. William Pearse is wrongly described as 'a commandant' and the most cursory inquiry would have revealed that he was nothing more than an aide de camp for his older charismatic brother.

The slender reasons advanced to justify the execution of Colbert, O'Hanrahan and Willie Pearse can be contrasted with the list of senior officers who were tried but not executed. Men such as de Valera and Ashe who outranked these men but were tried later. It is this factor that makes it clear that life or death depended less on evidence and more on the readiness of Asquith to exert control over the Army.

There are other more revealing insights to be gained from Maxwell's views on Constance Markievicz. The process of confirmation was designed to inject a degree of dispassionate reflection by a senior officer. Maxwell, like many men of his era could readily mitigate sentence on a woman purely on account of her sex. But he could forgive nothing once a certain boundary had been crossed and this was so with Countess Markievicz. Prior to her trial Maxwell had written to the Commander-in-Chief to inform him he intended to have Markievicz shot in the event that she was convicted. Maxwell's letter suggests he was preparing the ground:

```
'I intend to try her as she is blood guilty &
dangerous. I am of the opinion that this is the
case of a woman who has forfeited the privilege of
her sex.'[9]
```

Markievicz was tried and sentenced to death and of course there was never any doubt then or indeed since about her role. Maxwell's memorandum, written before she was tried, hardly has the ring of detachment that one might expect of a confirming officer.

In due course, her sentence was commuted by Maxwell. The trial record shows the death sentence was avoided 'solely on account of her sex'.[10] She was the beneficiary of prejudice on account of gender. Although the prejudice was not entirely that of the Army, as Asquith had made it abundantly clear that the execution of women was a sensitive political issue that required his personal clearance.[11] There are parallels with Casement's appeal for clemency later that year. While the appeal was in progress the Casement Diaries were passed round Westminster in order to undermine the campaign for clemency. This appeal to the prejudice against homosexuality fatally undermined the campaign for Casement's reprieve.[12]

Review by the Judge Advocate General

Part of the process of review and confirmation involved scrutiny by the Judge Advocate General. The scheme of the Defence of the Realm Act required that prisoners held for court martial be treated as soldiers subject to military law. Where a soldier was tried and sentenced to death under military law, his conviction was reviewed by the Judge Advocate General, who gave legal advice as to whether the conviction could stand.[13] One of the strengths of the office of the JAG was independence. In the United Kingdom, JAG staff were based in London and were therefore not susceptible to influence by local commanders. In the colonies, deputies were sometimes posted with the Army but a deputy JAG was answerable only to the JAG in London, not to the local commander. The task of the JAG was to provide independent scrutiny and legal advice. It was his constitutional role to advise the sovereign whether court martial proceedings should be confirmed or not and in fact, the sovereign always followed the advice of the JAG.

It has already been observed that Maxwell had no 'legal chief'. Nor was there any representative of the Judge Advocate General in Dublin. Where Maxwell needed lawyers to prosecute trials, young men like Wylie and Longworth were plucked from front-line service and assigned court martial duties. The only other lawyer in the Army Headquarters was Lieutenant Bucknill. Hitherto, it has been thought that the role of Deputy Judge Advocate General was filled by Lieutenant Bucknill but his service record shows that he did not assume this post until September 1917.[14] His father, Tommy Bucknill had been a daring amateur steeplechase jockey until his legal skills had taken him onto the bench. As an Old Bailey Judge, he had famously sobbed when passing sentence of death on a fellow Mason. His son was a diffident, clever but utterly conventional and un-athletic admiralty barrister. He was commissioned in the autumn of 1915 and posted to Egypt, under General Maxwell. After the Rebellion broke out, he arrived in Dublin as part of Maxwell's retinue. Bucknill was not in the best of health; he was suffering from severe sciatica. More cogently, he was not attached to the office of the JAG and had no independent powers.

Surviving correspondence shows that Lieutenant Bucknill perceived himself to be a junior member of the prosecution team. He provided assistance, not scrutiny. This finding is confirmed by examining the duties he actually performed. Bucknill took summaries of evidence,[15] he laid charges against the prisoners[16] and drafted memos for General Maxwell explaining and justifying the executions to Asquith.[17] He also assisted in drafting charges against those brought to trial in the months that followed.[18] For these services he was named in the honours list the following year.[19]

These actions are those of an officer concerned in the prosecution of offenders, not an officer providing the scrutiny and sometimes unwelcome oversight, which was, even then, the role of the office of the Judge Advocate General. This analysis is confirmed by a review of the Archives, suggesting that no officer from the office of the JAG was despatched to Ireland until mid-May.[20] It is therefore a safe conclusion that in the aftermath of the Rebellion the role of Deputy Judge Advocate General was not carried out by Bucknill or any other officer. These are critical findings because the office of the JAG provided a significant check on the power of the Generals. This safeguard was not present in these trials.

A little more needs to be said of the office of the JAG. In 1916, the Judge Advocate General was Sir Thomas Milvain KC,[21] then aged 72. He was in poor health and had begun to retreat to his family estates in Northumberland, where he died a few months later. In the spring of 1916 the office of the JAG was hard pressed under the weight of work generated by the Great War. Leadership and direction was lacking and the office of the JAG was effectively being run by Milvain's deputies. The most prominent deputy was Felix Cassel, who was of German parentage. It may be that the German dimension of the Easter Rising meant that Cassel did not feel able to assert the powers of the JAG in the spring of 1916.[22]

Later that year Milvain died and Cassel was appointed JAG and it is instructive to note that in 1921 when executions under martial law were again in prospect, Cassel was quick to intervene and insist that he personally review all death sentences. He explicitly declined to delegate this task to a deputy. This was the occasion of a notable row between Cassel and the General Officer Commanding in Ireland. Cassel argued that his right to review convictions by courts martial was 'part of my duty to His Majesty under the Letters Patent which I hold to tender my advice personally'.[23] On that occasion the Army Council sided with the JAG and his opinion prevailed. The contrast with what took place in 1916 is stark.

The Royal Prerogative

Every citizen sentenced to death was entitled to seek the protection of the royal prerogative of mercy.

This discretionary power was vested in Wimborne, the Lord Lieutenant and Governor General of Ireland by virtue of the Letters Patent granted by the sovereign. The power was extra – judicial and non-legal: 'mercy is not the subject of legal rights. It begins where the law ends.'[24] In essence it was open to every condemned citizen or his family to petition the Lord Lieutenant to exercise the power. The Lord Lieutenant usually took advice but was free to make his own decision.

This prerogative power was not ousted by the Defence of the Realm Act. We can see that this constitutional protection was for the most part scrupulously observed during the War of Independence in respect of trials under the Restoration of Order in Ireland Act.[25] In the 1916 trials, this protection was simply swept away when Maxwell arrived in Dublin on 28 April and asserted martial law powers granted to him by the Cabinet.

This issue came to a head on 7 May when John Dillon approached Lord Lieutenant Wimborne to seek clemency for prisoners awaiting execution. Wimborne acknowledged his power had been usurped by Maxwell[26] but agreed to raise the matter. Wimborne dined that night with Maxwell at the Royal Hospital Kilmainham. The next morning Wimborne wrote a courteous but furious note to Maxwell railing against the latest round of executions:

> 'After our conversation last night I was, I must admit, dismayed to learn that three comparatively unknown insurgents were executed this morning...'[27]

But for the implementation of martial law, it is likely that Wimborne would have exercised the royal prerogative at least in respect of those who were not signatories to the Proclamation of Independence. Wimborne's letter recognised that his power to consider appeals for clemency had been seized by the military. This letter offers the most compelling evidence that the prisoners were not tried by due process of law.

This point is reinforced by the fact that some months later a small number of prisoners, who were not executed, petitioned the government for clemency. These men, Tobin, Clancy and McNestry had taken part in the siege at the Four Courts. Their petitions were rejected on the ground that nothing could be done which might undermine the position of General Maxwell as military governor exercising martial law.[28]

Promulgation

Following confirmation, an officer appeared in the prisoner's cell and formally read out the findings and the sentence imposed. In the Dublin trials the gap between conviction and promulgation was usually a day or two. Gerald Doyle recalled promulgation. Four officers entered his cell and ordered him to stand to attention. The senior officer began to read:

```
'You Gerald Doyle did take part in an armed
rebellion against His Majesty the King and having
been tried by Courts Martial are found guilty and
sentenced to death.'
```

The officer stopped there, remembered Doyle.[29] After a lengthy pause the officer announced sentence had been commuted.

The theatrical pause between announcing sentence of death and commutation of sentence was part of the ritual and it was a familiar theme in the recollection of prisoners.[30] Liam Tobin recalled an officer entering his cell and informing him he had been sentenced to death. The officer then left and returned to the cell shortly after to inform him the death sentence had been commuted. It was just a joke.[31]

Last meals for prisoners awaiting execution were provided by Mrs Callender of the Lucan Restaurant at Sarsfield Quay.[32] This had nothing to do with any desire of the prisoners to eat well. Kilmainham had been defunct as a prison for many years. There was no furniture and no cooking facilities.

Prisoners were given access to family and friends before execution. And it appears that the Army made every effort to ensure final visits took place. Although in relation to Pearse, his mother was unable to get through, being delayed at an army checkpoint.[33] The Army were also unable to collect MacDonagh's wife because of sniping.[34] Plunkett was permitted to marry. A particularly distasteful aspect of what took place was the practice of allowing prisoners awaiting execution to be held within earshot of the firing squads.

Execution

Much has been written about the executions, some of it thoughtful[35] but much of it not. It was later said that Thomas Kent faced his death without a care: 'not a feather out of him'.[36] These words came from an ex-soldier seeking to ingratiate himself in Republican circles and they are hardly worth taking seriously. The official account at Westminster gave a more sombre perspective, stating that the prisoner needed to sit on a chair because of his nerves. Other lurid accounts sought to venerate the prisoners, demonise the British Army and sustain propaganda.

The truth is rather more difficult to discern and although it may be considered prurient to dwell on the way men were executed, it is relevant to this study because the executions were part of the trial process and cannot be exempted from scrutiny.

The evidence comes from a number of distinct sources. First, an Assistant Provost Marshal gave a sketchy account to a fellow officer.[37] Another can be gleaned from a second-hand account given by an ex-DMP officer, Sergeant Soughley, who served at Kilmainham but was not present at the executions. There is also an account of one execution by an officer who commanded a firing squad.[38]

A fourth source can be found in accounts given by other prisoners at Kilmainham, where a few were able to hear the volleys, with varying degrees of clarity. Kilmainham was an eighteenth-century gaol with thick stone walls and what a prisoner might be able to hear would depend very much on the location of his cell and so these accounts are difficult to evaluate.

A fifth source is provided by members of the clergy who attended the later executions and gave first-hand accounts. But these accounts tend not to be revealing because they dwell more on the spiritual aspects of the executions and were careful to spare the feelings of families. A final source comes from the records created after the executions.

In order to understand what happened at these executions, it is necessary to explain how the process worked.

In the Army there was a procedure for everything, and this included the process of execution. By tradition, execution took place at dawn or as early as possible in the day. There was no prescribed number for a firing squad but in 1916, it consisted of 12 men marshalled by an NCO and commanded by an officer. The squad fired from a range of 10 paces.[39]

Pearse, MacDonagh and Clarke were all executed within minutes of each other by a single firing squad commanded by a junior officer under Major Rhodes, an Assistant Provost Marshal.[40] He was a curious choice for this difficult duty as we will see.

There were a number of odd features attached to these executions. The use of a firing squad to carry out more than one execution was a significant departure from existing convention and a direct contravention of orders issued by General Staff.[41]

A second odd feature was that no clergy were permitted to be present at the executions of Pearse, MacDonagh and Clarke. This was also a significant departure from convention and a protest was made by the clergy who were ministering to the prisoners.[42]

Third, the certificate of execution named Captain Lynch as the medical officer present at the executions (although it is an odd fact that the death certificate was signed by Captain Stanley of the Royal Army Medical Corps (RAMC)).

One final, quite curious detail emerges. Major Rhodes was relieved of further execution duty immediately after the executions of Pearse, MacDonagh and Clarke and assigned far less onerous tasks.[43] If Major Rhodes had carried out his duties correctly, it is unlikely that he would have been relieved. A clue may lie in what happened to Major Rhodes next. Before the year was out he was permitted to relinquish his commission on the ground of ill health. This was due to partial blindness, said not to arise from his service in the Army. The record of the Medical Board shows: 'left eye practically blind and less than 6/36 in right eye with glasses'. In May he was supervising the executions and by November he was nearly blind, a rather sudden deterioration on the face of it. He was found to be 'unfit for general service at home and abroad and also for office work'. There is, however, another more revealing entry in his file, stating that Major Rhodes was 'not fit for a post necessitating much nervous strain'. There is sufficient evidence to infer that it was his mental state, rather than his eyesight, that required his retirement.[44]

It is inconceivable that Major Rhodes would have been ordered to oversee the execution of the rebel leaders if there had been any doubt about his mental fitness. It follows therefore that the concerns about his psychiatric state arose after May 1916 and referred to the manner in which he carried out his last stressful duty, which was the executions of Pearse, MacDonagh and Clarke.

Rhodes was replaced on execution duty by Major Heathcote who was another territorial officer. He was an architect in civilian life.[45] Heathcote issued new and very detailed orders for the next round of executions. The detail of the new orders suggests Heathcote had prior experience of execution duty and that is probably why he was chosen.[46] The fact that detailed new orders were necessary also implies that the procedures the night before had not been satisfactory. One of Heathcote's new measures was to require a separate firing squad to be convened for each prisoner.[47] He also permitted clergy to be present at execution if the prisoner wished.

The task of execution was more difficult than might be imagined. A volley of bullets from a firing squad armed with Lee Enfield rifles from a range of 10 paces could wreak terrible damage but did not always kill. On the Western Front this was sometimes due to the reluctance of men on the firing party. Men chosen for this duty were often resentful, insubordinate and occasionally refused to take part,[48] fired wide or failed to shoot.[49] Sometimes the Army got round this difficulty by not informing the firing party of the nature of their duty until the moment of execution arrived, so that the troops could not confer.[50] Sometimes officers explained to firing parties that it was in the interest of the prisoner that they shoot straight. Even these measures were not enough to prevent some men firing wide. There are a number of well-documented examples in other theatres of war where a prisoner survived the blast and had to be finished off with a pistol at close range.

The Army used a number of strategies to ensure that the executions were effective and swift. The rifles were loaded out of sight of the firing party. Eleven were loaded with 'ball' and one with blank. This encouraged men to take part in the execution in the hope they might be one who fired the blank.[51]

The natural disinclination to shoot down an unarmed man was strong, even where the prisoner had been convicted of murder or deserting his post.[52] Did this reluctance extend to the shooting of rebels who had recently fought against the Army? All of the executions were carried out by the Foresters who had suffered such heavy casualties at Mount Street and it may be that this is why they were chosen for firing squad duty. One of the firing squads was commanded by Second Lieutenant A.A. Dickson, who reported no lack of enthusiasm for the task. He based his view on comments made by a few men, although bravado by a few may not have reflected the feelings of the majority of the firing squad. Nearly all of the Foresters were still raw recruits. They were church-going conscripts from villages and farms who had become a part of the newly formed 59 Division. This was the first time that they would have been called on for execution duty.

It should be remembered that after an execution there would be no post mortem and the body of the prisoner was buried in minutes. In Dublin, immediately after execution, the bodies were moved by horse-drawn ambulance to Arbour Hill and buried in quicklime after a short service.

For all these reasons, the Army needed to impose supervision on the conduct of executions. This was achieved by requiring an Assistant Provost Marshal to be present to ensure that the prisoner executed was the prisoner who had been sentenced and that the orders laid down were carried out. After the execution the Provost would write a certificate of execution confirming the bare details of the execution, identifying the prisoner and stipulating the time and date of execution.

The second method of supervision was the presence of an officer of the Royal Army Medical Corps. This officer was required to pin a white card over the prisoner's heart to give the men a clear target. After the execution he was required to write a certificate of death setting out the bare facts and that death had been 'instantaneous' which was the standard on which the Army insisted.[53] Courts martial records of soldiers of this period show that very occasionally the doctor would record 'death was practically instantaneous' which the Army did not consider to be an acceptable standard. Rarely, the doctor's report might record that 'death was not instantaneous. The coup de grace had to be administered by the officer in charge of the firing party.' [54] But in all cases the Army expected a finding that 'death was instantaneous'.

The certificate of death for Pearse, MacDonagh and Clark, however, reads:

```
'The prisoners were dead before the commandant
disposed of the bodies.'⁵⁵
```

It should be added that in executions of this era, it is unique to find a death certificate that pertains to more than a single prisoner. The inference is that for at least one of these prisoners, death did not come swiftly and a bland composite certificate was written to disguise that fact. Whatever took place, it is a fair inference that Major Rhodes's mental state began to deteriorate after that.

What took place in respect of the other prisoners who were executed? An officer of the Foresters later wrote an account of an execution that he maintained was properly carried out. A few members of the clergy also wrote about these events but their accounts are framed in terms of spiritual deliverance and promoting the faith. There is a good deal of third-hand hearsay[56] but a paucity of hard evidence. Markievicz was also a prisoner in Kilmainham and very soon after reported that some of the executions required 'repeated volleys' but this may have been said for propaganda reasons and must be treated with considerable scepticism.[57]

There are two first-hand accounts of the executions on 8 May, when Ceannt, Colbert, Heuston and Mallin were executed. One was written by the officer who commanded a firing squad:

```
'The thirteen rifles went off in a single volley.
The rebel dropped to the ground like an empty sack
. . . I was glad there was no doubt the rifles
had done their work and there was no need for me
to do what the old Major had told me, about the
officer going back and finishing the job with his
revolver.'⁵⁸
```

Here is an account of another execution the same morning written by Rose McNamara, who had been vice-commandant of Cumann na mBan at Marrowbone Lane. McNamara was being held in Kilmainham. She kept a diary in which she recorded an entry for 8 May:

> 'Loud reports of shots at daybreak. We say prayers for whoever it was; heard terrible moans; then a small shot. Then silence.'[59]

Captain Stanley (the medical officer) later let slip: 'the rifles of the firing party were waving like a field of corn'.[60] After these executions on the 8 May, Captain Stanley asked to be excused attendance at further executions.[61]

Something of value might be gleaned from the death certificates for these prisoners. But an examination of the prisoners' courts martial records shows that the death certificates have been removed in respect of Willie Pearse, Plunkett, O'Hanrahan, Daly, MacBride, Mallin, Ceannt, Heuston, Colbert, MacDiarmada, Connolly and Kent.

There is no doubt that the death certificates existed and were placed on the courts martial record in the usual way, as they are referred to in the files. It was the practice of the Army to place the death certificate and certificate of execution on the prisoner's file which was then sent to the Office of the Judge Advocate General. The practice was uniformly observed in relation to all prisoners and there are many examples from executions on the Western Front in 1916[62] and subsequently in respect of executions carried out by military courts in Ireland in 1921.[63] In the case of MacBride, by way of example, Major General Sandbach forwarded the papers to the JAG in London with an express reference that the death certificate is 'Enclosed'. [64]

The absence of a death certificate in respect of just one or two prisoners might be attributable to misfiling or an omission by a clerk. The absence of the certificate in respect of all these prisoners suggests that the certificates were deliberately removed after the event. There is evidence that copies of the certificates were gathered together in a central file but the certificates are absent from this file also.[65]

The question is whether this was done for a proper administrative reason – it is difficult to imagine one – or because the contents might be a source of embarrassment. One would tentatively suggest that embarrassment could only arise if the certificates suggested that one or more of the executions had not been carried out properly and there was a danger of the files being made public.

The potential for embarrassment was certainly present. By mid-May the circumstances of Connolly's execution began to leak out and it was a moment of acute embarrassment for the government. At Whitehall civil servants claimed that nothing was known at Westminster about Connolly's wounds; the execution was 'purely a local affair'.[66] This was quite untrue; Asquith had been informed in writing.[67] Even then the full truth did not emerge. The official account that he was shot sitting in a chair was untrue. He was lying stretched out, feet forward, head rolling back, almost prone and according to the Provost Marshal 'quite unconscious'.[68]

It should be remembered that events in Ireland were part of a wider debate about army courts martial. The Army resisted scrutiny into trials and executions of soldiers on the Western Front. At first, in order to quell public disquiet, Asquith made a commitment to publish the trial records in unequivocal terms: 'I will arrange for this to be done'.[69] It seemed then, that disclosure was a foregone conclusion. However, the Permanent Secretary of State for War, Sir Reginald Brade, and the Army Council orchestrated opposition to this process.[70]

Asquith's administration disintegrated in December 1916 and the new Lloyd George government declined to disclose trial records on the ground that it was not in the public interest.[71] In response to individual requests from widows and family, the JAG refused access on the ground that the entitlement of a prisoner to a copy of his trial record did not extend to executors and family and that in any event the Army Council claimed privilege on the ground of public policy.[72] Ceannt's widow, for one, tried to get hold of the trial record of her late husband without success. But there was a window of some months when it seemed that the trial records would be made public and that there was considerable disquiet that this would have an adverse impact on the war effort. The trial records could not be made to disappear but the death certificates could be destroyed or simply removed from the files.

CHAPTER EIGHT

Due Process

The primary question is not whether the prisoners were innocent or guilty, whether they were fairly tried nor whether the conviction rate was significantly high or not. All these are interesting and important questions which because of the passage of time and the destruction of most of the trial records can never be satisfactorily answered. Even where trial records exist, they are not sufficiently detailed to provide reliable answers to these questions. The primary question is, applying the standards of the time, whether the prisoners were tried by due process.

Right at the heart of this question lies the fact that these trials were conducted in private. No press, public or lawyers were admitted. The year after the Rebellion, George Gavan Duffy, a campaigning solicitor, brought an action for a writ of habeas corpus challenging the legality of the trials on this ground.[1] General Maxwell swore an affidavit stating that he gave the order for the trials to take place 'in camera' because it was 'necessary for the public safety and for the defence of the realm'.[2] Maxwell's contention that he gave such an order and did so for the reasons he specified, was never challenged or tested.[3] The legal argument focused on the legality of the 'in camera' order.

The central argument for the prisoners was that the rules of procedure governing Field General Court Martial did not permit the exclusion of the public. Further, that if such a power existed it was for the government to show that 'necessity' required exclusion of the public. Gavan Duffy briefed Ferdinand Schiller Kings Counsel,[4] one of the foremost advocates of that era although the German–Irish connection may have carried an unwelcome echo of recent events.

Counsel for the Crown was the Attorney General, F.E. Smith. In court, Smith was an outstanding advocate. Out of court he was arrogant and a heavy drinker but was reckoned to be the cleverest and sometimes the rudest man of his generation. 'F.E'. was certainly the only man known to the public simply by his initials. Also appearing for the Crown was the Solicitor General, Sir Gordon Hewart. This was the strongest legal team the government could field and the message about the importance of the case was clear. If the prisoners' action was successful then it meant that the trials had been unlawful: the leaders of the Rebellion had been unlawfully executed and the surviving prisoners would have to be freed. Linked to this case were so many other unresolved issues: Asquith's pledge to publish the trial records; whether a general amnesty might be granted to the prisoners; whether conscription in Ireland might still be possible. A great deal rested on the decision of the Court.

F.E. Smith was in all respects the best choice to defend this difficult position. Smith privately conceded the government case was fraught with difficulty. His view was shared by the JAG who took the view that the 'in camera' order could only be justified as an act of martial law. The government law officers expressed a similar opinion.[5]

Because of the importance of the issues raised, the case was put before the Lord Chief Justice. In that era, the role of the Lord Chief Justice was closely linked with the executive and Lord Chief Justice Reading's determination to contribute to 'the national effort' has been well documented in David Foxton's outstanding study of this era.[6] F.E. Smith, who was a member of the Cabinet, must have understood only too well where the sympathies of the Lord Chief Justice lay. Smith simply needed to muster a credible argument that the Court might accept without embarrassment.

His argument may be distilled to this: that the decision to sit in camera was 'necessary for the public safety and for the defence of the realm'. F.E. Smith argued that there was an undoubted power in the High Court to exclude the public and therefore 'it must a fortiori be possessed by a general court martial and still more by field general court martial'.[7] This argument was accepted by the Court. The finding of the Court has since been criticised on the ground that although the High Court has an inherent jurisdiction to regulate its own proceedings, a court martial is a creature of statute, so if the power is not conferred by statute it does not exist.[8]

A subsidiary argument advanced by the prisoners was that if there was a power to sit in camera, then that power had to be exercised judicially by each court martial. The circumstances in which the first trial held on 2 May might well be different from a trial the following day or the following week. The court disposed of this argument quickly:

```
'we  must  assume  that  the  field  general  courts
martial  convened  by  him,  which  he  was  the  proper
person  to  convene,  and  which  sat  in  consequence,
held  the  same  view.'
```

There is a question here as to whether these trials took place in camera because the Commander in Chief ordered it or because the officers who were carrying out trials in the same building all exercised an independent judicial judgement and came to the conclusion the court must sit in camera. This latter argument is hardly persuasive.

In the course of his judgment, Lord Chief Justice Reading explored the possibilities that might arise if the trials were held in public. The first possibility was that people might enter and shoot witnesses. Second, he surmised, witnesses might be exposed to retribution. L.C.J. Reading's first observation hardly bears scrutiny. Richmond Barracks was a heavily guarded fortress. The Rebellion had been crushed and most of the population were entirely loyal or at least acquiescent.

The possibility that witnesses might suffer retribution for giving evidence is an argument that deserves the most careful consideration. In fact, in most of the trials, the witnesses were soldiers, most of whom had come to Ireland after the Rebellion had started and would depart as soon as order was restored. There were a handful of police officers and civilian witnesses who would be at risk and this should be acknowledged. Three DMP officers who gave evidence at the trials were later shot dead during the War of Independence. Curiously, the obvious inference is not the correct one. A close examination of those cases shows that these officers were killed for reasons unconnected with their role in the trials.[9] Other civilian witnesses were not harassed in any way.[10]

Even if witness protection was a live issue, it is doubtful that this factor could justify the court to sit in camera. Witness protection is an issue in most jurisdictions and it has long been an issue in Ireland's troubled history but this factor has never before or since justified trials in camera. It should be pointed out that a few years later during the martial law era of 1921, the press and the public were admitted to trials under martial law without difficulty.[11]

Finally, although the 'in camera' order was upheld in *ex parte Doyle*, the court did not acknowledge the mischief that this caused. The observations of Mr Justice Darling crystallised the thinking of the court:

> 'the Court was not open to the public. That is all the complaint comes to.'[12]

There was a little more to it than that. These courts were convened at dates and times which were not publicly known and with such speed and secrecy that it was not possible to test the legality of the proceedings by a writ of habeas corpus. It was hardly surprising that witnesses were unavailable or that families were unable to organise legal advice – in fact some lawyers were turned away from Richmond Barracks. All these difficulties hinged on holding the trials in secret.

Inevitably *ex parte Doyle* was decided against the prisoners. There are some legal disputes which can never be divorced from the political context in which the argument takes place. While the lawyers argued, allied troops from all over the Commonwealth were fighting and being killed on the Western Front. It was hardly likely that the Lord Chief Justice would forsake the government at such a crucial juncture. The case might be viewed on the one hand as a cosy establishment conspiracy or an example of the way standards in law inch forward. Sir Gordon Hewart, counsel for the Crown in *ex parte Doyle*, later became Lord Chief Justice and achieved lasting fame in another case when he ruled that 'Justice should not only be done but should manifestly and undoubtedly be seen to be done'.[13]

The scope of the ruling in *ex parte Doyle* needs to be defined. Maxwell's contention that the trials were conducted under DORA was not challenged for tactical reasons. Gavan Duffy preferred to avoid a factual dispute and confine the argument to law. Therefore the issue of whether the trials were in fact conducted under DORA or martial law was never the subject of argument. Second, a court can only rule on the material that is placed before it. The only witnesses to the trials were the officers who prosecuted or sat in judgment in these trials. The only other potent source of evidence lay in the trial records of those who had been executed. But only a prisoner could require the Army to release his trial record.[14] Efforts to secure trial records made by the families of executed prisoners had been successfully resisted by the Army Council. Ultimately, *ex parte Doyle* failed because of the determination of the military and a small group of influential politicians to suppress the trial records and the readiness of the courts to support the executive at a time of crisis. So it is that the decision in *ex parte Doyle* did not resolve the question of whether the prisoners were tried under the Defence of the Realm Act or not. It is that issue we now address.

The evidence thus far reviewed shows that the government intended to limit Maxwell's powers to conduct trials to the statutory regime under DORA. The evidence, however, also shows that the entire country was under martial law from the moment of Maxwell's arrival: the suppression of the Rising, the arrest of the prisoners, the deportations, round ups and internment of thousands of prisoners were not carried out under any statutory or common law power; they were carried out under martial law. The numerous martial law proclamations requiring the surrender of arms, restrictions on movement and association bear witness to this.

After the first few days of May the continuance of martial law could hardly be justified by necessity. The reason why the extension was permitted was summed up by the government law officers: martial law allowed the army to take steps 'where there may be no appropriate regulation under

DORA'.[15] In other words, General Maxwell could do what he thought necessary without needing to consider what the law permitted. It is unrealistic to suggest that the suppression of the Rebellion was effected by martial law but the prisoners were tried under statutory powers granted by Parliament.

Although Maxwell adopted the formal language and proformas of trial under DORA, the evidence suggests that the prisoners were tried under a trial regime of Maxwell's creation and there are a number of other factors that support this analysis. First, for reasons set out in the last chapter, the prisoners did not receive the usual protection afforded by the Judge Advocate General.

The second is that the Lord Lieutenant was not permitted to exercise his constitutional duty to consider the exercise of the royal prerogative of mercy.

Third, the rules of procedure entitled the prisoner the time to prepare his defence, have free communication with his witnesses and any friend or legal adviser he wished to consult. These protections could be removed by the convening officer where 'military exigencies rendered it impossible or inexpedient'. [16] There is no evidence that General Maxwell gave any order removing these protections. But a review of the surviving trial records suggests that these provisions were largely bypassed. A comparison with trials on the Western Front shows that soldiers on trial by FGCM were usually represented by an officer who would have access to a copy of the rules under which the trials were conducted. The Dublin prisoners did not have representation or access to the rules under which the trials were carried out.

The trial records, to the extent that they can be traced, are set out in the chapters that follow. To a great extent they provide the evidence that underlies this analysis and others are free to make an informed judgment.

CHAPTER NINE

The General Post Office

Once seen, never forgotten. Archive images of the charred ruins of the GPO remain an iconic reminder of a turbulent century. After all these years the bullet marks in the columns of the facade bear silent witness to a brazen assault on the Empire.

The heart of the Rebellion was at the General Post Office, which was seized on Easter Monday 1916. The GPO acquired a number of outlying posts designed to impede a frontal infantry assault. The anticipated assault never came and the outlying units retired to the GPO. In the end, it was the fires caused by an artillery barrage that began to overwhelm the building. On the Friday evening, the remnants of the garrison relocated to Moore Street before the surrender the following afternoon. At the most, the GPO garrison numbered 460.[1]

As far as can be established, at least 23 GPO prisoners were tried by courts martial.[2] Fifteen were sentenced to death and of these six were executed.[3] The balance had their death sentences commuted to prison terms.[4] Seven others were sentenced to prison terms.[5] One prisoner was acquitted.

Where trial records can be traced they are set out in the chapters that follow. In respect of some prisoners, the record of trial has not been preserved but a fragment here and there survives[6] and it is possible to piece together some of the more extraordinary events.

John R. Reynolds was one of the prisoners held at the Rotunda overnight and marched up to Richmond Barracks the following day. He was seen arriving at the barracks on the point of collapse. Here, he was relieved of his wristwatch in exchange for water. When his trial was called on a few days later he had recovered his wits. He told the court that on Easter Monday his daughter had been buying stamps at the GPO when the building was stormed. He went in to look for her and both he and his daughter were held captive all week. In fact Reynolds was a Volunteer. He belonged to a company that did not drill because of the age or work commitments of the men. It may be for this reason he was not known to the G men of the DMP and no rebuttal evidence could be called. His daughter Molly was in the Cumann na mBan and they had both spent a busy week in the GPO.[7] He was the only GPO prisoner to be acquitted.[8]

CHAPTER TEN

P. H. Pearse

Pearse was tried at Richmond Barracks on 2 May. Brigadier General Blackader presided.[1] Pearse was charged that he 'Did an Act to wit, did take part in an armed rebellion and in the waging of war against His Majesty the King such act as to be calculated to be prejudicial to the Defence of the Realm and being done with the intention and for the purpose of assisting the enemy.'

The trial record is set out below:

'2nd Lt. S.L. King 12th Royal Inniskilling Fusiliers (12th Battn) being duly sworn-
I was on duty at the Rotunda Dublin on Saturday 29th April. The Sinn Fein was firing at the soldiers. The accused came from the neighbourhood from which the shots were being fired. The accused was in the same uniform in which he is now, with belt sword and revolver on and 3 containers with ammunition. The accused surrendered to General Lowe.
The accused cross examines the witness-
Q Where you a prisoner in our hands and how were you treated?
A I was and was very well treated.
Constable Daniel Coffey Detective Department Dublin Metropolitan Police being duly sworn states-
I was present when the accused Pearse was in custody at Irish Command HQ at about 5pm Saturday 29th April. I identify him as a member of the Irish Volunteers. I have seen him several times going through the city with bodies of men and acting as an officer.
The accused does not cross examine this witness.
Sgt. G. Goodman Military Police (Prov) at Staff Corps being duly sworn states
I was on duty at Arbour Hill Detention Barracks on the 1st May.

I saw the accused writing the letter now produced
to the Court. He handed it to me. The letter is
marked X and attached and signed by the President.
(Author's note: the letter to his mother contained
a full admission of his part in the rebellion and
a short crucial postscript: 'I understand that the
German expedition on which I was counting actually
set sail but was defeated by the British.')
The accused does not cross examine this witness.
Prosecution closed.
The accused calls no witnesses in his defence.
The accused makes the following statement.
My sole object in surrendering unconditionally was
to save the slaughter of the civil population and
to save the lives of our followers who had been
led into this thing by us. It is my hope that the
British government who has shown its strength will
also be magnanimous and spare the lives and give
an amnesty to my followers, as I am one of the
persons chiefly responsible, have acted as C in C
and president of the provisional government. I am
prepared to take the consequences of my act. But I
should like my followers to receive an amnesty. I
went down on my knees as a child and told God that
I would work all my life to gain the freedom of
Ireland. I have deemed it my duty as an Irishman
to fight for the freedom of my country. I admit
I have organised men to fight against Britain. I
admit having opened negotiations with Germany. We
have kept our word with her and as far as I can
see she did her best to help us. She sent a ship
with arms. Germany has not sent us gold.'

There is no doubt that Pearse expected to be executed more or less
immediately after capture and that he desired that fate.[2] If he had a fear, it
was that execution might not take place; that he would be treated as nothing
more than a dangerous crank.

Curiously, had the prisoners been tried in the civil courts they would have
had no defence in law to a charge of treason, rebellion or murder and the
death penalty was available for each of these offences. The central problem
for the Army was that the Proclamation of 25 April[3] revoked the right to

trial by jury. The proviso to section 1 of DORA[4] prevented a court martial from imposing a death penalty, save where the breach of the regulations was carried out 'with the intention of assisting the enemy'.

Lieutenant Bucknill and the Attorney General Lord Campbell spent some fruitless hours grappling with the difficulty of proving an intention to assist Germany. By 1 May, it appears the whole courts martial process had stalled. Pearse wrote the letter to his mother that day. It was passed by Sergeant Goodman to a junior officer and then to Lieutenant Alfred Bucknill.[5]

Bucknill later remarked with considerable understatement, that 'the prosecution' would have been in some difficulty without this postscript'.[6] In fact the postscript was all that the Army needed. A charge was drafted against Pearse within hours. Pearse was moved from Arbour Hill barracks to Richmond Barracks later that day and tried the following afternoon, 2 May. The letter and the damning postscript formed the cornerstone of the prosecution case. There is a question here: did Pearse write the postscript as a careless afterthought or was it his intention to provide the Army with the evidence that would result in his prosecution and execution?

Confined alone at Arbour Hill, awaiting trial, it is likely that Pearse agonised over the countermand, the lost arms shipment, the German fleet that failed to materialise and the many casualties among his own men and the people of Dublin. In his enforced isolation he may have felt an overwhelming need to confide his thoughts about the Rising and why it had failed. He had been kept incommunicado since the Saturday afternoon. Although on the Sunday, he did have an opportunity to speak briefly to Volunteer officers who had been allowed to come up from the country to confirm the surrender. Two officers had come up from Wexford[7] and one from Ashbourne but there was no opportunity to speak in private. It may be therefore that Pearse was driven to write the postscript by a desire to confide his thoughts.

On the other hand, it is unlikely that Pearse believed his mother was remotely interested in whether the German fleet had sailed or not. Pearse was a barrister by training, and although he had barely practised, he understood only too well the legal consequences of assisting the enemy in time of war. And he must have understood the legal effect of the postscript to his letter. The trial regime under the Defence of the Realm Act had received considerable publicity in Ireland and a number of Volunteers had been tried under the DORA regime in 1914 and 1915.[8] But even if Pearse had not understood the nuances of DORA, it is difficult to avoid the conclusion that the postscript to the letter was written to ensure that he faced the death sentence. This inference is reinforced by two factors. First, that he placed the postscript at the top of the first page, knowing that it would be read by his captors. Second, Pearse's closing address in his trial, in which he emphasised German involvement.

In the final hours before his execution Pearse expressed the hope that what he had said in his closing address would not be used against other Volunteers.[9] It was a pious hope; he must have known that his admission might have consequences for others, which would prove fatal.

What is remarkable is that although the Army acknowledged the need for proof that Pearse had acted with 'the intention of assisting the enemy' this requirement was simply overlooked or ignored in relation to many of the trials that followed. Both standing courts at Richmond Barracks took the same approach. There is no record of their deliberations, only the results of their discussions and it is therefore a question of inference. It seems likely that the courts took the view that if it was proved against Pearse that he had acted with the intention and for the purpose of assisting the enemy, that could be inferred in respect of the other prisoners.

CHAPTER ELEVEN

Thomas Clarke

Thomas Clarke was tried on 2 May at Richmond Barracks and Brigadier General Blackader presided.[1] Clarke faced what became the standard charge, taking part in an armed rebellion 'with the intention and for the purpose of assisting the enemy'.

The prisoner denied the charge. The trial record is set out below as it appears in the archive.

> 'Prosecution
> 1st witness 2nd Lieut S.L. King 12th Inniskilling being duly sworn states -
> Between 10 and 11am on Tuesday 25th April 1916 I was in Sackville Street. 2 men rushed across from the direction of the Post office, and took me prisoner taking me into the main entrance of the post office. While I was detained there I often saw the prisoner. He appeared to be a person in authority although he was not in uniform.
> Some of the men obtained a key from him at different times and some wore uniforms. I have no doubt he was one of the rebels.
> Cross examined:
> Whilst I was in the post office I was very well treated.
> Prosecution closed.
> The accused does not call any witnesses and makes no statement.'

Clarke was convicted and sentenced to 'death by being shot'.

The proceedings and sentence were confirmed that day by Maxwell. The prisoner was moved to Kilmainham the same evening. In the parlance of the Army, sentence was 'promulgated the same day'. That is, the prisoner was officially informed of his fate.

At 4.15am the following morning, Clarke was shot. MacDonagh and Pearse were also shot the same morning.

He was described by prosecuting counsel in this way: 'He looked about 65. He did not defend himself either and was perfectly calm and brave throughout the proceedings.'[2]

Clarke was one of the first prisoners to be charged and noted the wording, which required proof of an intention 'to assist the enemy'. He told another prisoner the same day, that this provision allowed him to contest the charge without behaving dishonourably.[3] In fact, although he entered a not guilty plea, he did not take part in the trial to any extent nor did he use the opportunity, as Connolly and Pearse did, to make a speech for posterity.

Before he was executed he was given the opportunity to see his wife, who was brought up from Ship Street Barracks where she was being held with the other women prisoners. He described the trial as a 'farce'. It may be that he realised when his trial began that there was only one outcome and decided not to engage with the process for that reason.

CHAPTER TWELVE

Joseph Plunkett

Plunkett was tried on 3 May at Richmond Barracks and Brigadier Maconchy presided. Plunkett was charged with rebellion 'with the intention and for the purpose of assisting the enemy'. The prisoner entered a not guilty plea.
The trial record is set out below.[1]

'1st Witness Major Philip Holmes 5th battn (attached to 3rd battn) R. Irish Regt states after being duly sworn:-
I identify the prisoner as a man who was one of the leaders of a large company of Sinn Feiners who surrendered on the evening of 29th April. They surrendered at the bottom end of Sackville St. In the area in which the Sinn Feiners who had been in the Post Office for several days had retired when the Post Office was burnt. The Sinn Feiners in the Post Office had been firing on the troops for several days and had killed and wounded a number of soldiers. He was dressed in the green uniform he is now wearing with a captain's badges of rank on his sleeves when he surrendered.
The party at the head of which he surrendered was armed.
2nd Witness. Sergeant John Bruton, Dublin Metropolitan Police states
I know the prisoner Joseph Plunkett.
The Headquarters of the Irish Volunteer movement are at No 2 Dawson Street.
I have seen him on two occasions entering and leaving No 2 Dawson Street, dressed, as well as I could see, in the Uniform of the Irish Volunteers on at least one occasion.
His name appears on the Proclamation issued by the Irish Volunteers and I believe him to be a member of the Executive Council of that body.

Cross examined by the prisoner
How do you know the Proclamation was issued by the
Irish Volunteers?
Answer. I know the names of the men which appear
at the foot of the Proclamation are connected with
the Irish Volunteers.
They include P.H.Pearse, Edmund Kent, Thomas
MacDonagh, John McDermot, who are members of the
Council of the Irish Volunteers and who constantly
attended meetings at No 2 Dawson St.
3rd Witness Lt Colonel H.S. Hodgkin D.S.O. 6th
Battalion Sherwood Foresters states:-
I saw the prisoner when he surrendered on the 29th
April. He was wearing a sword & pistol.
Defence
The prisoner in his defence states.
I have nothing to say in my defence but desire
to state that the proclamation referred to in
Sergt Bruton's evidence is signed by persons
who are not connected with the Irish Volunteers
& the Proclamation was not issued by the Irish
Volunteers.'

The last witness for the Crown, Lieutenant Colonel Harry Sidney Hodgkin
might have regarded his service in Ireland as an interesting diversion from
the Great War. He had been a professional soldier, seeing service against
the Boers but by the outbreak of the Great War he was retired with every
prospect of a quiet life. He was re-called in 1914 and proved to be an officer
of some ability. He was decorated and mentioned in despatches three times.[2]
He took his battalion of Sherwood Foresters to France in the summer of
1916. By early 1917 he was leading his men in desperate fighting near
Arras.[3] He was posted missing in action the following year. As it turned out,
he been captured and was repatriated after the Armistice and was able to
return to his retirement.

The Rebellion having been so completely crushed, the other witnesses
called by the Crown might reasonably have regarded the trials as the end of
the affair. It was of course just the beginning and the 'G Men' of the DMP
would be in the front line of the War of Independence. Sergeant Bruton's
close colleagues, Smith, Hoey and Barton were all shot and killed in the
streets of Dublin. Bruton became a recluse in Dublin Castle. After the Truce
he disappeared to England and was not seen again.[4]

The principal witness, Philip Holmes was as Irish as Plunkett. He was a veteran of the Western Front. He had been wounded and gassed twice. He returned to France later that year and was wounded again. He joined the RIC, following in the footsteps of his father and grandfather. In 1920 he was appointed Divisional Commissioner of police in Cork. Holmes was killed in an ambush in County Cork, in 1921.[5]

As to the prisoner, General Maxwell confirmed conviction and sentence within hours. Plunkett was of course gravely ill. He and his fiancé were married that night in Kilmainham Prison. He was shot a few hours later. Notice of execution was carried in *The Irish Times* the following day. A marriage notice was also carried:

'Plunkett & Gifford. May 3, 1916 at Dublin, Joseph Plunkett to Grace Gifford.'

A few hours after execution, the trials at Richmond Barracks re-commenced. Plunkett's younger brothers George and Jack were in the line of prisoners awaiting trial that morning.

CHAPTER THIRTEEN

George Plunkett

George Plunkett was tried on 4 May 1916 at Richmond Barracks. Colonel Sapte presided.[1] Plunkett was charged with taking part in armed rebellion 'with the intention and for the purpose of assisting the enemy'. He faced a second charge of inciting disaffection among the civilian population.

The prisoner denied the charges.

'Private James Murray 3[rd]Battn Royal Irish Regt states:

I identify the Accused as a man I saw in the General Post Office on Tuesday, Wed and Thurs the 25th to 27th April 1916. I saw him walking about doing nothing in particular. He was dressed in uniform as he is now (3 badges on each cuff) and bore a revolver. There was a lot of firing going on, on these three days, apparently from the roof, as far as I could judge, of the Post Office. I did not see him act as if he was an Officer, but he was dressed as one.

Cross examined by the accused

Q: Do you remember what sort of a revolver I was wearing, large or small or the pattern?

A: It was a middling size revolver in a tan pouch. I don't know whether it was blued or bright.

2nd witness for prosecution: 2nd Lieut. W.H. Ruxton 3[rd]Battn Royal Irish Regt. States: I identify the Accused as one of a second armed party that came up to me at the top of Sackville Street Dublin on (I think) Saturday last (29th April) and surrendered. They came from the direction of the General Post Office. He was dressed as he is now. I am not certain whether he was armed or not.

3rd witness for Prosecution Constable Daniel Hoey, detective, Dublin Metropolitan Police states: I

identify the Accused, one of the Plunketts - I
frequently saw him before this occurred at the Hd
Qrs. Of the Irish Volunteers, 2 Dawson St, Dublin.
Defence. The Accused in his defence states:
I did not attempt to cause disaffection among the
civilian population. I have nothing to say except
that I was in a military organisation and merely
carried out my orders.'

Plunkett was convicted on the first charge only. He was sentenced to death.
Sentence was commuted to ten years' imprisonment.

Unlike his better known brother, George Plunkett was not a signatory
to the Proclamation and he was not well known to the 'G Men' although
he had become a familiar sight leading his company through Dublin when
parades were held.

Had the full extent of his involvement been known, it is unlikely he
would have been spared. In 1916, George Plunkett was about 21 years
old. He was captain of a company in the Fourth Battalion of Volunteers,
based at his father's estate at Larkfield, Kimmage. At the estate a disused
mill was taken over by the Volunteers. The company grew up almost by
chance. Over a period of months men from England had gathered. These
men, mainly from Liverpool, Manchester, Glasgow and London were liable
to conscription and service in France. Faced with this prospect and knowing
that rebellion was brewing in Ireland, they made the choice to fight against
the Empire. These men numbered not less than 64.

In the weeks leading up to the Rebellion they were engaged in making
shotgun cartridges and hand grenades. There was little else to do and the
men sometimes worked a 24-hour shift.[2]

On Easter Monday George Plunkett mobilised his company. Each man
had a haversack, a shotgun, pike and sometimes a rifle and a handgun. One
of the men later recalled, they caught a tram to the city centre. George
Plunkett paid the fares.[3] This company of men took over the GPO.

During the course of the week George Plunkett remained at the GPO.
When Connolly was wounded in the street, it was George Plunkett who
pulled him to safety.[4] On the Friday after the evacuation of the GPO, the
garrison became trapped at Moore Street by machine gun fire. On the far
side of the road a British soldier was badly wounded and it was George
Plunkett who crossed the street and brought the man to safety.[5]

CHAPTER FOURTEEN

Jack Plunkett

Jack Plunkett was tried on 4 May at Richmond Barracks, the trial being conducted by Colonel Sapte. Plunkett was charged of taking part in armed rebellion 'with the intention and for the purpose of assisting the enemy'. He faced a second charge of inciting disaffection among the civilian population.[1]

Pleas: Not Guilty to both charges.

'Private James Murray 3rd Battn Royal Irish Regt states:
On the 25th April 1916 I was taken as a prisoner by the Irish Volunteers to the GPO. I was confined in an upper room but was often taken down on fatigue work elsewhere. I saw the accused walking about the building on that date and the two following days. He was dressed in uniform and carried a revolver. There was a large number of armed Irish Volunteers in the building and much firing took place apparently from the roof of the building. I did not hear the Accused give any orders.
Cross examined by the Accused.
Q   On what days exactly do you allege you saw me in the GPO?
A   On Tuesday Wednesday and Thursday
Q   Were you captured at Ballybough?
A   Yes
2nd witness for prosecution Detective Sergeant John Bruton Dublin Metropolitan Police states: I know the Accused John Plunkett - I have seen him about twice marching through the streets with the Irish Volunteers. I cannot remember the dates but it was some time ago. It is part of my duty to watch these Volunteers. He was dressed in uniform and marched at the head of some men - he appeared to be in authority.

```
Cross examined by the accused
Q. Are you quite sure I was in uniform on these
occasions and dressed as an Officer
A To the best of my belief - You were certainly
in uniform.
3rd witness for the Prosecution    2nd Lieut Patrick
Joseph O'Brien   7th Battn Royal Munster Fusiliers
states:
I identify the Accused as a Prisoner handed over
to me by capt. Cherry of the North Stafford Regt
on Sunday 30th April 1916. He was in a party stated
to have come from Sackville Street. I am Prison
Commandant at Richmond Barracks Dublin.
4th witness for the prosecution 2nd Lieut W.H. Ruxon
3rd Battn Royal Irish Regt states:
I identify the Accused - he was in a second party
of prisoners brought from the direction of the
GPO to me at the Parnell Monument in Sackville
Street.  All this party appeared to be armed.
Defence:  The accused in his defence says:
I was fighting for Ireland, if I was fighting
not for Germany - I had no intention of helping
any enemy of England, unless Ireland is an enemy
- I absolutely deny that I attempted to cause
disaffection among the civilian population.
If detective Sergt. Bruton saw me marching in the
streets as he alleges, I was not in uniform as I
had no uniform before the Saturday before Easter -
nor did he see me marching as an officer or giving
directions as I was not an Officer then.'
```

This case throws up a curious detail about Sergeant Bruton's evidence. Jack Plunkett was an engineer. Prior to the Rebellion, he did not have a uniform or hold any rank.[2] He certainly did not march at the head of Volunteers. He was still only in his late teens. It seems likely that Sergeant Bruton had confused him for his older brother George, who held the rank of captain and would certainly have been seen leading Volunteers through the streets. This crucial error placed Jack Plunkett at risk of execution.[3]

It can be seen from the transcript that Jack Plunkett refrained from saying anything to draw attention to his brother George. Context, as always is vital. George and Jack were tried only hours after their eldest brother Joe was executed.

Jack Plunkett was convicted on the rebellion charge. He was acquitted on the lesser count of causing disaffection. He was sentenced to death.

On the day that George and Jack Plunkett were convicted, Maxwell was recalled to Westminster to justify the execution policy. The Cabinet required him to curtail the executions. On his return there were many cases awaiting review and confirmation and sentence of death was commuted in respect of most prisoners. Sentence on both the surviving Plunkett brothers was commuted to ten years' penal servitude.

CHAPTER FIFTEEN

William Pearse, John McGarry, J.J. Walsh and John Dougherty (McGallogly)

William Pearse, John McGarry, J.J. Walsh, Dougherty (aka John McGallogly) were tried on 3 May at Richmond Barracks. Brigadier Maconchy presided. The prisoners were charged with taking part in an armed rebellion 'with the intention and for the purpose of assisting the enemy'. McGarry, Dougherty and Walsh entered not guilty pleas. Pearse pleaded guilty.

The trial record is set out below.[1]

'1st Witness Lieutenant S.L. King 12th Battn R. Inniskilling Fusiliers states:- On Tuesday 25th April at 11am I was seized by two armed men outside Clery's shop opposite the General Post Office.

John Dougherty was one of the two. He held a revolver at me and told me if I did not put my hands up he would blow my brains out.

He took me to the General Post Office where I was held as a prisoner till Friday night.

I was in uniform.

I saw each of the other prisoners in the G.P.O. while I was there and during that time the Post Office was held against His Majesty's troops by men firing against the troops.

There was another officer there Lieutenant Chalmers who was wounded, also in uniform.

I know that William Pearse was an officer but I do not know his rank.

Cross examination[2]

I do not know what McGarry's position was. He was not in uniform.

J. Walsh did not appear to be in any authoritative
position but was dressed in uniform.

I saw Pearse, McGarry and Walsh wearing equipment,
belts and pouches. Dougherty had a revolver but no
equipment.

It was Dougherty who threatened to blow my brains
out not the man with him.

I am quite certain that I saw McGarry with equipment
on.

John Dougherty states:-

I did not say that I would blow Lieut King's
brains out.

William Pearse states

I had no authority or say in the arrangements for
the starting of the rebellion. I was throughout
only a personal attaché to my brother P. H. Pearse.
I had no direct command.

John McGarry states:-

I had no intention of assisting the enemy. I had
no position or rank of any sort. I was employed as
a messenger. I did not know of the rebellion until
the Post Office was taken. I had no rifle.

J.J. Walsh states:-

During the past 18 months I have had no official
position big or little in the Irish Volunteers or
any other national movement and my whole attention
was confined to business.

I gave it up at the time of the split between the
Redmondites and the Irish Volunteers. I mean my
official position. I remained in the Volunteers
as a private & on being mobilised on Monday I
knew nothing whatever of the intention of the
mobilisation.

I fired on nobody during the time at the Post
Office. I had no arms whatever. I was told off to
attend to the water and sand arrangements in case
of fire.'

The trial lasted about 15 minutes.[3] The prisoners were found guilty and
ordered 'to suffer death by being shot'. McGarry was recommended to
mercy on the ground that he was 'misled' by his leaders.

There is a note on the file signed by General Byrne asking the age of Pearse. An answer was given the same afternoon: he was 33 years old. Maxwell confirmed the death sentence on Pearse the same day. Sentence was promulgated that evening and he was shot in the early hours of the following morning.

Pearse was described in Maxwell's *'A Short History of rebels'* as a commandant. In fact he held the rank of captain, although he was not much more than a runner for his brother. He was quite a naïve man in thrall to his older brother's compelling personality.

Sentence was commuted in respect of the other three. J.J. Walsh and McGallogly received ten years' imprisonment. McGallogly was 17 years old, a fact the court might have established before imposing a death sentence.

McGarry was the only one recommended for leniency and received the shortest sentence. He was not in uniform[4] and his case, that he was 'misled' by the leaders was accepted by the court. This prisoner was in fact Seán McGarry, a member of the Executive Council of the IRB. McGarry had been advised by Tom Clarke that the charge alleging 'intent to assist the enemy' could be honourably defended and he intended to take that course.[5] McGarry took that advice. Some of the other leaders suggested that the followers simply assert they were misled into the rising. McGarry took that advice also.

The account given by Walsh was a mixture of truth and fiction. He had been prominent in the Volunteers in Cork until 1915 when he was served with a government order banning him from living in Cork. He went to Dublin where he ran a shop and remained on the fringes of the Volunteers. He mobilised on Easter Monday with full knowledge of what was afoot.[6]

Walsh, McGarry and McGallogly were moved to Mountjoy and then to Portland Prison. They were escorted by soldiers of the Notts and Derby regiment, who were more than friendly. McGallogly later recounted that the prisoners gave what money they had to the Tommies as a gift. The Tommies generously used the money to buy food and cigarettes for the prisoners.[7] The men were moved to Portland where governor Denty ruled with a strong arm: 'Denty's Inferno' quipped Walsh.[8] Walsh remained in prison until 1917. He was elected MP for Cork and tried again in 1918, this time for sedition.[9]

McGarry also went to prison. He was released the following year but was interned in 1918 when he was linked with 'the German Plot'. He escaped from Lincoln prison with Seán Milroy and de Valera.

John McGallogly [10] emerges as a gauche and taciturn young man who was used to privation. He was a coal miner from Bothwell in Lanarkshire. In early 1916 he and his elder brother became involved in the Glasgow Volunteers and took part in a raid on a local colliery, taking two hundredweight of explosives. Their involvement was suspected by police and in order to avoid capture they caught a tram to Paisley and a train to Ardrossan where they crossed to Belfast and travelled down to Dublin. They knew a rebellion was brewing in Ireland and were determined to take part. They spent some weeks living in dire poverty before being sent to Larkfield, where they joined the other émigrés from London, Manchester, Glasgow and Liverpool. Both brothers served in the GPO. In McGallogly's account written many years later he did not dispute the evidence of Lieutenant King. At the surrender they gave false names because of their involvement in the explosives affair in Glasgow – as if they were not already in the worst of trouble.

CHAPTER SIXTEEN

Harry Boland

Harry Boland was tried on 9 May at Richmond Barracks. Colonel Sapte, presided. Boland faced the standard charge of rebellion 'with the intention and for the purpose of assisting the enemy'. Boland faced a second alternative charge that he 'Did attempt to cause disaffection among the civil population of His Majesty.' He denied the charges.[1]

> 'First Witness for Prosecution No 57769 Sergeant
> E Henry R.F.C., states:-
> (Instructor at school of Musketry Dollymount)
> On the 25th April 1916 I was proceeding with
> Sergeant Hyland about 5:30 a.m. to the School of
> Musketry Dollymount when near Fairview, the accused
> who appeared to be a sentry and was armed, called
> out to me "Halt! Hands up or I'll shoot" He kept
> us covered with the rifle - 3 or 4 other armed
> men then joined him. We were made prisoners and
> confined. Eventually we were handed over the same
> morning to the rebels at the GPO.
> Cross examined by the accused
> I am satisfied he used the words "I'll shoot" I
> was reasonably well treated throughout.
> DEFENCE
> The accused in his defence says:-
> I was totally unaware that a rebellion was going to
> take place. I had been irregular in any attendance
> at parades lately and was much interested in Gaelic
> athletics which kept me fully occupied. I found
> myself under orders and had to obey. I was delegate
> for an athletic conference on 23rd April and got
> order for mobilisation on that date. I ignored it
> owing to the athlete conference. I was not in on
> the secrets of the organisation and had even made

> engagements which the rebellion upset. I deny that
> I attempted to cause disaffection.'

Sergeant Henry was a former RIC man and at the time of his capture he was seconded to the training school on Bull Island in Clontarf. It was an easy posting, rudely disturbed by events of Easter Week. Sergeant Henry's evidence was truthful and quite restrained in the circumstances. The trial record does not capture the full absurdity and drama of the Rising. Harry Boland, having captured Sergeant Henry took him to the GPO, travelling most of the journey by cab.[2] Sergeant Henry was held there until the Friday evening when the prisoners were released. After his release from the GPO, Sergeant Henry had run and taken refuge in the ruins of the Coliseum theatre, where he remained hidden. When he finally emerged from hiding, weak with hunger and thirst, he found that the surrender had taken place some days earlier.[3] This leant an extra piquancy to the moment when he identified Boland: 'He who laughs last, laughs best,' said the Sergeant. To which Boland replied, 'Yes chum, I am laughing. I am not whinging as you were when I took you prisoner.'[4]

Boland's account to the court was a mix of fact and fiction. He was a GAA man; he had been a hurler of considerable ability. It appears he was aware of the rising on Easter Monday. Boland lived at 15, Marino Crescent, Fairview (birthplace of Bram Stoker). On Easter Monday he set off from home to join the Rebellion, picking up his prisoner en route and eventually arriving at the GPO on the Tuesday. He and others occupied the Metropole Hotel on Sackville Street, defending the approaches to the GPO. On Friday, as the Metropole blazed, they evacuated their positions and joined the GPO garrison, which was attempting to break out to Moore Street. On the Friday evening he took his place in a line of men with orders to bayonet charge the barricades at the end of the street. This suicidal enterprise was abandoned by the leaders at the last moment and the men were stood down. Boland surrendered with the GPO garrison the next day.

He was sentenced to ten years' penal servitude, which was reduced to five by General Maxwell. The lenient sentence may be attributed to the fact that Boland was plainly not an officer and he was tried at a late stage because Sergeant Henry had hidden in the rubble for some days after the surrender. Boland was shipped off to Dartmoor where he and his fellow prisoners proved to be a troublesome and determined lot.

Boland was released the following year. He was elected by South Roscommon to Parliament in 1918. Like others he declined to take his seat and took his place with the First Dáil Éireann the following year. He engineered de Valera's escape from Lincoln Prison the same year and later accompanied de Valera to the USA to raise funds. During the trip the Irish delegation frequently encountered a Bolshevik mission. Both the Bolsheviks and the Irish were seeking international recognition of their respective countries. In the course of their dealings, Boland acquired four pieces of the Russian crown jewels as security for a loan, which was redeemed by the Russians decades later. The jewels remained hidden by Boland's mother up the chimney at Marino Crescent or behind a sliding door in the hot press, where they stayed safely hidden during the War of Independence.

After the Truce, Boland opposed the Treaty but worked hard to prevent civil war, but having failed he set in motion a plan to import a shipment of Thompson machine pistols from the USA.[5] In the early stages of the civil war, Free State troops raided the Grand Hotel at Skerries where Boland was staying. What happened next is unclear. He was certainly unarmed but he was mortally wounded at close range. While he lay dying he admitted to his sister that he knew the man that had shot him. He was a friend who had been in prison with him. Boland refused to give the name of his killer and asked that there be no reprisals.

CHAPTER SEVENTEEN

Seán MacDiarmada

MacDiarmada was tried at Richmond Barracks on 9 May. Colonel Sapte presided.[1] MacDiarmada faced the standard charge of rebellion and a lesser alternative of 'inciting disaffection among the civilian population of His Majesty'. He denied the charges.

On the long walk from the Rotunda to Richmond Barracks, MacDiarmada limped in a long way behind the other prisoners. A number of prisoners recall MacDiarmada at the barracks in a batch of men who had been picked out for trial as early as 30 April.[2]

As the days passed the leaders were brought up for trial. There were executions on 3, 4 and 5 May. More and more prisoners of junior rank were tried but the Provost Marshals still did not come for MacDiarmada, although he confided in other prisoners that some men had to be executed and he expected to share their fate.[3] The strain on MacDiarmada must have been immense as he waited to be called up for trial.

The explanation for the delay may lie in the fact that the Provost Marshals had a strong case against many prisoners and they concentrated on these prisoners. But they had problems assembling a case against MacDiarmada. He was far less well known than the other signatories and there were difficulties proving that he was a signatory to the proclamation or even a senior and active Volunteer. When he surrendered at Sackville Street he was not armed nor wearing a uniform. Although he was a key member of the IRB, he held no rank in the Volunteers. He was physically disabled and could not walk any distance without a stick. A mobilisation order was found during the search in the gymnasium but the investigating officers were unsure it could be attributed to him. Finally, although his name appeared on the proclamation in the Irish form, he was in custody under the name John McDermott and he had withheld his current address.

The DMP did not even know where he lived. There was an attempt by an officer of the G Division to trick a Cumann na mBan girl into leading them to his home.[4] This was Molly Reynolds who came up to Richmond Barracks on 6 May to give evidence for another prisoner. When she left the court she found a number of 'G Men' waiting in the corridor. She was approached by one with a story about a lame GPO prisoner who needed to send a message to his family. This attempt to induce her into leading the detectives to MacDiarmada's house was unsuccessful and they continued to hunt around for other evidence.

There were four more executions in the early hours of 8 May, including Ceannt, another signatory. Of the signatories only Connolly and MacDiarmada were left alive. He must have felt the net was closing. There is no evidence as to how, but later that morning MacDiarmada slipped away from his captors and got into a large group of men on the square. These men were about to be deported. They had been issued with tins of bully beef and were ready to march out. It was a long walk from Richmond Barracks to the North Wall and MacDiarmada's wasted leg would hardly take the strain. He was surrounded by friends and men he knew and no doubt they would have helped him. At this point a detective appeared and picked MacDiarmada out from the ranks.[5] On one account this was Detective Hoey who remarked: 'You can't slip away that easy, Seán.' MacDiarmada was tried the following day.

'1st Witness for prosecution – Constable Daniel Hoey, detective department, Dublin Metropolitan Police says,-

I have known the accused by the name of John McDermott, and in the Irish form Sean McDiarmada, for 3½ years. The accused associated with the leaders of the Irish Volunteers, Thomas Clarke, P.H. Pearse, Joseph Plunkett, Frank Fahy, Joe McGuinness, PJ Duggan and others. They held executive meetings once a week and general council meetings once a month at the Hd Qtrs 2 Dawson Street. The accused and those mentioned attended these meetings. The accused visits an office at 12 D'Olier Street, Dublin, frequently. It has the name Sean MacDiarmada on a plate. I have seen some of the others mentioned visiting there. Thomas Clarke had a tobacconist shop at 75a Parnell Street. This shop was frequented by leading members. I have seen the accused there frequently. I did not see the accused at Liberty Hall, the Headquarters of the General Transport Workers Union.

Cross examined by the accused

I have only known the accused to associate with Irish Volunteer leaders during the last twelve

months. I have known him for 3 ½ years but at first
he did not so associate as far as I know. I do
not know all the objects of the Gaelic League but
I understand the Irish language is one of them. I
do not know his connection with the Gaelic League,
I have not inquired into it. I have not seen the
accused at the Hd Qtrs of the Gaelic League.
The subject of the Central Executive meeting of
the Irish Volunteers is published in the "Irish
Volunteer." I produce a copy- (marked X. Signed
and attached to proceedings). A paper known as
Nationality is published at 12 D'Olier Street.
This is the accused principal means of livelihood.
There are several offices at 12, D'Olier Street.
Clarke's shop sells papers etc as well as tobacco.
He did a good business there. I have seen the
accused visit many public houses and remain there
a considerable time.
2nd Witness for Prosecution- 2nd Lieutenant W.H.
Ruxton Royal Irish Regiment states:-
I was on duty at Parnell Street on 29th April 1916.
3 parties of rebels, two armed, one partially with
knives & some ammunition, surrendered. The accused
was one of the two armed parties who surrendered
between 6 & 7pm. The accused spoke to me and said
he would not be able to march far on account of
his leg. I asked him why he could not march.
One of the others told me his leg was paralysed.
I asked the accused "how did he get into this
affair?" The accused replied to the effect that
he had his place in the organisation. The parties
came from the direction of the General Post Office
- they were sent on to the Rotunda. I am positive
the accused is the man I spoke to.
Cross examined by the accused
I should imagine there were about 200 men in the
accused's party. They were not all armed. I did
not notice any arms in the accused's possession.
3rd Witness for the Prosecution S.A.L. Dowling 3
Irish Regt. States:- I was on duty on 29th April
1916 in Sackville Street. I took the names of

about 23 of the rebels after they laid down their
arms. I identify the paper as my list (marked Y
signed & attached). The accused was in that party
and is shown on the list, but I do not know if he
actually gave the name.
Cross examined by the accused
I did not pay particular attention to the surrender
of arms and did not see the accused with any arms.
4th Witness for prosecution Lieutenant colonel H.F.
Frazer 21st Lancers states-
I was present in Richmond Barracks on 30th April
1916, and I identify the accused as one of those
confined there, but not necessarily on that date.
All papers taken from the prisoners on this occasion
were handed to me. I identify the paper produced
as one of those handed in to me in the gymnasium
on that day. This paper is marked D signed by the
president and attached.[6]
5th Witness for the prosecution states – Edward
Gannon clerk warden Mountjoy Prison Dublin, I
identify the accused as John McDermott who was
confined in Mountjoy Prison Dublin in May and June
1915. I produce the cash and property book in which
the accused signed his name Sean MacDiarmada. The
spelling is the same on the document marked D now
shown to me. Except for the S there is a strong
resemblance between the signatures.
Cross examined by the accused
I am not a fluent Irish scholar.'

(**Author's note:** A sixth witness for the prosecution was Captain Henry
de Courcy Wheeler. His evidence and that of a seventh witness does not
survive. MacDiarmada's closing address does not survive.)

MacDiarmada was convicted on the primary charge and acquitted on the
lesser alternative.

The prisoner's fate hung in the balance. Shortly before the trial,
MacDiarmada's house was traced. The house, in Monkstown, was raided
by Captain Orchard and ten men of the Leicester regiment. Entry was
forced. Captain Orchard later wrote 'It was a nice large house and obviously
furnished by eccentric people.' An application to join the Volunteers was
found together with a minute book of the Gaelic League and Volunteers.

This book yielded many names and addresses. Also found were a number of mobilisation orders, addressed and ready to send. In the confusion over the Easter Weekend they had never been delivered. Captain Orchard set about delivering the mobilisation orders and making arrests. At some point the seized documents were despatched to Richmond Barracks. 'That should settle a few arguments...' wrote Captain Orchard.

The seized mobilisation orders did not arrive in time for MacDiarmada's trial but they were put before General Maxwell when he was considering confirmation. The seized mobilisation orders tied up neatly with the mobilisation order put before the court martial. Maxwell's '*Short History of rebels*' makes an explicit reference to the seizures: 'he wrote and sent despatches and mobilisation orders for and to the rebels during the rebellion'.[7] Maxwell confirmed conviction and sentence the next day but the execution of Connolly and MacDiarmada was suspended pending consideration by Asquith.

In the great debate at Westminster on 11 May, Asquith justified the forthcoming execution of MacDiarmada on the ground that he was a signatory to the proclamation.[8] He was executed the following morning.

CHAPTER EIGHTEEN

James Connolly

Connolly was tried in the Hospital Wing at Dublin Castle on 9 May. Colonel Sapte presided.[1] He faced the standard charge contrary to DORR Reg 50, taking part in the Rebellion and a lesser alternative of 'inciting disaffection among the civilian population of His Majesty'. He denied the charges.

The record of the trial is now set out.

'First witness for the prosecution 2nd Lieut. S. L. King 12 Res Battn. Royal Innis. Fus.
In Sackville Street Dublin about 11am on the 25th April 1916 I was taken prisoner by the rebels and taken upstairs in the General Post Office. There were two other officers confined in the same room. There were many armed rebels in the building. I saw firing from the Hotel Metropole.
I saw the accused, in uniform and equipped with a revolver etc. Going across to the Hotel Metropole. I saw him pointing out as if to order a window to be broken in the hotel which was done, and fire opened from the window. I saw the accused on 3 or 4 occasions near the General Post Office.
Cross examined by the accused
I was in the Post Office from 25th to 28th when I was marched out of it by one of the rebels. We were very well treated generally by the rebels. The window broken gave a good field of fire across Sackville Street. The uniform the accused wore was the green Volunteers uniform with rings on his arms and a wide awake hat. I cannot remember any feathers in it.
Re - examined by the Prosecution
When we were put out of the Post Office we were told to run for our lives and we were fired on by

the rebels, and 2 of us hit. I cannot state whether
the British troops were firing at the time.
2nd witness for the prosecution Capt, H. E. Dec
Wheeler Reserve of officers states:-
I saw the accused, James Connolly in bed at the
Dublin Castle Hospital on the 29th April 1916 between
3 & 4pm. I had previously seen the rebel leader
P.H. Pearse surrender at the top of Moore Street
off Great Britain Street. I produce a document
which I brought to the accused from Pearse, which
he signed in my presence. (Marked x Attached).'

(Author's note: the order of surrender.)

'3rd witness for prosecution 2nd Lieut S. H. Jackson
3/R Irish Regt. states:-
On the 1st May 1916 I searched the rebel John
MacBride and found on him the document I produce
to the court. It purports to be signed by James
Connolly and I consider the signature the same as
that shown to me by the Court.'

(Author's note: this was a note signed by Connolly announcing the setting
up of the Republic.)

'2nd Lieut A.D. Chalmers 14th Royal Fusiliers
states:-
About 12.10pm on 24th April 1916 I was in the
General Post Office Dublin when about 300 armed
rebels entered and seized the Post Office and made
me prisoner. I saw the accused present among them.
The accused ordered me to be tied up in the telephone
box. This was done. I was kept there about 3 hours.
One of the rebels came and asked me how I was getting
on. I replied I was about suffocated. Apparently the
man went to the accused. I then heard the accused
say "I don't care a damn what you do with him." The
words were obviously concerned with me.
I was kept in the General Post Office until 28th
April 1916. On the 25th and 26th April   from the

window of the room I was in, I saw the accused
giving orders about firing from the Hotel Metropole.
I heard him give orders for firing on more than
one occasion.

Cross examined by the accused.

I think I saw the accused on the 26th April. Up
to that I had frequently seen him. The rebels
did their best for us whilst we were in the Post
Office.

The accused was in a dark green uniform with a
distinctive hat with cock feathers in it. The
distinctive uniform was very noticeable from the
other volunteer uniforms. I saw the accused close
while he was in the post office. I did not actually
hear the accused order me to be tied up in the
box. One of the rebels went up to the accused and
on his return I was tied up.

Defence — the accused in his defence says:-

I do not wish to make any defence except against
charges of wanton cruelty to prisoners. These
trifling allegations that have been made in
that direction if they record facts that really
happened deal only with the almost unavoidable
incidents of a hurried uprising, and over throwing
of long established authorities, and no where
show evidence of a set purpose to wantonly injure
unarmed prisoners.

We went out to try and break the connection
between this country and the British Empire and to
establish an Irish Republic.

We believe that the call we thus issued to the
people of Ireland was a nobler call in a holier
cause than any call issued to them during this war
having any connection with the war.

We succeeded in proving that Irishmen are ready to
die endeavouring to win for Ireland their national
rights which the British Government have been
asking them to die to win for Belgium. As long as
that remains the case the cause of Irish freedom
is safe. Believing that the British Government

```
has no right in Ireland, never had any right in
Ireland, and can never have any right in Ireland,
the presence in any one generation of even a
respectable minority of Irishmen ready to die to
affirm that truth makes that government for ever
a usurpation and crime against human progress.
I personally thank God that I have lived to see
the day when thousands of Irishmen and boys and
hundreds of Irish women and girls, were equally
ready to affirm that truth and seal it with their
lives if necessary.
The accused desires that a copy of these proceedings
shall be given to his wife.
He is directed to make a formal application to Hd.
Qtrs. Irish Comd.'
```

Connolly was convicted of the first charge. On the second alternative charge, he was acquitted.

On the question of whether Connolly was fit to be tried, in the prisoner's file there is a certificate signed by two doctors, including Dr Tobin, who had care of Connolly. His mental condition is described as 'unimpaired'. Both Doctors certified 'he is fit to undergo his trial'.

Connolly devoted a good part of his closing address – more than he would have wished – to refuting allegations of ill treatment made by Lieutenant Chalmers, who was the only prisoner to allege any sort of ill treatment while in custody. His comments were described by another GPO prisoner as 'malicious lies'.[2]

Connolly's execution was briefly delayed while Asquith considered the position. In the early hours of 12 May, Nora Connolly and her mother were summoned from home by the army. According to Nora Connolly, they were told the prisoner was 'very weak' and wished to see his wife and daughter. They went by car to Dublin Castle and up the stairs where there were six soldiers with fixed bayonets and twelve more on the landing. In an alcove, two more soldiers with fixed bayonets guarded the door to a last meeting.[3]

They had harboured a hope that execution might be delayed because of his wounds. Connolly was having none of that: 'I remembered Sheepers,' he replied – a reference to the Boer commando who was nursed back to health before being shot in 1901.[4]

Connolly must have realised that the court's refusal to release a copy of the proceedings to his wife meant that the record of his trial would be destroyed or at least remain buried in the archive. He managed to pass to his daughter a hidden copy of the closing statement he had made at his trial.[5]

Connolly was taken by stretcher to an ambulance and moved to Kilmainham Gaol, where he was executed later that morning.[6] His speech survived and reached a wide audience. It was an emotionally-charged address written while awaiting execution, and at a time when most of Europe was locked in a war sustained by nationalist feeling. But the central point advanced by Connolly, was that any small group of men could impose their views on society by force of arms. That was one of the legacies of this era and it has not quite gone away.

CHAPTER NINETEEN

Desmond FitzGerald

Desmond FitzGerald was tried at Richmond Barracks on 16 May 1916. Colonel Sapte presided. The prisoner faced the standard charge of rebellion 'with the intention and for the purpose of assisting the enemy'.[1]

FitzGerald was a writer who settled in Kerry with his wife. He became a Volunteer organiser in 1914. He was later the subject of a special powers order banning him from the county. In the autumn of 1915 he was convicted of sedition and imprisoned for six months. He emerged from prison on 31 March 1916. He became aware of the rising on Easter Monday when his wife told him about firing in the centre of Dublin. This gave him some pause for thought but after dinner at the Globe Hotel, he went to the GPO to help out. Once there his primary duties were caring for the wounded and organising food for the garrison. He remained there until late on Friday. As the GPO blazed, FitzGerald evacuated the wounded through a passage fashioned through a line of buildings leading to the Coliseum theatre on Henry Street. He was taken prisoner during the round-up but talked his way out and walked to his home in Bray.[2] He was arrested there and taken before the Assistant Provost Marshal, Major Rhodes, at Kingstown.

The trial record is now set out.

    '1st Witness for prosecution
    2nd Lieut S.R. King 12/Royal Inniskilling Fusiliers
    states:-
    I was taken a prisoner on Tuesday 25th April 1916
    by the rebels and detained by them in the General
    Post Office until the night of the 28th April, I
    saw many armed rebels and heard much firing. I saw
    the accused in the Dining Hall of the Post Offices
    during that week - He seemed to be in charge of the
    commissariat, I generally saw him at mealtimes. I
    did not see him armed nor in uniform. He seemed to
    be there of his own free will.
    CROSS EXAMINED BY THE ACCUSED

```
I did not see you take part in any fighting. All
your energies seemed to be devoted to the food
supply. You treated us very well indeed.
The Accused hands in a statement:-'
```

(Author's note: the accused then handed in two documents in which he
made full admissions to taking part in the Rising to Head Constable Mulligan
and the APM Major Rhodes. Those documents included admissions to all
that he had done, including possessing a handgun, a fact not alleged by the
prosecution. Neither of these documents were put before the court by the
prosecution and the prisoner would have been better off saying nothing.
This prisoner was an intelligent and articulate man who was plainly out of
his depth in the conduct of his defence. The explanation for his conduct
lies in his decision to give a full account of all that he did and hope that
the court would limit any sentence accordingly. Having handed in these
documents and made his situation a good deal worse, the accused sought
to undo the damage he had done to his own case by further explanations as
set out below.)

```
'The Accused in his defence further says:-
With reference to the automatic pistol I took it
off a man who had fired a shot from it by dropping
it on the floor. Not knowing the mechanism, I spoke
to the O'Rahilly about it. He told me to keep it
safe for the present, until he could attend to it.
I did not have it to use myself but merely for
safe custody. I did not do any actual organising
work owing to circumstances beyond my control -
I object to the statement of Hd. Constable Mulligan
appended to my statement - It is incorrect as far
as I can remember. The immediate reason I went to
the PO was to convey reply to a message which I
had taken for the O'Rahilly.'
```

FitzGerald was sentenced to twenty years' penal servitude, reduced by
Maxwell to 10 years. He was returned as Sinn Féin MP for Dublin in 1918.
The following year he was appointed Director of Publicity for Dáil Éireann.
He edited *The Irish Bulletin* during the War of Independence. After the
Truce, he favoured the Treaty. He became Minister of External Affairs and
later Defence Minister. He held his seat until 1938.

CHAPTER TWENTY

The Four Courts

The Four Courts dominate the north bank of the river Liffey to the west of Dublin city centre, a legacy of the late eighteenth century, when Ireland had last enjoyed a measure of self government. The great drum-shaped dome and the grand neoclassical lines of its facade – the work of architects Thomas Cooley and James Gandon – were intended to evoke the power of the state and the majesty of law.

It took just a few minutes for the Volunteers to take control of the Four Courts complex. It was not just a gesture, because in the context of the Rebellion, the Four Courts had some strategic value: it overlooked the western approaches to the city. This allowed the Volunteers to prevent army reinforcements moving from the Royal Hospital and Richmond Barracks to the city centre. The operation was carried out by the First Battalion of the Volunteers under the command of Ned Daly. The building was fortified with furniture and law books and readied to repel an assault.

The Four Courts garrison numbered about 300.[1] It included outposts at Church Street, North Brunswick Street and up as far as the North Circular Road. It also included North King Street, which had no particular strategic significance but it so happened that an army commander marked a line on a map showing a new perimeter. It happened to traverse the rebel positions in North King Street and it was with this sweep of a pencil that the most bitter fighting of Easter Week was precipitated.[2]

After the surrender, the prisoners were moved to the Rotunda where the officers were separated from the men.[3] The result of this elementary step was that nearly all of those who held positions of command in the Four Courts area were tried on 2 and 3 May, apart from Nicholas Laffan, who was wounded and not tried.[4] A number of prisoners who held no rank were also tried. Thomas Bevan was one of these. He had been responsible for guarding prisoners taken during the Rising. Although in the confusion following the surrender, he was regarded by the Army 'as a prisoner of some importance'.[5]

In the trials that followed, 19 men were sentenced to death[6] and of these one was executed.[7] Eighteen prisoners had their death sentences commuted to penal servitude.[8] Three prisoners were sentenced to prison terms.[9]

Only the trial records for Ned Daly, James Dempsey and O'Donovan and Shouldice can now be traced and these are now set out.

1. Major General Maxwell (*centre*) and his staff officers at the Royal Kilmainham Hospital after the suppression of the Rebellion. *2nd left* Brig Gen Hutchinson (chief of staff) *3rd left* Lt Bucknill (legal advisor) *6th from left* Prince Alexander of Battenberg (Aide de Campe) *7th from left* in civilian attire Brig Gen Joseph Byrne (Deputy Adjutant General). Courtesy of Top Photo.

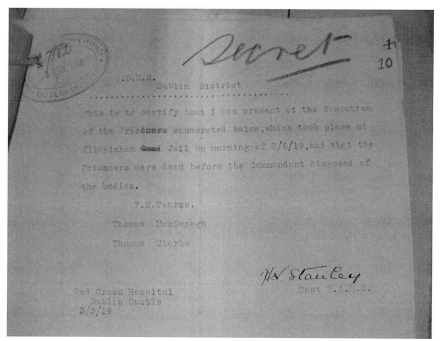

2. The death certificate provided by Captain Stanley. Courtesy of the National Archives (TNA): Public Record Office PRO.

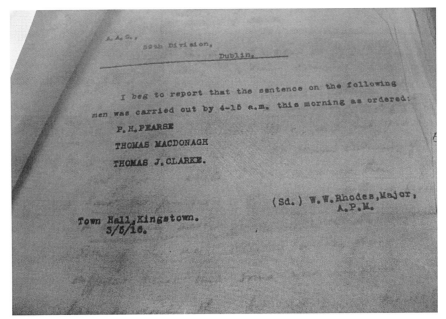

3. The certificate of execution provided by W.W. Rhodes. Courtesy of the National Archives (TNA): Public Record Office PRO.

4. Sackville Street, Dublin (Bachelor's Walk Corner) in ruins. Courtesy of Kilmainham Gaol Museum (17PC-1B14-10).

5. Two Republican prisoners being taken to Kilmainham. Courtesy of Kilmainham Gaol Museum (17PC-1B14-20).

6. Photograph showing Major John MacBride (in a long dark coat) being marched off under escort after his arrest. Courtesy of Kilmainham Gaol Museum (17PD-1A14-23).

7. Photograph taken inside the GPO during Easter Week. Courtesy of the Irish Military Archives.

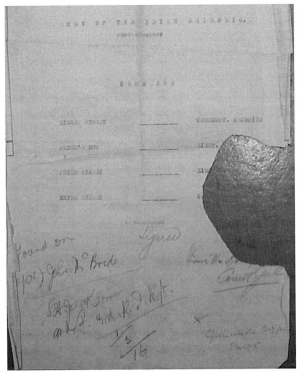

8. The MacBride document. MacBride handed this document to an army officer after his arrest. It showed his appointment to a position of command at Jacob's. That part of the document showing the names of others who held a position of command at Jacob's has been cut away. Courtesy of the National Archives (TNA): Public Record Office PRO.

9. Asquith visits prisoners at Richmond Barracks on 12 May 1916. Courtesy of Pádraig Óg Ó Ruairc.

Irish Rebellion – May 1916.
Liberty Hall, Dublin, the Rebel Headquarters, after the storming.

10. Liberty Hall Dublin in May 1916, after the building was shelled and captured.

11. Lieutenant Colonel Cecil Fane, DSO. Colonel Fane led the Foresters at Mount Street Canal Bridge where he was wounded. He is seen here recuperating at the Royal Hospital Kilmainham. He was awarded the Order of St Michael and St George for his part in the supression of the Rebellion.

12. Major C.H. Heathcote of the Sherwood Foresters, who supervised all the executions barring Pearse, MacDonagh and Clarke. Courtesy of the Foresters Museum.

13. Captain (later Lieutenant-Colonel) Martyn M.C. of the Sherwood Foresters, who led the assault on the South Dublin Union. Courtesy of the Foresters Museum.

14. Brigadier General Blackader (front row seated on left with peaked cap and dark moustache). Blackader tried Pearse, MacDonagh, Clarke, Ceannt and many other prisoners. Courtesy of the Leicestershire County Archive.

15. Colonel Douglas Sapte (front row, third from left, seated with monocle and pith helmet). Sapte tried Connolly, MacDiarmada, Harry Boland and Joseph Plunkett amongst others. Courtesy of the Fusiliers Museum of Northumberland, taken Rawalpindi, 1908.

16. Liam Cosgrave speaking after his by-election win in Kilkenny in the summer of 1917. After the Rebellion he narrowly escaped execution. A few years later, during the Civil War, he was President of the Executive Council of the Irish Free State. In this period 77 men were executed by Military Tribunals authorized by his government. Courtesy of the Irish Military Archives.

CHAPTER TWENTY ONE

Ned Daly

Edward Daly was tried on 3 May at Richmond Barracks, Brigadier General Blackader presided. The prisoner was charged with taking part in an armed rebellion 'with the intention and for the purpose of assisting the enemy'. The prisoner denied the charge.[1]

'1st witness
Lieutenant Halpin. 3rd Sherwood Foresters.
Having been duly sworn states.
I was arrested opposite the Four Courts on Monday April 24th & I was taken into the Four Courts & detained in custody until the Saturday following. I first saw the accused on Thursday April 27 he was armed & in uniform.
I don't know if he was in authority. There was firing from the Four Courts while I was there.
Cross examined by the accused.
I first saw the accused in the room in which I was being detained. He asked if I was being properly treated & on the second occasion he told me there was a danger of the building in which I was being shelled and he had me removed. On the third occasion he asked me if I had my meals and bedding allright.
The witness withdraws
2nd witness Lieutenant A.P. Lindsay 5th Bn Inniskilling Fusiliers being duly sworn states.
I was arrested on Tuesday April 25 by the rebels at the Four Courts & was fired on prior to arrest. Another officer with me was wounded (Lord Dunsany).
We were both taken into the Four Courts and confined there.

I saw the accused during my confinement. I did
not see the accused give any orders. I saw him on
Thursday, Friday & Saturday and had conversation
with him. On Saturday I was informed that Commandant
Daly wanted to see me - and I went down to see
him. Commandant Daly is the accused. He said he
intended to make a counter attack as the position
was hopeless. I told him that it was hopeless and
that he had better surrender. He said that he could
not surrender without orders from his superiors.
Cross examined by the accused
He told me he had had a conference with the officers
and that a counter attack had been decided upon. He
also said he did not expect anyone who took part
in this counter attack would come back alive. He
said the object of making this counter attack was
to save the lives of as many people as possible in
the building.
The witness withdraws
Prosecution Closed
The accused calls no witnesses and makes the
following statement.
The reason I pleaded "not guilty" was because I
had no dealings with any outside forces. I had no
knowledge of the insurrection until Monday morning
April 24. The officers including myself when we
heard the news held a meeting and decided that the
whole thing was foolish but being under orders we
had no option but to obey.
Statement ends.'

Daly was convicted and sentenced to death by being shot. Maxwell confirmed
the proceedings and sentence the same day. Daly was shot in the early hours
of 4 May.

Daly's assertion that he did not know about the Rebellion until Easter
Monday was plainly untrue. His denial that he intended to assist the enemy
was true. This was another case in which the question 'intention to assist
the enemy' was put squarely in issue by the prisoner. There was no evidence
of an intention to assist the enemy and it must be presumed that the court
simply took 'judicial notice' of German involvement.

There is no doubt that most army officers believed that there had been German involvement, which went beyond the attempt to land arms. One of the prisoners, Brennan-Whitmore,[2] recalled being repeatedly quizzed about the whereabouts of German snipers who the army believed were in the ranks of the Volunteers. The court does not seem to have been troubled by the absence of any actual evidence of an intention to assist Germany.

CHAPTER TWENTY TWO

Cornelius O'Donovan and John (Jack) Shouldice

O'Donovan and Shouldice were tried on 3 and 6 May at Richmond Barracks. Brigadier Maconchy presided. The prisoners were both tried on the standard charge of rebellion 'with the intention and for the purpose of assisting the enemy'. The prisoners denied the charge.

O'Donovan was 20 years old. He was a Volunteer. He was from Cork and had been studying agriculture in Dublin when the Rebellion started.

Shouldice was from a small village in County Roscommon. He was 34 years old. Contemporary photos show a lean cheerful figure with the thin moustache that had become fashionable at that time. He had been a civil servant for most of his adult life, mainly in London. He was also an IRB man. His circle meetings took place in Chancery Lane, with an apparently establishment-minded group of men who plotted revolution in the heart of the Empire. He returned to Ireland in 1913 and became a founder member of the Volunteers.

Both of these men fought in the Four Courts area at Easter. Curiously they were prosecuted on the basis they had been part of the GPO garrison. The trial record is set out below.[1]

> '1st Witness – Pte James Murray   10068 3rd Batt.
> R Irish Regt states:-
> I was arrested by a party of Irish Volunteers about 1 pm on Tuesday the 25th April. I was taken to the Dublin and Wicklow Manure Company first and then to the GPO. I was kept there till Thursday the 27th April. I saw both the prisoners at the GPO. They were dressed in uniform as they are now. O'Donovan had a bandolier on. There was firing going on while I was in the GPO from the roof.
> I saw Shouldice with a revolver. The occasion on which I saw O'Donovan was as follows. I went to

get some coal in a bag at the GPO. As I passed
through the dining hall I particularly noticed
a man standing in the hall. I am sure it was
O'Donovan. On passing back with the coal I saw the
man again and I am absolutely certain it was the
prisoner O'Donovan.

The court here adjourns

ON THE 6TH DAY OF MAY 1916 AT 10:15 A.M. O'CLOCK the
Court reassemble pursuant to adjournment, present
the same members as on the 3rd day of May 1916.

Called on by O'Donovan, Mary Reynolds states:-

I was in the Post Office on Wednesday last week in
the dining room for my meals only. I was in the
room about 1 o'clock. I cannot say I saw most of
the men who were in uniform in the Post Office -
I never saw you in my life before. I was in the
dining room for about 1 hour from 1pm to 2pm.

1st witness for the prosecution recalled.

Private Murray recalled and examined by the prisoner
states:-

It was day time, shortly after dinner when I saw
you. I cannot state the time it was then, as there
was no clock going. I heard no bell. I am positive
it was you I saw. I don't know the names of my
escort who were with me when I went for coal.

CROSS EXAMINED BY JOHN SHOULDICE

I saw you on Tuesday Wednesday and Thursday in the
Post Office down in the very bottom of the Post
Office altogether, where there are two counters.
You were wearing a revolver. I cannot state exactly
what the times were when I saw you but it was in
the day time. You were speaking to some Volunteer
in uniform on Wednesday when I saw you, I am quite
certain it was you whom I saw.

Ist Witness for Defence, John Shouldice in his
defence calls Michael Brady.

Michael Brady states:

I did not see Shouldice in the PO whilst I was
there last week.

Cross examined by the Prosecutor

I was in the PO on Wednesday I cannot say how many
men were there and the prisoner might have been in
the PO without my seeing him.
Michael Brady called by O'Donovan states:
I was in the Post Office on Wed of last week, I
did not see O'Donovan there.
Cross examined by prosecution
I cannot say how many men were in the Post Office
and O'Donovan might have been in the PO without my
seeing him.
2nd Witness for Defence
John Shouldice calls Mary Reynolds 16 Clonmore
Road who states:
I did not see Shouldice at any time last week in
the PO.
CROSS EX BY THE PROSECUTOR
I went to the PO first on Easter Monday at about 1
pm to buy stamps and was kept by the rebels until
Friday. I never saw Shouldice before in my life he
might have been in another room in the PO.
Defence
O'Donovan in his defence states:-
I am ready to swear that I was not in the Post
Office at any time last week. I regret the truth
has not been brought out as to where I was. I am
firmly convinced that this is a case of mistaken
identity on the part of private Murray because in
my private life I have been mistaken for several
others.
Shouldice in his defence states:
I have been a member of the Irish Volunteers
practically since that body was formed. I turned
out with them on Easter Monday for mobilisation,
which was to have taken place the day before.
Once the thing started I couldn't very well get
out of it. We were ordered to surrender and we
surrendered.'

O'Donovan and Shouldice were convicted and sentenced to death. Sentence
was commuted to five years' penal servitude.

The trial record does not explicitly state why the trial was adjourned from 3 to 6 May but the likelihood was that the court were uncertain of the case against the accused and adjourned for further evidence.

It is not the case, as the trial record suggests, that Molly Reynolds was called by the prisoners. The day before the court reconvened, another prisoner John R. Reynolds was tried and acquitted. His case was that his daughter had been buying stamps in the GPO when the Post Office was seized and he had gone in to get her and both he and his daughter had been held captive at the GPO all week. The court accepted this explanation, although in fact Reynolds and his daughter had played a full part in defending the GPO. She was able to escape the night before the surrender.

The day after Reynolds was acquitted, a DMP officer went to the Reynolds house and brought Molly Reynolds to Richmond Barracks, where the trial of O'Donovan and Shouldice had been reconvened. Plainly the officers running the trial did not suspect that she was a member of the Cumann na mBan and brought her to the barracks to test the case being made by the prisoners.

She told the court she had been a prisoner at the GPO all week and knew none of the rebels there. Her attention was directed to Shouldice (whom she knew) but did not identify. She was shown a number of other prisoners (one of whom must have been O'Donovan) but she made no identifications.[2]

It is highly likely that the same procedure was adopted in respect of Brady, the other witness.

These were akin to dock identifications but the trial record wrongly shows these individuals as defence witnesses. It follows that these trial records are inaccurate in a very significant way. This conclusion must raise a question mark about the accuracy of the trial records in general.

Years later, Jack Plunkett cast an interesting light on this trial. Plunkett wrote of a 'Tommy' who was a prisoner at the GPO and helped out in the kitchens. That Tommy was Private Murray. After the surrender Private Murray was prevailed upon to give evidence against the GPO prisoners. It seems he had been altogether too helpful to the rebels in the GPO and he was led to believe that he was at risk of prosecution himself and was held in custody by the Army. In the circumstances Murray became a compliant and dangerous witness. His evidence that he had seen the prisoners at the GPO was entirely mistaken at the very least.

O'Donovan had never been at the GPO but he had been at the Four Courts. By Easter Saturday, he had become aware, without ever being directly told, that there was a rebellion afoot. He turned out on Easter Monday fully equipped:

'I carried a short Lee Enfield, two revolvers and
ammunition for all three as well as the Howth
rifle.'

His battalion occupied the Four Courts.[3]O'Donovan and seven others were
detailed to fortify an upper storey of the Four Courts, overlooking the river.
Piling up law books and barricading windows, they exchanged fire with the
troops until the Thursday when an artillery gun was brought up onto the
south side of the Liffey and fire was opened on the Four Courts:

'There came a shattering explosion, and the room
trembled.'

This was one of the 18 pounders brought up from Athlone. It spelled the
beginning of the end for the defence of the Four Courts.

Shouldice had not been at the GPO either.[4] He was in the forefront of
the most bitter and sustained fighting around North King Street.

O'Donovan and Shouldice were sent to Dartmoor Prison. Shouldice's
abiding memories were companionship, cold, hunger and fog rolling across
the moor towards the prison. Both men were later transferred to Lewes
and were released in 1917. They both survived the War of Independence.
O'Donovan finished his college studies and settled in Glasnevin. Shouldice
returned home to Fairview and became prominent in the Gaelic Athletic
Association (GAA).

CHAPTER TWENTY THREE

James Dempsey

James Dempsey was tried at Richmond Barracks on 5 May, Brigadier Maconchy presided. The prisoner was charged with the standard charge of rebellion and attempting to cause disaffection. He denied the charges.[1]

'1st Witness No. 3568 Pte. P. Cullen 3rd. S. Lanc Regt states:-
I was taken prisoner on Tuesday 25th April by the rebels in Kirwin's Yard. The prisoner now before the Court was amongst those who took me in Mendicity Institution. He was actually sentry over me in the Institution and threatened to shoot me several times. He was armed with a rifle.
EXAMINED BY THE COURT
The Prisoner was taken off being sentry over me some time before I was released
DEFENCE
The Prisoner in his defence states:-
The Witness statement is incorrect. I surrendered in Cabra[2] Road and was not in Mendicity Institute at all. I had no idea what sort of parade I was about to take part in. I thought it was for ordinary manoeuvres.'

The prisoner was convicted on both charges. This is the only case that can be traced where the prisoner was convicted of rebellion and incitement to disaffection.

He was sentenced to death on the rebellion charge. His sentence was commuted to three years by General Maxwell.

There is reason to believe that the prisoner was not part of the Mendicity garrison. The names of those who were at the Mendicity are well documented[3] and Dempsey's name is not among them.

CHAPTER TWENTY FOUR

The Mendicity Institute

The Mendicity Institute was an established charity for the relief of poverty. The original building had been a gracious three-story Regency residence which was pulled down and replaced by a grim, two-story red brick structure, behind gates, railings and a substantial wall. The Mendicity overlooked the quays. It was half a mile west of the Four Courts and a few hundred yards from army headquarters at the Royal Barracks.

On Monday 24 April, J.J. Heuston left the GPO in command of a small group of men. He had orders from Connolly to 'seize the Mendicity'.[1] The strategic value of the Mendicity lay in the fact that it interrupted the movement of troops moving from the Royal Barracks along the quays to the Four Courts and the city centre. The occupation of the Mendicity was designed to give Daly's battalion time to fortify the Four Courts.[2]

According to an account by one Volunteer many years later, some of the men were 'astonished' when Heuston ordered them to take the Mendicity.[3] A side door was forced and front rooms on both floors were then occupied by the rebels.

A sapper party was allowed to pass in front of the Mendicity. A large party of the 10th Royal Dublin Fusiliers followed. At this moment the garrison were 'putting out a tri-colour'. This caught the attention of the Fusiliers: 'we saw the officer in front drawing his sword and pointing'.[4] Firing began.

An army officer was killed in the first few seconds. He was Lieutenant Gerald Neilan, a veteran of the Boer War, and the son of a well-known Dublin family. In a painful irony, his brother was fighting on the other side. Nine other ranks were wounded. The Fusiliers regrouped, attacked but were repulsed and a stalemate ensued. On the following day the Mendicity was subjected to sustained machine gun fire. A bayonet charge failed and the Fusiliers shifted tactics to containment and snipers.

The original task was to hold the Mendicity for a few hours to allow the garrisons in the city to fortify their positions. This task had now been accomplished, but for reasons which are not clear the Mendicity was not evacuated. The same evening the Mendicity was reinforced by ten men from Swords. It became another redoubt from which there could be no escape. James Crenigan from Swords, who was then only sixteen, recalled the intense fighting on the Tuesday night and Wednesday: 'there was no relief – you just slept at your post'.[5]

On Wednesday 26 April, there was another assault by the Royal Fusiliers. Backed up by machine gun fire and grenades the Royal Fusiliers overwhelmed the Mendicity:

> 'the place was just plastered with machine gun and rifle fire and we seemed to be surrounded.'[6]

Heuston tried to evacuate the building but was caught in the open and forced to surrender. One of the garrison, Peter Wilson, was killed at the point of surrender. Two of the garrison were wounded, William Staines and Richard Balfe who was left for dead until picked up by an army medical orderly. Both were too badly wounded to be tried. A total of 23 unwounded men surrendered. All were tried by courts martial. It was later said by one of the men that this reflected the casualties that the garrison had inflicted on the Army.[7] This was partially true. General Maxwell was certainly determined to try those who had inflicted such casualties.

There was another dimension. The Mendicity was the third rebel stronghold to fall. The first was City Hall, where few prisoners were taken. The second was the newspaper offices, which were evacuated before the final assault. The Mendicity was next. By the Sunday of that week the Army would be overwhelmed with prisoners. But on Wednesday 26 April there were only a handful of prisoners and the Army were able to log the captured men. There was also an abundance of evidence. The search of the Mendicity yielded a number of key documents, including an order signed by Connolly: *'seize the mendicity at all cost'*. There was also a notebook attributed to Heuston, showing his full name and rank. One wistful entry reads 'I hope we shall be able to do better next time.' Also found in the Mendicity were a number of duty rosters, which left little room for manoeuvre by the prisoners.

The men were brought to trial at Richmond Barracks. They were tried in groups, no more than four at a time, which reflected the cramped rooms in which the trials were held. A number of trial records can be traced. The evidence is broadly the same in all the surviving trial transcripts and only the trial of Heuston and his three co-defendants is reproduced. All 23 prisoners from the Mendicity were tried on 4 May.

By the time the trials were called many prisoners had been advised by their leaders to say that they were ignorant of the plans for rebellion.[8] Because they could not give sworn evidence, their accounts could not be tested in cross-examination. In particular, no hard questions could be asked of any prisoner as to what part he had played in the siege, which had lasted from Monday to Wednesday lunchtime.

Many of the Mendicity prisoners advanced the 'dupe' defence.[9]   James Marks told the court 'I did not know what was going to happen.' William Wilson also insisted he was a dupe.[10] Fred Brooks told the court he was mobilised for manoeuvres and thought there was to be 'a prize for the best equipped company'.[11]

The probability is that many of the rank and file who occupied the Mendicity on the first day were unaware a rebellion was planned. Others who joined on the second day could hardly have been ignorant of the Rebellion. Crenigan[12] was one of the Swords company who joined the garrison on the second day. Despite his youth he knew very well what he was getting into. He and his brother, who was killed at Ashbourne, were both active Volunteers. Thomas Peppard[13] and the others who had come down from Swords, plainly knew what they were getting into.

The trial date, 4 May, was a pivotal day. Willie Pearse, O'Hanrahan, Daly and Plunkett were all executed that morning and as a result Maxwell was recalled to London to justify his actions. At the Cabinet meeting on 5 May, Maxwell was encouraged to bring the executions to a swift conclusion and to confine sentence of death to a small number.

Maxwell did not return to Ireland until the early hours of 6 May, when he began the process of confirmation in respect of all the men tried for involvement in the Mendicity siege. It seems likely Maxwell's actions were tempered by the views of Asquith and his Cabinet. Just as it suited prisoners to argue they were just dupes, it also suited the government to portray the rank and file of the rebels as 'dupes'. It avoided the need for wholesale executions and allowed the government to put forward a palatable explanation for an event that struck at the heart of the Empire.

Sentence of death on Heuston was confirmed and he was informed on 7 May and executed the following morning. Eighteen others had death sentences commuted to three years' hard labour. Four more teenage prisoners were given two years' hard labour. [14] The trial records suggest that where prisoners asserted they had been 'misled' into taking part in the rising, Maxwell acted on this and commuted sentence of death.

CHAPTER 25

Heuston, O'Dea, Kelly and Crenigan

John J. Heuston, William O'Dea, Patrick Kelly and James Crenigan were tried at Richmond Barracks on 4 May. Brigadier Maconchy presided. The prisoners were charged with taking part in an armed rebellion 'with the intention and for the purpose of assisting the enemy'. All denied the charge.

The record of trial is now set out.[1]

'1st witness Capt. A.W. MacDermot - 7th Batt. R Dublin Fusiliers states:-

On the 26th April I was present when the Mendicity Institution was taken by assault by a party of 10th Batn. Royal Dublin Fusiliers.

23 men surrendered on that occasion. I identify the four prisoners J.J. Heuston, W. O'Dea, P. Kelly and J. Crenigan.

They left their arms except their revolvers in the Mendicity Institution. When they surrendered some of them still wore revolvers.

One officer of the 10th Royal Dublin Fusiliers was killed & 9 men wounded by fire from this institute on the 24th April.

I searched the building when they surrendered. I found several rifles several thousand rounds of ammunition for both revolvers and rifles (.303).

I found 6 or 7 bombs charged and with fuses in them ready for use.

I found the following papers.

An order signed by James Connolly one of the signatories to the Irish Republic Proclamation, directing "Captain Houston" (sic) to " seize the mendicity at all cost." It was dated 24th April 1916. James Connolly signed as "Commandant General

Dublin Division"

Also papers detailing men for various duties in the Mendicity Institute.

All these papers are headed

"Army of the Irish Republic"

Also two message books signed by Heuston "Capt."

One contains copies of messages sent to "Comdt. General Connolly" giving particulars of the situation in the Institute.

The other message book contains copies of messages commencing on 22nd April two days before the outbreak. One message contains a reference to MacDonagh who is stated to have just left Heuston. Another is a message to " all members of D Co. 1st Batn." Stating that the parade for the 23rd is cancelled and all rumours are to be ignored.

Another message dated the 23rd states "I hope we shall be able to do better next time."

These documents are all attached to the proceedings by the court

Examined by the court Captn. MacDermot states:-

Heuston commanded the party of men who surrendered.

2nd witness Lieutenant W.P. Connolly 10th R. Dublin Fusiliers states:-

I was present when 23 men surrendered on the 26th April at the Mendicity Institute.

I identify the four prisoners before the court as being amongst them.

The leader was J. J. Heuston.

I was present when the troops were fired on from the Mendicity Institute on the 24th April, when Lieutenant G.A. Neilan was killed and 6 men wounded to my knowledge.

Heuston was without a hat when he surrendered. He was not in the uniform of the Irish Volunteers.

I was present when the building was searched and found arms and ammunition and also the documents now before the court.

Cross examined by J.J. Heuston

I cannot say exactly where I found the message books but they were in the building.

Examined by the court
Among the arms there were some old German mausers.
Among the ammunition there were two cases of
"Spange" German ammunition.
Defence
W. O'Dea states - I was perfectly ignorant of
what was going to occur. I understood it was an
ordinary route march when I was called out as we
had been told some time previously that the best
equipped company was going to get a prize at the
Easter manoeuvres. It was to have taken place on
Easter Sunday but was postponed. I do not know why
it was postponed. I turned out in full uniform but
I took it off when we were about to surrender.
J.J. Heuston states -
The message in the notebook produced saying "I
hope we can do better next time" is not mine.
The order from Connolly addressed to "Captain
Houston" is not addressed to me as my name is
"Heuston".
I had no intimation of the nature of the charge
against me until this morning.
P. Kelly states -
I did not know anything about the rebellion
beforehand or what I was coming out for. I came
out because I was asked to. I thought it was for
manoeuvres. I did not fire any shots.
J. Crenigan states-
I did not know what I was called out for. I thought
it was for manoeuvres. I am 16 years old.'

Heuston's defence, such as it was, amounted to a denial that he had been in command. He had one other point of significance to make: that he had not been given the time or the means to prepare his defence.

It might be remembered that Asquith and Maxwell insisted that these trials were conducted according to law. This trial was conducted in secret. The prisoner (then aged 22) was unrepresented and had no opportunity to prepare for trial. He had no access to the rules under which the trial was conducted. It is in cases such as this that Asquith's argument wears thinnest.

CHAPTER TWENTY SIX

Jacob's Factory

Jacob's biscuit factory was situated in south Dublin, a few hundred yards from Saint Stephen's Green. It was seized by the Volunteers on Monday 24 April. It was intended that the factory should act as a supply depot, providing provisions for the Volunteers and population in the south of the city.[1]

The factory comprised of a series of Georgian terraces, one added to another over many decades until it formed a block, which was in parts six storeys high. The industrial chimneys behind the Georgian facade became an odd but familiar sight on the Dublin skyline. The factory covered some acres and though it was a formidable complex, it would have been impossible to defend against a frontal assault.

There were barely enough rebels to secure the factory – about 170 men and women.[2] Neither were there enough guns or ammunition for a sustained fight.[3] The garrison were amply provisioned, mainly with biscuits and cake.

The commandant at the factory was Thomas MacDonagh. He and his officers suffered from a dearth of military experience. A single exception was Major MacBride, who had joined the Volunteers that morning. His experience of combat was limited to guerrilla war on horseback in the Boer War. His military experience proved useful but it was hardly any preparation for urban street fighting.

The factory employed over 3,000 men and women. When the Volunteers went into action on Easter Monday they were forced to confront a mob of hostile local people. Many factory workers rightly reckoned that if the factory did not open, then workers would not be paid. In the affray that followed, the Volunteers were hard pressed and shot and bayoneted a local man.[4] The mob dispersed in appalled silence.

Troops from Portobello Barracks engaged the Jacob's garrison on the Monday and then withdrew. Snipers were placed on the roof and throughout the week there were exchanges of fire between the garrison at Jacob's factory and troops from both Portobello and Wellington Barracks. The fighting quickly tailed off.

Later in the week MacDonagh sent reinforcements to the College of Surgeons. Another patrol was sent to reinforce the Volunteers who were holding up the Sherwood Foresters at the canal bridge at Mount Street but this foray was not pressed home. There was little other fighting and casualties were light on both sides.[5]

Perhaps the most significant engagement took place on Sunday 30 April when two battalions of the Staffords arrived at Saint Patrick's Park a few hundred yards from the factory. The Army were anticipating that Jacob's would follow the orders issued by Pearse and surrender. Two of the officers present were Lieutenant William Wylie, who had been tasked with guiding the troops to their destination. With him was Major James Armstrong, the Provost Marshal.

Despite advice from Wylie, Colonel Taylor, a 'short and slightly pompous'[6] officer allowed the Staffords to file into the park and rest in the open. This lazy and arrogant disposition attracted immediate fire and snipers opened up from the roofs. Wylie recalled 'we lost about 12 men in as many seconds'.[7] The shooting continued as the soldiers scrambled for cover.[8]

The surrender followed later that afternoon although some of the Jacob's garrison had already walked off into the crowd. The remainder were marched to Patrick's Park and laid down their weapons. The South Dublin Union garrison followed shortly after and fell in behind the prisoners from Jacob's. Major Armstrong, the Provost Marshal took the surrender and Lieutenant Wylie noted down the names of the prisoners and who was armed and who was not.

After the surrender, some of the police officers held prisoner at Jacob's declined to identify their captors.[9] Little other evidence was available and the Army was compelled to rely on two central strands of evidence. First, the evidence of Major Armstrong about the firing from the direction of the factory. Second, his recollection of who the officers and NCOs were and who was armed and who was not. His recollection was bolstered by Wylie's notes, which detailed the names and ranks of those surrendering. Curiously, Wylie prosecuted many of the trials. In some instances Wylie's recollection was better than Armstrong's but Wylie was prosecuting counsel and could give no evidence.

It was a shambles, but despite all this, the Army brought to trial most of the officers and NCOs at Jacob's. They did so in large part because the prisoners made no effort to conceal their identities.

As far as can be established nine members of the factory garrison were tried. Of these, six were sentenced to death and three were executed.[10] Three others were sentenced to prison terms, including Richard Davis, a first aider who held no rank. When the sift was taking place at Richmond Barracks, Detective Hoey appears to have mistaken Davis's first aider uniform for that of an officer. Davis was a big, bearded forthright man. When asked by Detective Hoey 'Don't I know you?' Davis bellowed 'No but I know you.'[11] He was selected for trial.

MacDonagh, O'Hanrahan and MacBride were tried on the 2, 3 and 4 May. They were executed on 3, 4 and 5 respectively.

MacDonagh was a signatory of the Proclamation and commandant at the factory, so his execution was unsurprising by the standards of the time. Michael O'Hanrahan was a junior Volunteer officer. He was executed but Thomas Hunter who was second in command at Jacob's garrison was spared.

A small number of trial records can be traced and these are now set out in the following chapters.

CHAPTER TWENTY SEVEN

Thomas MacDonagh

The prisoner was tried on 2 May at Richmond Barracks, where Brigadier General Blackader presided. He was charged with taking part in an armed rebellion 'with the intention and for the purpose of assisting the enemy'. A not guilty plea was entered by the court.

The trial record is set out below.[1]

```
'1st witness
Major J.A. Armstrong 1st Royal Inniskilling Fusiliers
- Provost Marshal 176th Brigade. States:
I was present at St Patrick's Park on 30th April
1916.
There were British troops there & I saw them
fired on. I was under fire myself. The shots came
from the direction of Jacob's Factory. There were
several casualties among the British troops. At
a later hour I saw the accused coming from the
direction of Jacob's Factory under a white flag.
He made several journeys through our lines. About
5pm he surrendered with over 100 others to General
Carleton. He was acting as an officer when he
surrendered.
I made a list of the unarmed men & the accused was
not on that list.
He made a statement to me that he was a commandant.
He was subsequently sent under escort to Richmond
Barracks.
Cross examined by the accused:
I did not know that the accused came out at the
invitation of General Lowe.
The accused made the statement to me that it was
no use my searching for papers as they had all
been destroyed.
The witness withdrew.
```

```
Prosecution closed
The accused calls no witnesses in his defence.
The accused in his defence states - I did everything
I could to assist the officers in the matter of the
surrender telling them where the arms & ammunition
were after the surrender was decided upon.'
```

MacDonagh was convicted and sentenced to death by being shot. He was described by Lieutenant Wylie who prosecuted him as 'a poet, a dreamer and an idealist'. Wylie's recollection was that MacDonagh had taken no part in the trial: 'He was the only prisoner who said absolutely nothing.' The trial record supports that almost completely. Shortly after the trial a leaflet was sold in the street purporting to be MacDonagh's final speech at his trial. Even his family were taken in.[2] It was not until the trial records were released over 80 years later that it was exposed as fake, written for propaganda purposes.

General Maxwell confirmed finding and sentence the same day. MacDonagh was shot in the early hours of the following morning.

CHAPTER TWENTY EIGHT

Michael O'Hanrahan

Michael O'Hanrahan was tried on 3 May at Richmond Barracks. Brigadier General Blackader presided.[1] O'Hanrahan was charged with taking part in a rebellion 'with the intention and for the purpose of assisting the enemy'. The prisoner denied the charge.

The record of the trial is set out below.

'Prosecution
1st witness Major J.A. Armstrong being duly sworn states:-
I was present at St Patrick's Park on 30 April. The British troops were fired on and there were several casualties. The fire came from the neighbourhood of Jacobs Factory.
The same day a surrender was arranged by Mr MacDonagh and over 100 men arrived from Jacobs Factory as a result of the surrender and another large body arrived as a result of the surrender. The accused belonged to one of the parties. He was in uniform and armed. After the surrender he was removed in custody to Richmond Barracks. He said he was an officer.
Cross examined by the accused
All the officers appeared to be armed with pistols or revolvers.
I cannot say whether he was armed or not but all unarmed men were placed on a separate list and the accused is not on that list. The shots which caused the casualties came from the immediate neighbourhood of Jacobs Factory.
The Witness withdraws
Prosecution closes
The Accused in his defence makes the following statement

> As a soldier of the Republican Army acting under
> the orders of the Provisional Government of that
> Republic duly constituted I acted under the orders
> of my superiors.
> Statement ends.'

It is plain that Major Armstrong had no idea from which garrison O'Hanrahan had come. Nor did he know whether he was armed. The list relied upon by Armstrong had been compiled by Wylie.[2] It was in all probability accurate but it was entirely hearsay and inadmissible.

Perhaps the most damaging evidence against O'Hanrahan was his own statement to the court.

General Maxwell confirmed finding and sentence within hours of the trial. O'Hanrahan was executed the following morning.

CHAPTER TWENTY NINE

John MacBride

MacBride was tried on 4 May at Richmond Barracks. Brigadier General Blackader presided. MacBride was charged with taking part in an armed rebellion 'with the intention and for the purpose of assisting the enemy'. The prisoner denied the charge.[1]

Blackader and MacBride served on opposite sides during the Boer War. General Blackader was one of the garrison at Ladysmith and MacBride was one of those who laid siege. He took part in a cavalry charge of the British guns at Colenso where his horse was shot from under him. He had pursued the war as a means of fighting against Britain on the only front available. MacBride was known to Blackader at least by reputation.[2] It does not seem to have occurred to Blackader that he should have excused himself from sitting on this trial.

After the Boer War, MacBride married Maud Gonne but the marriage quickly failed. It may be that MacBride was simply unable to adjust to civilian life and the marriage broke up in a welter of allegations of violence and drunkenness.

MacBride returned to Ireland where he was still a legend. But he slipped slowly into penury, heavy drinking and occasionally ridicule. In 1908 a confidential police report described him as unemployed and living in 'straightened circumstances'. He lodged with Fred and Clara Allen for some years[3] and when the post of water bailiff came free, the nationalists on Dublin Corporation went out of their way to ensure he got this post.[4] MacBride prospered and occasionally spoke at public meetings, and was a vociferous opponent of conscription in Ireland. In 1916, he was a few days short of his fifty-first birthday, portly, unfit, with a reputation for heavy drinking. By chance he was in Saint Stephen's Green on Easter Monday and joined the Rebellion. Those who remembered him at Jacob's factory recall a steady, calm figure.[5]

The trial record is set out below.

        '1st witness Major J.A. Armstrong
        Inniskilling Fusiliers
        Duly sworn states

I was present at Patricks Park Dublin on April 30. The British troops were fired on on that occasion & there were casualties. The fire came from the neighbourhood of Jacob's Factory. I was present when the prisoners from Jacob's Factory surrendered at 5pm.

I recognise the accused as one of them. He gave his ranks as an officer. I had a list of the unarmed men made before the party was disarmed and the accused does not appear on that list. I was present when a summary of evidence was taken and I gave the same evidence as I have given now to the best of my belief. The accused did not cross examine me. The accused was not in uniform.

Cross examined by the accused

I identify the accused as one of the party that surrendered. I do not produce a list with the accused's name on it.

The witness withdraws.

2nd witness 2nd Lieutenant S.H. Jackson 3rd Royal Irish Regiment.

Duly sworn states.

I recognise the accused as John McBride. He gave his name as Major John MacBride.

I was in charge of a searching party in the gymnasium. The accused handed his notebook to me there, the date being 1-5-16. Papers attached marked X were found in the notebook.

(**Author's note:** these documents included a typed note naming MacBride as Commandant at Jacob's and a despatch dated 25 April.)

The accused declines to cross examine the witness.

The witness withdraws.

3rd Witness Inspector Richard H. Boyne. Dublin Metropolitan Police.

Duly Sworn. States.

I am an inspector of the Dublin Metropolitan Police. On May 2nd at about 11am I visited the lodgings of the accused and I found (Evidence of this witness disallowed).[6]

Prosecution closed.

Defence

1st witness Mrs Allen 3 Spencer Villas, Glenageary duly sworn states

I have known the accused 25 years.

I remember you leaving my house last Easter Monday Morning dressed in civilian clothes. I remember receiving a letter from the accused's brother Dr McBride saying he was coming up from Castlebar and asking the accused to meet him at the Wicklow Hotel Dublin. I remember the accused saying that he was going to lunch with his brother and would be back around 5 o/c. I remember Dr McBride was to be married the following Wednesday and that the accused was to be best man.

I have never seen him in uniform. Nor has he got such a thing as far as I know.

The prosecutor asked no questions.

The accused in his defence states

On the morning of Easter Monday I left my house at Glengeary with the intention of going to meet my brother who was coming to Dublin to get married. In waiting round town I went up as far as St Stephen's Green and there I saw a band of Irish Volunteers. I knew some of the members personally and the commander told me that an Irish Republic was virtually proclaimed. As he knew my rather advanced opinions and although I had no previous connection with the Irish Volunteers I considered it my duty to join them. I knew there was no chance of success and I never advised nor influenced any other person to join. I did not even know the positions they were about to take up. I marched with them to Jacob's Factory - after being a few hours there I was appointed second in command and felt it my duty to occupy that position. I could have escaped from Jacob's Factory before the surrender had I desired but I considered it a dishonourable thing to do. I do not say this with the idea of mitigating any penalty they may

```
impose but in order to make clear my position in
the matter.
Statement Ends.'
```

MacBride was convicted and sentenced to death. Sentence was confirmed by Maxwell the same day and MacBride was shot by firing squad the following morning. His body was immediately removed for burial at Arbour Hill.

MacBride and Liam Cosgrave had gravitated towards each other during their confinement. Cosgrave had helped MacBride secure his job with Dublin Corporation. According to Cosgrave, who appears to be a reliable narrator, MacBride asked if he might get his job back as a water bailiff. If this was said, it may have been MacBride's dry humour. They were both in the most imminent danger of being shot. Over 450 people had been killed during the Rebellion and a good part of the city centre lay in ruins. But this may have been a crucial few days for MacBride. He had recaptured that moment in his life that had defined him and it had vanished with the surrender. He realised that he faced a long prison sentence, to be released in late middle age, facing poverty and long-term unemployment.

As a result of Liam Cosgrave's request, a barrister was allowed to enter the barracks and see a few of the prisoners. These included Cosgrave, Ceannt and MacBride. Although, as Cosgrave put it, MacBride 'did not seem to be too keenly interested in his own case'.[7] MacBride's conference with counsel 'was a short one'. Liam Cosgrave later related 'there was no more unconcerned prisoner in Richmond Barracks, either, as to his fate or the discomforts prevailing'.[8]

What emerges is a man who had made up his mind to face the firing squad. A number of men based at Jacob's Factory slipped away before the surrender.[9] This opportunity was available to MacBride but not taken up. He had the opportunity to discard his weapon before the surrender but did not do so. When asked his name, he volunteered his rank at Jacob's Factory and the title, Major, by which he had been known for years. The day before his trial he gave evidence for Ceannt, a course of action which hardly endeared him to Blackader.

Furthermore, although MacBride had ample opportunity, he did not discard a key document that showed his rank. It is unlikely that this was because MacBride had forgotten about the document. The evidence of Lieutenant Jackson shows that the document was not found on MacBride: it was one of three incriminating documents handed over by the prisoner.

Most revealing of all, the crucial document, which showed MacBride's rank at Jacob's also listed the name and rank of three other Volunteer officers. But an examination of that document shows that the names of the other three Volunteer officers have been carefully cut out by hand, so that only MacBride's name and rank remained visible. It is difficult to resist the inference that this was done by MacBride and that he intentionally kept hold of the document so that it would be found and used against him.

MacBride did not offer any defence at his trial and seems to have courted the death sentence. He appears to have been concerned only to delineate the circumstances in which he came to be involved. This appears to have been Blackader's impression also: 'the accused wished to die'.[10]

After the trial MacBride emerged from the courtroom into the square at Richmond Barracks. He was carrying a dustcoat on his arm. He joined the other prisoners. He was asked how his trial was, and if he had received his sentence and his reply was:

```
'I looked down their rifles during the Boer War
and I will do the same tomorrow morning.'11
```

At this point he was recognised by a British officer who had fought against the Boers. Two of the escort party were asked to stand back and a photograph was taken.[12]

He was seen later that day in the Barracks square by Seán T. O'Kelly and called out:

```
'Nothing will save me Seán. This is the end.
Remember this is the second time I have sinned
against them.'13
```

Laying responsibility on his captors was disingenuous to say the least. MacBride had engineered this outcome. He was making the supreme sacrifice but he was also creating a legend.

A question arises as to why he called Mrs Allen, his long-standing landlady, to give evidence. She said nothing that mitigated his position. The truth may be quite straightforward: he wished to see her and this was the only way in which it could be managed. There is some contemporary evidence of a romantic attachment.[14]

CHAPTER THIRTY

James Melinn

James Melinn was tried at Richmond Barracks on 3 May. Brigadier General Blackader presided. The prisoner was charged with taking part in rebellion 'for the purpose and with the intention of assisting the enemy'. He denied the charge.[1]

```
'Prosecution
Ist Witness
Major J.E. Armstrong, Inniskilling Fusiliers duly
sworn states:-
I was present in St. Patrick's Park on the 30th
April last and the British troops were fired on
and several casualties occurred. The shots came
from the direction of Jacob's factory. A large
party from Jacob's Factory surrendered on the 30th
April 5 pm. The accused was one of the party. He
was armed. He gave his rank as a Sergeant in the
Irish Volunteers and was in uniform
CROSS EXAMINED
I did not examine the arms to see if it was clean.[2]
I touched no arms myself.
The arms were laid down by order of the Commanding
Officer of the rebels and were then collected and
taken away in a cart. I had a list made of the
unarmed men prior to the disarming of these men.
He is not on that list.
WITNESS WITHDRAWS
PROSECUTION CLOSES
The accused makes the following statement
I understood that we were going to Easter Manoeuvres
as we usually have them, and inspection, notice
of which had appeared in the Irish Volunteer for
weeks prior to Easter.
```

```
I went to the Manoeuvres and did not know we
were to take action. I repudiate entirely that I
had any intention of assisting the enemy. I never
fired a shot.'
```

Melinn was sentenced to death but 'recommended to mercy as the Court understand he may be a dupe'. Sentence was commuted by General Maxwell to ten years' penal servitude.

CHAPTER THIRTY ONE

The South Dublin Union

It was a foundling hospital and later a workhouse, the largest in Ireland. It sprawled over 50 acres in the south west of the city. The southern aspects dominated the South Circular Road and the Rialto Bridge on the Grand Canal.[1]

Inside the complex lay a maze of alleys and buildings, including a dinner hall, a church, the nurses' home, and a hospital with living accommodation for over 3,000 residents and staff. The hospital remained fully occupied during the Rebellion.

The Union was occupied at about midday on Monday 24 April by Éamonn Ceannt and the Fourth Battalion Volunteers, drawn from south-west Dublin. There were three outposts – at Marrowbone Lane, at Ardee Street and at Mount Brown, a three-storey grain store on the north-west boundary of the South Dublin Union. The garrison numbered over 200 men and women.

The strategic importance of the South Dublin Union lay in that it commanded the western and southern approaches to the city. It prevented the movement of troops from Richmond Barracks to the city centre and it overlooked army HQ at the Royal Hospital Kilmainham, which was well within rifle range.

The main outpost was Marrowbone Lane, which was heavily defended. The defenders of this outpost had adequate arms and ammunition but they lacked provisions. Because, however, the building fronted onto the street, it was possible to step out and commandeer livestock being driven to slaughter. On the first day a messenger boy carrying three chickens to the Vice-Regal Lodge was dispossessed: 'My compliments to the Lord Lieutenant', he was told, as the chickens were carried off.[2] This scenario was repeated many times. Even a passing bread van was captured.[3]

That same afternoon the Army launched an assault on the guard at the Rialto Gate. This position was defended by Captain George Irvine, who was one of those men who had little prior notice of the Rebellion. A few days before Easter Monday he had issued invitations to a ceilidhe to take place on 30 April.[4] With Irvine were seven men: John Downey, John Traynor, Patrick and James Morrissey, Gerald Doyle, James Burke and William Corrigan, a partner in a firm of Dublin solicitors. These men took over a wooden hut overlooking the boundary wall and barricaded the doors with beds and mattresses.

Units of the Royal Irish Regiment formed up in Richmond Barracks and set off for the South Dublin Union immediately after the alarm was sounded. There was no pause to take stock.[5] Captain Alan Ramsey of the Royal Irish Regiment led a company of soldiers to reconnoitre the South Dublin Union. He hoisted himself up on a telegraph pole and was shot dead. Captain Ramsey was a veteran of the Western Front and a native of Ballsbridge. An unidentified soldier was also killed and another officer who forced a side door in the Union wall was shot down and lost a leg.[6] The first attack was beaten off.

The Volunteers relocated themselves in a stone building close by. Discovering there were patients inside, they returned to a hut, which afforded little protection.[7] A second attack was launched and Volunteer John Traynor was killed. Patrick Morrissey was severely wounded in the leg and William Corrigan received splinter wounds to the eyes and face. The hut was soon surrounded by troops from the Royal Irish Regiment who were firing freely through the thin wooden walls. Faced with the threat of grenades, Irvine and his men surrendered.[8]

While these events were taking place, the nurses' home, a three-storey building in the heart of the complex, was being fortified and boarded up. There were other fatalities that afternoon, including William McDowell, George Owens, Nurse Margaretta Keogh and a patient caught in cross fire. The Army casualties were heavy; Captain Alan Ramsey and Captain Warmington were killed along with five soldiers. Ten others were wounded.[9]

On the second day there was no significant fighting save that night, a Volunteer near a window was shot by an army sniper.

The next significant engagement took place on the Thursday afternoon. The Sherwood Foresters, having overcome resistance at Mount Street canal bridge, tried to force their wagons and infantry over the Rialto Bridge towards army HQ at the Royal Hospital.

At the Rialto Bridge the Foresters came under heavy fire from the South Dublin Union. The Foresters were forced to halt and carry out a major assault on the South Dublin Union to clear the way to cross the Rialto Bridge. They were joined by Sir Francis Vane who had come up from Portobello Barracks. Sir Francis, wearing a scout uniform, led a collection of 'Highlanders, sailors and policemen'. They too, joined the attack on the South Dublin Union.[10]

This time the attackers fought their way to close range and began to bore holes through internal walls. Grenades were thrown by both sides. The officer leading the attack was Captain Michael Martyn of the

Sherwood Foresters. A grenade thrown by one of Martyn's men dropped short of the target and rolled back to the feet of the attackers. The grenade was snatched up by Martyn and hurled through an aperture above the door-frame.

The man on the other side of the wall was Cathal Brugha, who sustained a multiplicity of grenade wounds. The other Volunteers had evacuated the nurses' home under the weight of fire. They were able to hear Brugha singing and on one account shouting orders to a non-existent garrison. He was delirious, one Volunteer guessed, but then the penny dropped: Brugha was playing out a charade to put off the attackers. With a rush the Volunteers returned to the Nurses home.[11] The fight for the South Dublin Union ended in a stalemate.

But the evening light was failing and the Foresters took their chance. The wagon drivers, brandishing a revolver in one hand and reins in the other, galloped their horse-drawn transports across the Rialto Bridge towards the city centre. With their wagons safely across, the Foresters at the South Dublin Union, conducted a gradual withdrawal and followed their transports across the canal.[12] Captain Martyn and Captain Oates were later decorated for their part in the assault.

The total number of Volunteer fatalities numbered nine.[13] Twelve soldiers were killed and ten wounded.[14]

On the following day, the defenders saw artillery spotters reconnoitring the South Dublin Union. That evening, General Maxwell wrote to Lord French promising that any strong points that continued to hold out would be 'blown off the face of the earth'.[15]

Mercifully, this prospect was overtaken by the surrender at the GPO. At the South Dublin Union, a stalemate prevailed. On the Sunday some of the outlying garrison slipped away before the surrender and went to ground. Most followed Ceannt into captivity.[16]

At least 12 of the prisoners from the South Dublin Union were tried. Two were executed[17] and another seven were sentenced to death but had their sentences commuted to prison terms. Three were sentenced to prison terms.

One of the men captured on the first day was hospitalised, escaped and avoided trial. The other six men captured on the first day at the Rialto gate were court martialled.[18] At this stage the Army only had a few prisoners. Their names were logged and Lieutenant Bucknill took a summary of evidence. Their trial was inevitable. They were all convicted and sentenced to death. Most of them were tried on 5 May, after General Maxwell's recall to London and this may help to explain why their death sentences were commuted to prison terms.

The position of those who surrendered at the end of the week is more complex. The surrender at the South Dublin Union was taken by Captain Rotherham. He and Ceannt marched the surrendering Volunteers to their last outpost at Marrowbone Lane. They collected the Marrowbone Lane garrison and marched to Saint Patrick's Park where they formed up behind the prisoners from Jacob's. Their names were taken by Lieutenant William Wylie under the supervision of the Assistant Provost Marshal Major Armstrong.

From this point they were marched to Richmond Barracks and the process of sifting prisoners for trial began. Some prisoners were picked out by the 'G Men' and put forward for trial. At this point the Army began casting around for other evidence that these men had taken a senior or active role in the Rebellion. The first port of call was Captain Rotherham who had taken the surrender at the South Dublin Union. When called upon to identify the prisoners, he said he did not feel able to identify them. His eyesight, he hinted, was no longer first class. Captain Rotherham was a polo player with a national reputation and this explanation seems unlikely.

In these circumstances the Army had to fall back on Major Armstrong, the Assistant Provost Marshal, who had to rely on lists drawn up by Lieutenant Wylie. Armstrong gave evidence against a number of prisoners who surrendered from the South Dublin Union. A review of surviving trial records suggests that his evidence amounted to little more than a formulaic account; that the prisoner was armed, had come from Jacob's and that there had been firing from that vicinity.[19]

Éamonn Ceannt was tried and executed. Other officers tried included Phil Cosgrave and Liam Cosgrave who were both sentenced to death. Liam Cosgrave's sentence was commuted to penal servitude for life. His brother, Philip Cosgrave, who was of comparable rank, had his sentence commuted to three years. A significant number of officers were never tried but a number of junior officers and men were singled out for trial. Seamus Murphy who was in command at Marrowbone Lane was not tried but a junior officer under his command, Colbert was tried and executed. Cathal Brugha who was second in command at the South Dublin Union was not expected to live. He was never tried. After the surrender he was removed to the Hospital Wing at Dublin Castle where he remained for many weeks.[20] Also wounded was Captain Ffrench-Mullen, who was third in command. He too, was not tried.

Peadar Doyle was tried and sentenced to ten years' penal servitude. Doyle was from Inchicore, a railway man with the Great Southern and Western Railway.[21] The decision to try this man was curious to say the least. The officer who gave evidence for the Army stated that Doyle did not appear to be in a position of authority and he could not say if Doyle was armed or not. Doyle was a prominent trade unionist and this may be the reason he was picked out for trial by the G men.

Finally, Charles O'Neill was also tried and sentenced to one years' imprisonment. The sentence suggests that he was very young.[22]

A selection of the surviving trial records are set out in the following chapters.

CHAPTER THIRTY TWO

Liam Cosgrave

Liam Cosgrave was tried at Richmond Barracks on 3 May.[1] Brigadier General Blackader presided. Cosgrave, like the other prisoners was tried under Regulation 50 of DORR; taking part in a rebellion with 'intent and for the purpose of assisting the enemy'. He denied the charge.

Cosgrave was first called before the court on 2 May for a pre-trial hearing. He was, perhaps, the only prisoner to question the legality of the court martial. His observations on this received short shrift. He also raised the question of legal representation and was told that he might have a prisoner's friend but not a lawyer.[2] Cosgrave asked that prisoners in his group be allowed legal advice. This concession, not extended to others, was permitted and later that day he was able to see John Ronayne, a barrister. Oddly, Ronayne was a National Volunteer – he had gone with the Redmondites at the time of the split. There followed a very short conference:

> 'Ronayne: What do you propose to say?
> Reply: There is no truth in the German charge. I accept responsibility for being in arms. A long sentence of imprisonment is not attractive.
> Ronayne: That will get you a long sentence. You will not get a firing squad. If you want to shorten your sentence admit nothing.'[3]

It is likely that the conference with counsel was rather longer than Cosgrave recalled. The advice to admit nothing was sound enough but Cosgrave's position was far more precarious than counsel suggested. Even then, the Rebellion had become known as the Sinn Féin Rebellion, although Sinn Féin had nothing to do with the Rebellion. But Cosgrave was a Sinn Féin Alderman. To the Army he may have appeared to be a leader rather than a junior officer of the Volunteers.

Wylie recalled: 'The next accused was waiting outside when the court closed to consider the verdict on the one just tried and I used to go out and ask them if they had any defence or were there witnesses they wished to be called.' On 2 May he went out and saw Liam Cosgrave, whom he recognised as a member of the Dublin Corporation.

Wylie went over and spoke to Cosgrave:

```
'I asked him if he had any idea of the position
he was in and he said he had not and asked me was
it serious. I told him the last three men who were
tried had all been sentenced to death and would be
shot in the morning.'
```

Cosgrave told him that 'when he marched out on Easter Monday morning he thought he was merely going out for a route march, that he was suddenly told to take 20 men into a hut in the South Dublin Union and hold it and before he knew what happened he was in the middle of a battle'.

Wylie had the case adjourned so that Cosgrave's character witnesses could be present and the trial commenced the following day, 3 May.

The evidence came from DMP Constable Patrick Walsh, who had observed Cosgrave at midday on Easter Monday at Dolphin's Barn when the Fourth Battalion mustered and set off for the South Dublin Union. Constable Walsh stated that Cosgrave had led the Volunteers as they moved out down Cork Street. Contrary to what Walsh had said in his deposition, he gave no evidence that Cosgrave was armed.[4]

Major James Armstrong also gave evidence that Cosgrave was one of many who had surrendered from Jacob's Factory. Armstrong observed that Cosgrave was not on the unarmed list and was therefore armed.

Returning to Wylie's recollection: 'I told the court that the accused wished to make a statement and call evidence and I turned and asked Cosgrave to say whatever he wished. "I would rather you made it for me" he said. So I then launched into a speech for the defence and then examined the three witnesses as regards the character of the accused.'

The witnesses included Sir James Gallagher, who was then Lord Mayor, Surgeon Macardle and Alderman Lorcan Sherlock. It was as distinguished a list of witnesses as might be found.

According to Cosgrave the trial lasted less than 15 minutes from start to finish.

After court closed to consider verdict, Blackader summoned Wylie back into the room and asked: 'Is that a decent man, Wylie, and was he in your opinion rushed into this?' Wylie replied 'I believe what he said.' 'Thank you', said the General. 'We will recommend a reprieve.'

This meant a death sentence with a recommendation for mercy. The papers then went to Maxwell for confirmation.

Cosgrave was taken back to a cell at Kilmainham. He still did not know the verdict or sentence. In the early hours of 5 May he heard MacBride, in the next cell being taken out:

> 'Through a chink in the door I could barely discern the receding figures; silence for a time then the sharp crack of rifle fire and silence again. I thought my turn would come next and waited for a rap on the door, but the firing squad had no further duty that morning.'[5]

Later that day Cosgrave was informed that his sentence had been commuted to penal servitude for life. In his report to Cabinet, Maxwell described Cosgrave as one of a number of 'important leaders'[6] who he had decided to reprieve. The notion that Cosgrave was then an important leader demonstrates how Maxwell was essentially out of touch. Cosgrave escaped execution by a very fine margin.

Cosgrave was 35, unmarried, a Sinn Féin member of Dublin Corporation since 1909. Wylie recalled him 'as a man always ready to help the poor of Dublin'. At the outset of Easter Week Cosgrave was not a committed revolutionary. On the boat to prison in England, he declared he had 'gone out' against his better judgment. The events at Richmond Barracks were a defining moment in his life and propelled him into revolutionary politics. Later that year, while still a prisoner, he was co-opted back onto the Dublin Corporation and won a seat in the First Dáil the following year. He became Minister for local government during the War of Independence and played an important role in enabling local government institutions to shift their allegiance and the reins of power to Dáil Éireann. Cosgrave later became the first President of the Executive Council of the Irish Free State.

CHAPTER THIRTY THREE

Éamonn Ceannt

Ceannt was tried on 3 and 4 May at Richmond Barracks. Brigadier General Blackader DSO presided. Ceannt was charged with 'taking part in an armed rebellion with the intention and for the purpose of assisting the enemy'. The prisoner denied the charge. The record of the trial is set out below.[1]

'1st Witness Major J.A. Armstrong Inniskilling Fusiliers states:

I was at Patrick's Park on the 30th April 1916. The British troops were fired on, the fire came from the neighbourhood of Jacob's Factory. Several casualties occurred. I was under fire. I was present about 5pm when the party from Jacobs Factory surrendered. I directed an officer to make a list of the unarmed men. The accused surrendered as one of the party and at the head of it, his name was not on the unarmed list. There was an armed list made and his name appears at the head of it and from information he gave he is described as commandant. I asked him to give orders and he did so, they were obeyed.

Cross examination by the accused

A list of all the men on parade was made. And that is the list of armed men. It does not follow that all men on parade were armed men. I have a perfect recollection of the time the list was commenced, it was commenced after the men were disarmed. I succeeded in making a list of all armed men after they had been disarmed because I had had a separate list of the unarmed men made before the disarming took place. I arrived at the list of armed men by a process of elimination only, and a recollection of men seen with arms, the accused was one of them. He had no rifle; either a revolver or automatic pistol, which he took out of his pocket, and laid on the ground.

Prosecution Closed

Defence

The Accused calls witnesses

1st witness John MacBride, sworn, states:

I know the accused intimately, I should be in no doubt as to his identity, I remember Sunday the 30th April 1916 and preceding days, I was in Jacob's factory, I left it on Sunday afternoon between 4 and 5pm. The accused was not in my company before I left. It was impossible for the accused to be in Jacob's Factory without my knowledge, he had no connection with the party that occupied Jacob's Factory.

Cross examined by the Prosecutor

I saw the accused in the neighbourhood of St. Patrick's Park when my party surrendered. I did not see the accused at any time between Easter Monday and Sunday the 30th April 1916. I have not the slightest knowledge that he is commandant of the 4th battalion. I saw him in uniform at the time the surrender took place drawn up in line.

The prisoner calls on Thomas MacDonagh who was not available as he was shot this morning.

The court adjourns this case for further evidence. At 12.45pm on the 4th May 1916 the court reopens.

2nd Witness

Richard Davys being duly sworn states:

I was in Jacob's Factory from Monday 24th April till Sunday the 30th. The Accused was not in Jacob's Factory during any part of that time. He was not of the party which surrendered from Jacob's Factory. I know the accused perfectly well. I don't think the accused could have been in Jacob's Factory or been one of the party surrendering from Jacob's Factory without my knowledge. I did not hear the accused's name mentioned at any time in connection with Jacob's Factory.

Cross examined by Prosecutor.

The party at Jacob's Factory surrendered at about

5pm on Sunday the 30th. The surrender took place
at Patricks Park. When I surrendered accused was
at the far corner of the same square. I could not
say if he was of the same party with me that came
to Richmond Barracks. I heard shots fired near
Jacob's Bakery but could not say who fired.

I saw a proclamation declaring Ireland a Republic
on Wednesday 26th April, I did not take any notice
of the names appended.

3rd witness Patrick Emmet Sweeney being duly sworn
states:

I was in Jacob's Factory from Easter Monday to
Sunday 30th April 1916. I never saw accused in
Jacob's Factory the whole time I was there.

The accused in his defence states:

Three witnesses who were in Jacob's Factory from
Monday the 24th April 1916 to about 5pm on Sunday
the 30th have sworn that I was not in Jacob's
Factory during any of that period and was not
one of a party which surrendered from Jacob's
Factory on Sunday the 30th April. Another witness
who was not available would have been able to
corroborate these 3. The evidence makes it quite
clear that I cannot have had anything to do with
the firing from the neighbourhood of Jacobs which
resulted in casualties to British troops at St.
Patrick's Park as referred to. I do not accuse
Major Armstrong of endeavouring to mislead the
court, but it is clear that he was deceived in
thinking that I was attached in any way to the
Jacob's party which as deposed fired on British
troops in the neighbourhood of Patrick's Park.
He has admitted that his plan of making a list
of armed men was by a process of elimination of
the unarmed men from the whole list on parade
and from recollection. He has admitted that the
list of armed men was compiled after all men
had been disarmed. I submit that this evidence
is not conclusive except insofar as it concerned
the unarmed men and is not evidence as to the

men who were armed. I claim at least that there
is reasonable doubt and the benefit of the doubt
should be given to the accused. In regard to
my carrying arms there is no positive or direct
evidence except that Major Armstrong believes I
carried a revolver or automatic pistol, which
he says I took from my pocket and laid upon
the ground. As to my having surrendered to the
military authorities this is sufficiently proved
by my presence at Richmond Barracks and is hereby
freely admitted. As to the accusation that I did
an act "with the intention and for the purpose
of assisting the enemy" I content myself with
a simple denial. The Crown did not even tender
evidence in this regard.
I gave away my automatic pistol.
The Volunteer uniform more often than not does not
indicate the rank of the wearer.
The witness I intended to call and could not be
found from the description I gave to the police
would have proved that I did not come from the
neighbourhood of Jacob's Factory.
I came at the head of 2 bodies of men but was only
connected with one body.'

The background to this trial begins on 1 May, when Ceannt was brought
up for the taking of the summary of evidence. The only witness for the
prosecution was Major Armstrong. He asserted that Ceannt had been one
of the leaders at Jacob's factory, which had inflicted casualties on the British
Army. In fact Jacob's factory had been commanded by MacDonagh and
Major MacBride. Ceannt had been in command at the South Dublin Union.

Where, following the taking of a summary of evidence, a charge was laid,
the prisoner was supplied with a copy. The form of the charge laid against
Ceannt was rebellion, contrary to Regulation 50 of the DORR, but owing to
the confusion arising from the surrender, the way the case was put against
the prisoner was that he had been one of the rebel officers at Jacob's Factory.

He was of course one of the signatories to the Proclamation of the
Republic and his life was at grave risk. But at this point Ceannt appears to
have realised that this was a charge he might rebut. He had already regretted
the surrender and he also had a wife and young child.

Following William Wylie's suggestion that prisoners could seek legal advice, a barrister and solicitor were sent for. The solicitor failed to appear but the barrister, John Ronayne, arrived at the barracks within the hour and was able to spend some time with Ceannt. Ceannt jotted down the strands of his defence on the back of the charge sheet.[2]

Ceannt's trial was reached on the morning of 3 May. By an odd coincidence the officer who had personally taken Ceannt's surrender was William Wylie who had been detailed to prosecute the case. At the surrender Ceannt had made quite an impression on Wylie. Twenty years later when Wylie wrote his memoir, he could still recall Ceannt at the point of surrender:

`'He was a big fine-looking man dressed in civvies with no collar or tie.'`[3]

The officer who was the only witness for the Crown was Major James Armstrong of the Inniskilling Fusiliers. Armstrong had been with Wylie at Patrick's Park when the surrender took place. His notes of who was armed and who was not armed had been compiled by Wylie. In Wylie's memoir he recalled that 'Blackader asked Armstrong did he take these particulars himself and Armstrong said no, but they were taken by a responsible officer. I was the officer.'

It was a long-standing rule of common law that a lawyer might appear as an advocate or as a witness but could never be both. Wylie was the one officer who might positively prove the case against Ceannt but could say nothing. The accuracy and reliability of the list produced by Major Armstrong was central to the prosecution case. Ceannt's cross-examination revealed some shortcomings in the list. The real point here is that Armstrong had not compiled the list himself. It follows that the bulk of Armstrong's evidence was probably accurate but it was hearsay and therefore inadmissible.

Ceannt's first witness was Major MacBride who had held a senior command post at Jacob's factory. MacBride had yet to be tried and any prisoner who drew attention to himself in this way ran the risk of being subject to special scrutiny or simply antagonising the Court. These considerations must have been in Ceannt's mind when he looked around for witnesses but it appears that MacBride had made his mind up that he would face the firing squad. At his own trial, the following day, MacBride would offer no defence, just an explanation and justification. He was therefore free to give evidence for Ceannt and did so. His evidence was true. Even his denial that he knew that Ceannt held high rank in the Volunteers may well have been true. MacBride was not a member of the Volunteers and only joined the Rebellion on Easter Monday.

The second defence witness called by Ceannt was Thomas MacDonagh who had been in command at Jacob's. Ceannt therefore called MacDonagh to rebut the prosecution case that he was present at Jacob's Factory. The trial record blandly records that this witness was 'not available' having been shot that morning. This aspect of the trials has caused many to comment in strong terms on the rush to judgment.[4] It cannot have been beyond the wit of Maxwell that the men being executed might have relevant evidence to give in some of the other trials.

There is another point to be made, however. When Ceannt called MacDonagh to give evidence, he already knew that MacDonagh had been executed.[5] It was common knowledge among the prisoners. Had MacDonagh been alive it is hardly likely that Ceannt would have called him. Because although he would have confirmed that Ceannt was not one of the Jacob's garrison, he would have been exposed to cross-examination about Ceannt's rank and the fact that Ceannt was a signatory to the proclamation. It comes down to this: Ceannt was trying to put the Court in an embarrassing position, which might make it draw back from a death sentence.

Why was Ceannt's trial adjourned overnight? Wylie recalls that Ceannt asked for other witnesses who could not be traced. This caused some delay in the trial on 3 May. It does appear probable that the absence of MacDonagh assisted Ceannt in securing an adjournment overnight until the morning of 4 May, while he found other witnesses.[6]

That evening Ceannt returned to his cell and talked over the events of the trial with Liam Cosgrave. The trial had raised points of admissibility which he barely understood. Ceannt is remembered by those who knew him as a big, quiet man, not socially adroit. He was more at ease speaking Irish than English. He had found his trial a difficult experience and was wise enough to know that he was out of his depth. Ceannt also confided in Cosgrave that he had not put his signature to the Proclamation. He had agreed to his name being used and 'did not repudiate it' but there was no signed copy on which the prosecution could rely so he feared the matter might be raised in evidence and how he might deal with the point. Ceannt asked that Cosgrave act as his 'soldier's friend'. Cosgrave was not a lawyer but in his work on the Corporation he had acquired some experience of court procedure. Cosgrave's trial had concluded that day. He had advanced no defence. Conviction was inevitable and Cosgrave was waiting to hear if he was to be executed. He agreed, even so, to act as 'soldier's friend' for Ceannt.

The following morning Ceannt applied for Cosgrave to act as the 'soldier's friend'. This request was refused by General Blackader on the basis that the prisoner 'had not availed of it on the first day of the court martial'.[7] This episode, which does not appear on the court record, remains unedifying. The trial then resumed and Ceannt was compelled to press on alone.

But Ceannt still had another card to play. He was able to find two other prisoners who could rebut the suggestion that he had been at Jacob's Factory.

Two of the witnesses he called had already been tried. Richard Davis had been convicted on the first day when trials took place.[8] Davis, was a tall, bearded Volunteer[9] in his 30s, a time-keeper at the Guinness brewery. His austere persona disguised the fact that he was a first aider, who held no rank.[10] There had been some amusement in the Volunteer ranks when Davis, 'Dickie' to his friends, was picked out by the 'G Men' as a leader and taken off for trial.[11] But Davis had been tried and sentenced to ten years. His sentence had been confirmed and so he was beyond the reach of retribution and could not prejudice himself by giving evidence for another prisoner.

The second defence witness, Patrick Sweeney, had been a founder member of the Volunteers. He had been a quartermaster and then a Lieutenant in the 2nd Battalion Volunteers.[12] Sweeney was then aged 38, an accountant married with three young children. Sweeney had been convicted on the morning of 3 May, when Ceannt's trial started. Confirmation of sentence of death in Sweeney's case was still pending when he decided to give evidence for Ceannt. At this stage the prisoners knew that executions were taking place but no one knew how many might be executed. It was a brave decision.[13]

The evidence of these prisoners was substantially true: Ceannt had been nowhere near Jacob's factory during the rebellion.

Wylie later wrote of the prisoner:

```
'He showed no sign of nervousness or faltering
before the court. I would say in fact he was the
most dignified of any of the accused.'14
```

Ceannt had no legal training but his closing address was remarkable in its clarity, although he made minor evidential concessions which were unnecessary.

In the muddle and confusion that surrounded the Rebellion, the newspapers published news that Ceannt had been convicted and sentenced to three years' imprisonment. The papers were read with relief by his family[15] but returning home to Dolphin Terrace, his wife Áine found the house utterly thrashed after a raid by the Army:

```
'tea and sugar were inches deep on the floor, our
tinned foods had been taken out and evidently a
```

```
bayonet run through each of them and doors and
windows were smashed.'¹⁶
```

Trailing around Dublin, Áine Ceannt was unable to find any information about her husband. She was eventually able to get access to Lord Powerscourt, the Provost Marshal[17] who was 'amiable'. He provided her with a pass and she went directly to Kilmainham where she found her husband: 'his Sam Brown belt was gone and his uniform was slightly torn'.[18] There was no chair 'and no bedding, not even a bed of straw'. He had no illusions about his fate.

Sentence was confirmed by Maxwell on 6 May and promulgated the following day. Later that week Maxwell wrote to Asquith setting out the grounds on which execution was ordered. In the case of Ceannt, Maxwell relied on the fact that could not be proven at trial: that he was a signatory to the Proclamation.[19]

Ceannt was shot at dawn on the morning of 8 May. Afterwards, his widow emerged from his shadow as a formidable lady. In the difficult years that followed she was active in the relief of poverty with the Irish White Cross. During the War of Independence, she was a District Councillor and a District Justice in the Dáil Courts. Her home was frequently raided. In later years she served with William Wylie on the Red Cross Committee. He remembered her as 'a good businesswoman without any "bitterness"'.

CHAPTER THIRTY FOUR

Con Colbert

Cornelius Colbert was tried on 4 May at Richmond Barracks.[1] Colonel Sapte presided. Colbert faced the standard charge of taking part in the rebellion 'with the intention and for the purpose of assisting the enemy'. He also faced a second charge of attempting 'to cause disaffection among the civilian population of His Majesty'. He denied the charges. The record of the trial is set out below.

> 'Major J.A. Armstrong Royal Inniskilling Fusiliers states On 30th April 1916 I was present at Bride St and Patricks Park when the British troops were fired upon. The accused was one of party which surrendered at about 5pm. He was dressed in Volunteer captain's uniform and was armed. These officers were armed with pistols or revolvers.
> These men who surrendered came from the direction in which firing had taken place.
> Defence – The accused in his defence states:– I have nothing to say.'

Colbert was convicted on the first charge and sentenced to death. A not guilty verdict was returned on the alternative charge alleging the causing of disaffection among the civilian population.

A letter smuggled out of Lewes prison the following year gave a different account of Colbert's trial. In this account Colbert stated that 'he could prove he was not at Jacob's'. The President of the court stated that 'this did not matter' and Colbert replied: 'If you say it does not make any difference, then I will not call a witness to prove it.'[2] It is likely that the court took the view that if he was a Volunteer officer and he was armed it did not matter which garrison he had surrendered from.

Confirmation was delayed because the executions on 4 May caused Asquith to recall Maxwell to London. Maxwell confirmed sentence on his return on 6 May and Colbert was informed late the following night. Execution took place at 3.45am on 8 May.

A story emerged later that his commanding officer, Seamus Murphy, who was married with a child, had somehow evaded trial and execution at the expense of Colbert. A theory was canvassed that they had swopped uniforms at Richmond Barracks.[3] In fact Murphy was a tall, heavily built man and Colbert small and compact. This theory was later rightly described as a 'canard'.[4]

Since then, two myths have attached themselves to Colbert. First, that he was 'in command' at Marrowbone Lane[5] and second that he was executed for this reason.

In fact there were nearly a dozen officers in Colbert's battalion who were of more senior rank.[6] Colbert was simply a junior officer in the battalion. Together with 15 men he was detailed by Ceannt to hold an outpost at Watkins's Brewery at Ardee Street. Here they remained until Tuesday 25 April, when it became apparent that the outpost was of no strategic value and late that night they gathered up their weapons and kit and crept in stockinged feet to Marrowbone Lane, another outpost of the South Dublin Union. Colbert's senior officers at Marrowbone Lane were Seamus Murphy and Joseph McGrath. One of the garrison later suggested that Colbert had assumed command from Murphy.[7] This was, one suspects, part of the process of lionising the executed prisoners. The notion that Colbert was in command at Marrowbone Lane has come to be accepted as fact although this account has been contradicted by so many other witnesses.[8]

No evidence was called at his trial that he held an independent command at Marrowbone Lane or anywhere else: the evidence given at his trial connected him (wrongly) with the Jacob's garrison. General Maxwell's *'Short History of rebels'* [9] set out the reasons for confirming the death sentence but did not in any way suggest that Colbert held an independent command.

The process by which historians have elevated Colbert to commanding officer at Marrowbone Lane has a good deal to do with trying to make sense of what happened: why else would he be executed? It obscures an important point, namely, that the system of selection for trial and confirmation of death sentences was capricious. When the prisoners were paraded at Richmond Barracks, Colbert was picked out by the 'G Men' because he was known to be active in the Volunteers. His commanding officer, Murphy, was not. As one of the other prisoners put it, 'Luck favoured Murphy' and he was deported the same day.[10]

Colbert was an accounts clerk at Kennedy's Bakery on Britain Street. He was the fourth youngest of thirteen children. He joined the Volunteers in 1913 and resisted Redmond's attempt to take over the Volunteers. When the split came he stayed with the Irish Volunteers. He was Chief Scout of the

Fianna scout movement and was also involved as a drill instructor. A short, strongly built young man, he did not smoke or drink. He was religious and like so many young men in a continent locked in war, he was intensely nationalistic in outlook. Colbert's last letters home hint at his fear of death and his hope that he would die bravely.[11]

CHAPTER THIRTY FIVE

Philip Cosgrave

Philip Cosgrave was tried at Richmond Barracks on 4 May. Brigadier General Blackader presided. The prisoner faced the standard charge of rebellion 'with the intention and for the purpose of assisting the enemy'. He denied the charge.[1]

```
'PROSECUTION
Ist Witness Major J.A. Armstrong, Inniskilling
Fusilers duly sworn states:
On Sunday April 30th I was at Patricks Park. The
British Troops were fired on.
I was present later in the day when a surrender
was arranged with Mr McDonagh.
The surrender was at 5 p.m. Two bodies surrendered
in adjoining streets. The accused was with one of
the bodies he was in uniform and he was armed. I
caused a list of prisoners to be made giving names
address and rank, his name appeared in the list
with the rank of Lieutenant. They were subsequently
removed in custody to Richmond Barracks.
CROSS EXAMINED BY THE ACCUSED
I made a separate list of the unarmed men and the
accused does not appear on that list. There was a
list also made of men who had arms.
The witness withdraws
Prosecution closed
DEFENCE
The accused declines to call witnesses
The accused in his defence stated
I was Commissariat Officer looking after the goods
of the men I had no arms but I had ammunition. I
did not take part in this thing for the purpose of
assisting the enemy. I had no communication with
anybody either directly or indirectly.'
```

CHAPTER THIRTY SIX

Gerald Doyle

Gerald Doyle was tried on 5 May at Richmond Barracks. Brigadier General Blackader presided.[1] Doyle was charged with taking part in rebellion 'with the intention and for the purpose of assisting the enemy'. The prisoner denied the charge. The record of the trial is set out below.

> '1st Witness 2nd Lieut JAMES WATSON, Royal Irish Rifles, duly sworn states:-
> I remember Monday April 24. I had a party of men at the South Dublin Union on that day - we were engaged in attacking a hut occupied by the rebels.
> The hut was divided into a number of wards. We suffered casualties from fire from the hut and an officer was killed.
> We rushed the hut and captured it. The rebels eventually surrendered. The Accused was one.
> I was there when he was taken, he was standing with his hands held up. He had no arms but there was a rifle lying a few feet from him but I couldn't say if it was his - he was handed over to the police station.
> The Accused declines to cross examine the Witness
> The Witness withdraws
> Prosecution closed.
> DEFENCE
> The Accused calls Witnesses
> 1st Witness WILLIAM P. CORRIGAN, duly sworn, states:-
> I knew the Accused. I cannot say if he was armed.
> The Accused is a very decent fellow.
> The Witness withdraws.
> The ACCUSED in his defence states:-

I joined the Volunteers two or three weeks ago
and on Easter Monday morning I got an order to
mobilize. I was told verbally by the man who
brought the message to bring some grub and that we
were going for parade for the day. I was told to
be in Kimmage at 10 o'clock.
After finishing my breakfast I went there and I was
marched from Kimmage to Emerald Square - we formed
up there and were told we were to parade through
the City. We left there and found ourselves in the
Canal and thence to the Union - as soon as I got
in I heard shots - I was sent with the others to
the hut where we were under fire - it got so hot
that we got out of it, but were driven into it
again. Two of my comrades were hit and I rendered
assistance as I had no arms.
As I was doing this the door was broken down and I
was captured and sent to Kilmainham Police Station.
The rifle that the Witness mentioned belonged to a
man who was killed - I knew absolutely nothing of
what was happening.'

Doyle was convicted and sentenced to death.[2] with a rider: 'Recommended
to mercy as the Court consider that he was a dupe.' In fact Doyle had been
a Volunteer for some years and knew only too well what he was doing when
he mobilised on Easter Monday. The findings of the court were confirmed
by Maxwell the following day. Sentence was commuted to three years' penal
servitude.

Doyle was then 19 years old, from Old Kilmainham. He was a plasterer
by trade, a clever young man with little formal education. He was the eldest
of seven children, the only one of whom was earning a wage. His father
had just joined the British army. In some ways this family was Dublin in
miniature; beset by poverty with competing claims on their loyalty. The
family had moved to Goldenbridge just before the Rebellion. When he was
captured, Doyle had the sense to give his old address at Kilmainham, which
was searched and ransacked.

Doyle called William Corrigan to give evidence as to character and fact.
Corrigan was a solicitor in a respected Dublin firm and his word might have
carried some weight with the court but for the fact that he was a Volunteer
also. He was Doyle's section leader, wounded in the face and captured with

Doyle on the first day of the fighting. He was next in line to be tried. If it were not so serious it might be considered ludicrous.

Doyle later gave a statement to the Bureau of Military History which threw an interesting light on his trial. Like many personal accounts written so many years later, there are parts which are redolent of what he later wished he had said, but here are two extracts:

'A soldier standing by my side whispered in my ear, "This is it, son and I wish you luck". (He was one of the Notts and Derbys). The door then opened and I was handed over to two Military Police. At the end of the room there were three high ranking officers sitting at a table. On the left facing me was another officer with a mass of papers on a small table and on the right was a lieutenant. He was the witness against me. I was marched up to the table where the three officers were. And I was placed in a chair.[3]

Captain Wiley then made a suggestion to the court that he be allowed to conduct my defence. I turned in my chair to look at him in surprise. (My mind at once sensed a trap.) The three officers consulted with each other and the President replied stating that he had no objection if the prisoner himself agreed to accept the generous offer. He then put a question to me, "Are you prepared to accept the generous offer of Captain Wiley, who is also a skilful lawyer and prepared to conduct your defence?" I replied stating while I wished to thank Captain Wiley for his offer I did not agree to accept. Captain Wiley then said he could understand my mind but that I did not realise the seriousness of my position. The President then picked up a Volunteer membership card and I immediately knew it was the one that had been taken from me when I was searched at the time when we were captured. It was only a new card which I had received only three weeks before the Rising and there was 1 & 6d contribution marked on it. I had lost my old card and received a new one from Willie Corrigan

```
who was my Section Leader. One of the officers
said "According to this card you are only a member
since three weeks before the Rebellion," and I
replied "That is the only card I have".'
```

Doyle was sent to Mountjoy with the other convicted prisoners. They were provided with prison uniforms and shipped to England. He was later sent to Lewes prison. He was seen there by George Gavan Duffy and agreed to allow his case to be used in a legal challenge to the lawfulness of the trials.[4] The test case was ultimately unsuccessful but it resulted in his trial papers surviving.

Doyle, along with the other convicted prisoners, was released in June 1917.

CHAPTER THIRTY SEVEN

William Corrigan

William Corrigan was tried on 5 May at Richmond Barracks. Brigadier General Blackader presided. Corrigan was charged with taking part in rebellion 'with the intention and for the purpose of assisting the enemy'. He denied the charge.

The evidence in his case was broadly the same as that given in the case of Doyle. Both were part of the small group of men captured at the Rialto gate of the South Dublin Union on the first day of the Rebellion. Corrigan's position was particularly hazardous because during the fighting which led to his capture, an officer had been killed and a number of soldiers wounded. He was also section leader in B Company of the Fourth Battalion of the Volunteers. He appeared before the court in uniform, still recovering from glass fragment wounds in the eye and face.[1]

Corrigan was fortunate to know people of influence. His father Patrick Corrigan had been a gangmaster[2] and 'a slum landlord and undertaker'.[3] He had made money and become an Alderman and put his sons through college. Corrigan was then aged 27. He was a newly-qualified solicitor who did a good deal of work in the Police Courts in Dublin. The senior partner in the firm was his elder brother who was allowed to visit Richmond Barracks and see his younger brother and perhaps provide some advice. He called in a favour from a well-connected Unionist King's Counsel who made representations to the Army.[4]

While standing in the corridor outside the court martial quarters he was approached by William Wylie KC who prosecuted many of the trials. They knew each other. The Dublin legal circle was a small one and it seems that Corrigan had briefed Wylie on more than one occasion. Corrigan later recounted Wylie's remark 'Remember if you do not think you are being fairly treated you can call on me.'

Wylie's recollection was a little different. He recalled going out into the corridor to see who the next prisoner was:

> 'I saw a man in uniform with bloody bandage round his head, went up to him, suddenly recognised him and said "My God Corrigan, what are you doing

here?"
  "Next to be tried," he said. "Have I any chance?"'

Wylie asked him how he came to be involved and Corrigan's response might have fitted many young men: 'There are Carson's Volunteers, Redmond's Volunteers, our Volunteers, the GR's... your OTC, besides the regulars. If you aren't drilling and marching you're not in it.'

In fact, Corrigan's trial was called on soon after and he found himself being prosecuted by Wylie. The record of the trial has not survived and Corrigan's account is limited to a single anecdote: 'A sergeant who had given evidence in my case wished to amend his evidence. Before he was allowed to do so Mr Wylie stated to him: "You have finished your evidence and you cannot add to or take from it unless it is in favour of the prisoner" and the Sergeant was not allowed to give any further evidence.'[5]

Corrigan's brother arranged for character witnesses. The Lord Mayor and Reverend Grimes gave evidence on the prisoner's behalf.[6]

Wylie, who seems to have forgotten he was prosecuting, examined Corrigan in his own defence 'and made an impassioned speech in his defence'.

After the evidence was heard and the prisoner returned to his cell, the deliberations of the court took an unexpected turn. Wylie, on being questioned by Blackader explained his connection with the prisoner:

> 'He is a solicitor and before this show started I got a case from him to advise one of his clients. There was a cheque for £5. 5. 0d with it which I haven't cashed yet. If you execute him that cheque might not be met.'

This response was met with silence and then laughter. We were all under 'strain' Wylie recalled. Blackader replied: 'Alright Wylie, your five guineas is safe. We will recommend a reprieve.'

Sentence of death was passed but a few days later commuted to five years' penal servitude and Corrigan was shipped over to England.[7] It had also been a testing week for his father Alderman Corrigan who had spent the week arranging character evidence and pulling in favours to save the life of his son. The same week Alderman Corrigan discovered that his undertaker's premises had been used by the rebels: among the cadavers they had stored a large quantity of explosives. The Alderman got hold of a hand cart and moved the explosives to a safe house before dumping his cargo, piece by piece, in the Liffey.[8]

After young Corrigan's release he returned to Dublin where he resumed practice as a solicitor. The Law Society had no professional conduct committee and although taking part in a rebellion might attract a death sentence, if the prisoner survived, there was no bar to legal practice.

The lives of Corrigan and Wylie crossed again in 1920 when the War of Independence was reaching a new pitch. It was a war being fought on many levels. The Ambush War was just one aspect of the conflict. Dáil Éireann had come into being and was gradually seizing control of local government and all the associated institutions and responsibilities, including health care.

Corrigan's firm acted for the Joint Committee of the Grangegorman Mental Hospital. The hospital had been part of the fabric of Dublin life for over a century dealing with the most intractable cases of mental illness. The Joint Committee ran the hospital but was required to submit their books for auditing to the Local Government Board in order to access funds. The Joint Committee declined to do so having sworn allegiance to Dáil Éireann. The Local Government Board declined to renew funding and a crisis loomed: if the patients could not be fed then they would have to be released within days. It was in these circumstances that Corrigan sought legal advice from Wylie.[9]

This bizarre meeting between Corrigan and the man who had prosecuted him and possibly saved his life, took place in Wylie's home at Clonsilla, then a small village to the west of Dublin. At that late-night meeting, Corrigan explained the dire circumstances and the imminent release of 400 mentally ill patients. Wylie remarked:

```
'This will be a nice town to live in with the
Black and Tans, the IRA and lunatics abroad.'¹⁰
```

The crisis was later averted but on Corrigan's account, the conversation turned to the war and how it might be ended. In due course Corrigan and Wylie later arranged for emissaries of Dáil Éireann and the British Government to come to the offices of Corrigan and Corrigan in late September 1920.[11]. Sir John Anderson, the senior civil servant in Ireland remained in one room and Arthur Griffith in another. Corrigan and Wylie shuttled back and forth between the two. It was in these circumstances, four years after the Rebellion, that these two men took the first tentative steps towards peace between Britain and the emerging state.

CHAPTER THIRTY EIGHT

James Burke

Burke was tried on 5 May at Richmond Barracks on the standard charge of rebellion with the intention and for the purpose of assisting the enemy. He denied the charge.[1]

'Prosecution
1st witness Lt Murphy, Royal Irish Regiment being duly sworn states:
I remember Easter Monday the 24th April 1916 about 2 pm. I was with a party of men entered the SDU we were fired on as a result of the fire Lieut Ramsey and one man was killed. The fire was coming from a shed, we entered the shed we arrested the accused with other prisoners in the shed. There were arms in the shed, rifles and revolvers. The accused was wearing uniform with sergeants stripes. They have been removed since. He was the first man I saw come out of the hut.
Cross examined by accused
The men in the hut surrendered, our party fired 5 volleys into the shed, the accused was of the party who fired at us.
2nd witness Lieut Watson Royal Irish Regt being duly sworn in states I recognise the accused as one of the men who was handed over to me at the SDU on Easter Monday the 24th April 1916. He was brought out under escort by Capt Warmington and handed over to me, he was brought out of the place the firing had come from. I was one of the party whose searched the shed and found arms there. I saw a man shot in the shed.
Cross Ex By accused
The man I saw shot in the shed was one of the inmates of the Union.

3rd Witness Sergt Taylor G.G.   M.P.S.C. not called
Defence
The accused in his defence states
I received a mobilisation order on the morning of
April 24th it was a verbal one. It was 25 mins
to eleven when I received it although the time I
had to attend was 10a.m. I understood it was for
a day's manoeuvre we were being called out, I
brought some rations and a rifle which I had got
at home which I got at Howth on 26th July 1914.
When I got to Kimmage I was told the Volunteers
had gone on and I was to follow them to Emerald
Square. When I arrived at Emerald Square there was
no sign of them. I was intending to return home
when I heard a section of the Volunteers had got
into the SDU grounds. I got over the wall into
the grounds and saw George Irvine who seemed to be
in charge of the section, I was informed that the
military were about to attack the place.
Shortly afterwards the place was riddled with
bullets and we retreated under the Captain's orders
to a stone building about 20 yards away, as this
was a hospital the Captain decided to return to
the original position in returning to that position
one of our men got a bullet through the thigh I
helped him upstairs into the hospital and with
the aid of another volunteer bandaged the wound.
I returned almost immediately to the wooden hut to
which the others had retreated.
I was just inside when I heard the Captain shout
"surrender" I had no ammunition with me and fired
no shots. We marched out Captain was in front till
he came within 5 or 6 yards of the forces when
he stopped and we were commanded by the Lieut in
charge of the British troop to hurry up and I
marched forward.'

The prisoner was convicted and sentenced to death. Sentence was commuted to three years' penal servitude.

Many years later Burke recounted his experiences.[2] He had been a founder member of the Volunteers. He had received a bayonet wound to the chest at Bachelor's Walk after the arms landing at Howth in 1914. He knew the Rebellion was in the offing and it was only by chance that he missed the mobilisation order.

CHAPTER THIRTY NINE

Saint Stephen's Green

Saint Stephen's Green was occupied by the Irish Citizen Army under Michael Mallin and Constance Markievicz. Before the occupation took place, a number of outposts were set up to delay the arrival of British troops coming up from Portobello and Wellington Barracks in the south of the city. One was at Davy's pub by Portobello Bridge, another at Harcourt Street Railway Station and at the railway bridge overlooking the South Circular Road. These outposts were required to hold out until the Citizen Army had settled into the Green.

While these events took place Michael Mallin established a position on the Green. A photo taken on the morning of the surrender shows a short, slightly built man with delicate features, clean shaven in an age when this was unfashionable. Mallin was a quietly spoken man, a father of five young children. His reputation in the Citizen Army was that of a disciplinarian: he court-martialled one of his officers for leaving his post during Easter Week. Mallin had served in the British army as an NCO for many years. Generations of historians have questioned his tactical acumen, perhaps unfairly, since street fighting was a new art and Mallin had served in the army as a 'Bandsman' rather than a front-line soldier. But his military service pushed him up the ranks of the Citizen Army to chief of staff – a post far beyond his capabilities.

On Easter Monday Mallin set his men to digging trenches on the Green. The road around the Green became littered with cars and traps pushed together to form makeshift barricades. There were then about 137 men and women mainly of the Citizen Army and a few stray Volunteers who had been unable to reach their units.[1]

Before MacNeill's countermand the plan included taking and controlling the building overlooking Saint Stephen's Green. On Easter Monday the turnout was greatly reduced and the need to occupy buildings overlooking the Green was even more pressing, but the opportunity was missed.

By early the next morning the Army had occupied the upper floors of the Shelbourne Hotel and the Services Club and opened machine gun fire on the Citizen Army positions. There were a number of casualties and the Citizen Army came perilously close to being run off the Green. Mallin got a bullet through his hat while pulling a wounded man to safety[2] and a bullet clipped the heel of Markievicz's shoe.[3] Gradually, Mallin was able to relocate his garrison in the Royal College of Surgeons, a substantial late Georgian building, fronted by railings on the west side of the Green.

The Royal College contained a shooting range for the Officer Training Corps and a search by Mallin's men yielded 89 rifles and over 24,000 rounds of ammunition.[4]

The British Army and the Citizen Army continued to dispute possession of the Green until the Saturday. Here, the Citizen Army women played a full part in the fighting.

News of the general surrender filtered through on Saturday night. That night a few members of the garrison simply made their escape. One of the garrison described Mallin as 'haggard' and 'Madame' (all the Citizen Army referred to Markievicz in this way) with 'her head in her hands'.[5] On the following day, Sunday, Mallin surrendered to Captain de Courcy Wheeler and a large force of soldiers.

In the course of the week the Irish Citizen Army had suffered six fatalities[6] and a number of wounded, including Margeret Skinnider, who suffered four bullet wounds. The British Army casualties are nowhere recorded. Constable Michael Lahiff was killed during the fighting. Also killed on and around the Green, were a number of civilians whose names are not known.

Mallin and approximately 110 others were marched to Richmond Barracks.

Mallin and Constance Markievicz were tried. William Partridge was also tried. He may have been particularly distinctive because he had suffered a head injury and was heavily bandaged. He was older than most of the garrison, aged about 43, a slightly built man, short in stature. Partridge was also a well-known trade unionist and evidence would later emerge linking him to the arms landing in Kerry.

Jim Joyce[7] was sentenced to life, commuted to five years by General Maxwell.[8] Joyce was an NCO, or a private according to one account, and it is curious that he was singled out for trial and most of his officers were not. Joyce was a thirty-five-year-old bottler washer who worked in the cellar of Davy's pub on Portobello bridge. His relations with the landlord 'Ould Davy' were strained on account of his connection with the Citizen Army. By chance, Joyce was one of the men chosen to seize Davy's Pub on Easter Monday and delay the arrival of troops coming up from Portobello barracks. Joyce and his men arrived at the pub. Joyce was promptly sacked by 'Ould Davy'. A free and frank exchange of views followed, before his boss was pushed out into the street.[9] Army units from Portobello Barracks were soon laying siege to Davy's pub. After a brisk exchange of fire, Jim Joyce and his men slipped away, leaving Davy's pub a blackened ruin.

The trial records of Michael Mallin, Markievicz and Partridge survive and these are set out in the following chapters.

CHAPTER FORTY

Constance Georgina Markievicz

Markievicz was tried at Richmond Barracks on 4 May 1916. General Blackader DSO presided.[1] Markievicz was charged with taking part in an armed rebellion 'with the intention and for the purpose of assisting the enemy'. She was also charged with attempting to cause disaffection among the civilian population of His Majesty. Markievicz pleaded not guilty to the charge of taking part in armed rebellion and guilty to the lesser charge of causing disaffection.

The record of the trial is set out below.

'1st Witness. Walter McKay duly sworn states-
My name is Walter McKay and I live in University Club Stephen Green and am employed as a page boy. I was 17 years old last Sept. I remember last Easter Monday April 24th and between 1 & 2 o'clock that day I was standing at the club door. From there I could see Stephen's Green and I saw a few rebels dressed in green uniform - they were putting the civilians out of the Green and as they were doing this the Accused drove up in a motor car, blew her whistle and leaned out of the car. She gave orders to a Sinn Fein after he had shut the gate of Stephen's Park. She then drove up towards the Shelborne Hotel - I saw her again about 1.15pm. She was then behind one of the Monuments in the Green. She had a pistol in her hand, which she pointed towards the Club and fired.
I ran upstairs and saw where the bullet struck. After firing she walked up towards the Shelborne Hotel dressed in knickerbockers and puttees. I was in the Club the remainder of the week and on Tuesday night there was firing from the Green.
CROSS EXAMINED BY THE ACCUSED
I was at the Meath Industrial School Blackrock.

I never saw the Accused in the Green before the occasion referred to.

I saw the Accused blow a whistle just one blast. I did not hear the order but I saw her say something to the man who went away.

THE WITNESS WITHDRAWS

2nd Witness. Captain Henry de Courcy Wheeler Reserve of officers attached to General Low's Staff duly sworn states-

I remember Sunday last April 30. I was in the Castle Yard that day. From there I proceeded to the College of Surgeons.

I met the Accused at the side door of the College of Surgeons in York Street. Commandant Michael Mallin of the rebels was with her. The meeting took place under a flag of truce.

Subsequently the rebels who were in the College of Surgeons marched out and surrendered - the Accused was one of the number. She was armed with a pistol and ammunition and Sam Browne belt. She handed her arms to me.

I offered to drive her in a Motor Car to the Castle, she refused and said she preferred to march with her men as she was second in command - About 120 rebels surrendered at the same time as the Accused.

The Accused declines to cross examine the Witness.

The Witness withdraws.

Prosecution closed

The Accused declines to call Witnesses.

The Accused in her defence states -

I went out to fight for Ireland's freedom and it doesn't matter what happens to me.

I did what I thought was right and I stand by it.'

Markievicz was found guilty and sentenced to 'death by being shot'. A rider to verdict was added by Blackader: 'The court recommend the prisoner to mercy solely and only on account of her sex.'

While this drama was being played out the prisoner's sister Eva Gore-Booth, who lived in London, was trailing around Horse Guards trying to get a pass to allow a solicitor get into Richmond Barracks and represent

Markievicz.[2] She had instructed George Gavan Duffy but no pass was ever issued.

Maxwell confirmed the finding and acted on the recommendation to mercy. This was a foregone conclusion. Even before the trial took place, Maxwell had pressed the Cabinet for permission to execute Markievicz, if she was convicted. Asquith had made it clear that such a sentence should be commuted.[3]

According to Wylie's Memoir it was thought that Markievicz might create a scene at her trial. When she entered the room for the trial

```
'I saw the General getting out his revolver and
putting it on the table beside him. He needn't
have troubled. She curled up completely.'
```

Wylie recalls what she said:

```
'"I'm only a woman. You cannot shoot a woman, you
must not shoot a woman". She never stopped moaning
the whole time....We all felt slightly disgusted.
She had been preaching rebellion to a lot of silly
boys, death and glory, die for your country etc.
And yet she was literally crawling. I won't say
anymore. It revolts me still'.
```

There was an account in circulation in the first week of May 1916 that the Countess had behaved badly at her trial. The source could only have been Wylie and this may at least show that his account was not recently fabricated.[4]

There is some circumstantial evidence that Markievicz was under extreme pressure at the time of her trial. She had been held at Kilmainham from 30 April until 4 May, the day of her trial. She was brought out briefly for a Summary of Evidence but otherwise was held in solitary confinement. Markievicz and some of the prisoners at Kilmainham could hear the rifle volleys. By the morning of the trial of Markievicz there had been seven executions. It was enough to dent the resolve of the strongest and if Wylie's account is right it might explain the Countess 'crawling' if that is what took place.

Wylie's account was described by one eminent historian as 'scurrilous distortion'.[5] Where a false accusation is made the motive is often obscure and personal, irrational and not open to analysis. Ultimately the question is whether Wylie's account is reliable or not. There are many aspects of the

Wylie memoir that can be demonstrated as unreliable by reference to other accounts.[6]

There are some questionable points in Wylie's account. First, the trial record shows that Markievicz's cross examination of the page boy is direct and purposeful. She establishes in cross examination that the page boy had been to Meath Industrial School, which had a relevance to the credibility of the witness which may have been lost on the officers trying the case. The Industrial Schools were established 'to care for neglected, orphaned or abandoned children'.[7] Many of these institutions were tough and discipline was hard. Meath Industrial School had a certain resonance in Dublin: a few years earlier eight boys from the school were tried for the manslaughter of an assistant master: they beat him to death with a scrubbing brush and hurling sticks.[8]

Markieviecz does not seek to suggest the witness has lied or was mistaken, she simply attempts to establish the extent of the evidence he was able to give. This purposeful cross-examination is at odds with Wylie's account.

Second, Brigadier General Blackader's note was contemporaneous; Wylie's account was written over 25 years later. It was Blackader's duty to write down the substance of what was said. Whatever criticism that might be levied at Blackader, failing to discharge his obligations to the Army cannot be sustained: it contradicts every known aspect of his character. If the prisoner made a plea for mercy he would be required to record that fact and he did not.

Third, the words that Blackader ascribes to Markievicz are those that she would have wished to be remembered by. Blackader could hardly have made them up and would certainly not have recorded words that reflect credibly on her and ignored comments to her discredit.

Markievicz made a different impression on other officers such as Lieutenant Bucknill, who vividly recalled Markievicz when she was brought to Richmond Barracks:

> `'She was standing gnawing an orange in the barracks square with a number of women prisoners behind her. She was dressed in dark green knickerbockers and puttees and tunic and had a green hat with cock feathers in it.'`[9]

Bucknill took the Summary of Evidence and recorded her response to the charge:

"We dreamed of an Irish Republic and thought we had a fighting chance." Then for a few moments she broke down and sobbed.'[10]

After the trial Markievicz was moved from Kilmainham to Mountjoy Gaol en route to England. It appears that she and Countess Plunkett (also in custody) declined to travel the journey in a cab with soldiers. According to Captain Dickson of the Sherwood Foresters, arrangements were made for the two women prisoners to walk from Kilmainham to Mountjoy. And so Countess Markievicz and Countess Plunkett walked the journey during curfew hours with an escort of soldiers. According ˙to Captain Dickson Markievicz and the recently bereaved Countess Plunkett walked in silence: 'two dignified and determined ladies'.[11]

Countess Markievicz, because of her lifestyle and a certain volatile quality has been an easy mark for some historians who have obliquely cast doubt on her veracity, reliability or even that she fought. It was said that when the Irish Citizen Army was occupying the Green she shot dead DMP Constable Michael Lahiff, who was unarmed and posed no threat.[12] If this were true, it was a wanton act.

But here is another account by Father Thomas O'Donoghue who fought at Saint Stephen's Green.[13] It concerns the death of Freddie Ryan who had been shot by soldiers occupying a building in Harcourt Street:

```
'Mallin gave orders that the body of the man who
had fallen was to be brought back. For this purpose
the Countess and Partridge returned to Harcourt
Street, the former armed with her parrabellum.
She (the Countess) kept up a running fire at 6,
Harcourt St, which enabled Partridge to bring the
body back.'
```

In 1918 she became the first woman elected to Westminster. She did not attend Parliament but took her seat in the First Dáil Éireann in 1919.

She remains an enigmatic and controversial figure.[14]

CHAPTER FORTY ONE

Michael Mallin

Mallin was tried at Richmond Barracks on 5 May. Brigadier Maconchy presided.[1] Mallin was charged with taking part in an armed rebellion 'with the intention and for the purpose of assisting the enemy'. Mallin was also charged with 'attempting to cause disaffection among the civilian population'. The prisoner denied both charges.

The trial record is set out below.

'1st witness 212c Police constable John O'Connell Dublin Metropolitan Police states:-
I know the prisoner Michael Mallin. There is a paper called the Workers Republic in which it has been stated that the prisoner is Chief of Staff of the Citizen Army. I have known the prisoner about 9 or 10 months. I have seen him marching with the Citizen Army and he has marched with James Connolly and the Countess Markievicz and has led them in company with James Connolly.
Cross examined by the prisoner
I did not know whether the prisoner was in command or James Connolly marching with the Citizen Army. I never saw him as a drill instructor or a band instructor. I never heard him make any speech at all. I have only seen it in the paper that the prisoner was the Chief of Staff of the Citizen Army.
Examined by the Court
The Citizen Army and the Irish Volunteers are two distinct bodies. The Citizen Army is under the command of James Connolly. There is a slight difference in the uniforms of the two armies
2nd witness No C128 police constable C. Butler Dublin Metropolitan Police states:-

I know the prisoner now before the court and have known him for 6 or 8 months. I have seen him marching with the Citizen Army wearing the uniform in which he is now dressed. On one of those occasions he wore a revolver on his waistbelt. He marched with James Connolly at the head of the army and also with the Countess of Markievicz.

I saw him on Easter Monday about 11.50am He was in front of Liberty Hall dressed as he is now.

He seemed to be busy generally organising the Citizen Army & there was a large crowd present.

Cross examined by the prisoner:-

He led a section across the footbridge as far as I can remember.

He has been on friendly terms with the police and I know nothing against his character.

Re examined by the prosecutor.

He was facing in the direction of St. Stephens Green and the College of Surgeons when he crossed the footbridge.

3rd Witness Captain H.E. Wheeler Reserve of officers states:-

I was on duty on 30th April outside the College of Surgeons. A body of prisoners surrendered to me between 12.30pm and 1 pm. The prisoner and the Countess of Markievicz came out of a side door of the College. The prisoner was carrying a white flag. And was unarmed but the countess was armed. The prisoner came forward and saluted me and said he wanted to surrender and this is the Countess Markievicz.

He surrendered and stated he was the commandant of the garrison.

I took over the garrison which consisted of prisoner, Countess Markievicz, 109 men and 10 women. I found them in the College and they laid down their arms under my direction.

Defence

The prisoner states:-

I am a silk weaver by trade and have been employed by the Transport Union as band instructor. During

my instruction of these bands they became part of
the Citizen Army and from this I was   asked to
become a drill instructor. I had no commission
whatever in the Citizen Army. I was never taken
into the confidence of James Connolly. I was under
the impression I was going out for manoeuvres on
Sunday but something altered the arrangements and
the manoeuvres were postponed till Monday. I had
verbal instructions from James Connolly to take
36 men to St. Stephens Green and to report to the
Volunteer officer there. Shortly after my arrival
at St Stephens Green the firing started and the
Countess of Markievicz ordered me to take command of
the men as I had been so long associated with them.
I felt I could not leave them and from that point
and from that time I joined the rebellion. I made it
my business to save all officers and civilians who
were brought into Stephens Green. I gave explicit
orders to the men to make no offensive movements
and I prevented them attacking the Shelborne Hotel.
1st Witness Mr L.J. Kettle states:-
the prisoner prevented my death by shooting.
I was treated with every possible consideration
and also I saw he did the same for any other
prisoners who were brought in.
Cross examined by the prosecutor:-
I was taken prisoner on Monday afternoon 24th April
and was taken first to Stephens Green and Mallin
appeared to be in command. I heard a good deal of
firing but actually did not see the firing myself.
On Tuesday morning I was taken to the College of
Surgeons and kept there till Sunday. I could have
been released any day during that time but was kept
there till Sunday. I was released at the time of
surrender and handed over. I heard firing whilst I
was at the College. From the sounds it appeared to
me that the firing was coming from the College. I
knew the College was being fired at.
The prisoner continuing in his statement says:-
I indignantly repudiate any idea of assisting
Germany.'

Mallin was convicted and sentenced to death. He was executed on 8 May.

The implication of Mallin's evidence was that Markievicz was in command at Saint Stephen's Green. This was untrue. It must be surmised that Mallin banked on the army not executing a woman. Markievicz had been tried the day before and was awaiting confirmation of sentence when Mallin was tried on 5 May. Mallin had five young children and his wife was pregnant and it is probable that these factors influenced the conduct of his defence.

The witness called by Mallin was Laurence Kettle, head of the Dublin Corporation Electricity Department. Kettle's car had been commandeered on the first day of the rebellion as he drove through Stephen's Green. He was recognised as a frequent visitor to a local army barracks and held as a suspicious character. In fact, Kettle's brother Tom, was an officer with the Royal Dublin Fusiliers.[2] According to subsequent accounts, Kettle was on good terms with his captors and there is no hint that his life was ever at risk. It is worth remembering that he had been involved in the arms landing at Howth in 1914. One suspects that the passage in his evidence '*the prisoner prevented my death by shooting*' was probably exaggerated or even made up to assist the accused.

CHAPTER FORTY TWO

William Partridge

William Partridge was tried at Richmond Barracks on 17 May and Colonel Sapte presided. Partridge faced the standard charge of rebellion with an alternative charge, that he 'Did attempt to cause disaffection among the civilian population.' Partridge denied the charges.

Partridge was a labour councillor, a poet and a founder member of the Irish Citizen Army,[1] which was set up in 1913 to protect strikers from the excesses of the DMP and the hired strike-breakers. Partridge was a slightly built man, barely five foot five tall and was prone to bouts of extreme ill health. He was a powerful public speaker and an active trade unionist, campaigning against sectarianism and for better housing and healthcare for people living in unrelenting poverty. The failure of the Trade Union movement to relieve poverty led him inexorably down the path of revolution.

He was one of the last prisoners to be tried by FGCM. He would have known about the execution of his senior officers, Mallin and Connolly and that Markievicz had narrowly escaped being shot. Although the execution policy had been discontinued, he probably would not have known that. He was in fact, still uniquely at risk because he was one of the few prisoners who might be linked with the failed arms landing in Kerry. The main parts of the trial are now set out.

'Accused: William Partridge, 3 Patriotic Terrace, Brookfield Road, Kilmainham
1st witness for prosecution
Captain H.E. de C. Wheeler Reserved Officer states:- I was outside the College of Surgeons Dublin about 1:30 p.m. on the 30th April 1916 when a surrender of rebels was made to me. Among those who surrendered were Michael Mallin, Countess Markviewicy (sic), they were the leaders of their party. I ordered them to disarm in the College, which was done and then to form up in Stephen's Green. This also was done. I handed them over to Lieut Orelim and an

escort. There had been fighting between the rebels in the College and his Majesty's troops outside.

2nd Witness for Prosecution:-

2/Lieut A.C. Orelim 10th Hussars (Reserve Cavalry) states:-

On the 30th April 1916 I took over about noon a party of rebels who had surrendered to Capt. Wheeler from the Surgeons, Dublin. The leaders were Countess Markiewicy (sic) and Michael Mallin. I marched the party eventually to Richmond Bks where I handed them over to 2/Lieut. O'Brien. I saw their names taken down by a NCO at the Gymnasium door. There was one man with his head bandaged in the party and only one. The accused appears to have a wound on top of his head. On the 15th May 1916 I saw the accused and he told me he was wearing a bandage on the 30th April 1916.

Cross examined by the accused.

The party had already been disarmed when I took them over. He made the statement voluntarily about his wearing a bandage but I did not caution him first it would be used as evidence against him.

3rd Witness for Prosecution

Constable Christopher Butlin, DMP 128C states:-

I have known the accused for about 10 months as a member of the Citizen Army Liberty Hall. I have seen him with them on a few marches also at Liberty Hall with a rifle and bayonet when he was at an upper window apparently on guard about the middle of April before the Rebellion I have seen him with Connolly, O'Brien and P.T. Daly at labour meetings in the Custom House Square, he used to address the meetings.

On 30th April 1916 I was on the Richmond Bks Square Dublin when a party of rebels were marched in. I identify the accused as one of them. Mallin and the Countess Markievicy (sic) were among the party. The accused had a bandage round his head.

Cross examined by the accused.

The Accused is well known as a member of the Labour Party in Dublin. The other Connolly, O'Brien and

P.T. Daly are also well known Labour men. I have not known the accused take part in any meeting other than Labour meetings. The Citizen Army is a Labour Organisation. The accused was, I believe a private in this Army.

4th witness for prosecution

Constable John O'Connell C.212 DMP states:

I have known the accused for about 10 months. I have frequently seen him at Liberty Hall. Sometimes he had a rifle with him. This was before the rebellion. He sometimes marched as a private in the Citizen Army.

Cross examined by the accused

Liberty Hall is the HQ of the Irish Transport Worker's Union.

5th Witness for Prosecution

Detective constable Francis J McKenna RIC states:

I am stationed at Tralee Co Kerry I have known the accused for about six months. I have seen him in Tralee on several occasions. He associated there with the Labour Leaders and some of the Sinn Fein leaders there. I last saw him there on the 21st April 1916. I saw him about noon on that day, I had seen him come off the 10:56 a.m. train on the 20th April 1916.He was not living in Tralee then. He was met by Patrick J. Hogan a publican and a prominent Sinn Feiner and also by Michael O'Connor the local secretary of the Tralee Transport Union. The members of the Tralee TU are nearly all Sinn Feiners. The accused stayed at Hogan's that night. On the 21st April 1916 I saw him leave Hogan's and entered Spincer's stationery shop about 12 noon. He was with Thomas O'Gorman, President of the Tralee Trades Council. I do not know what he did until he left by the 7:30 p.m. night mail for Dublin.

Cross examined by the accused

I believe there are other branches of the TU in Kerry. The accused was generally with the Transport Union officials when I saw him in Tralee.

(Other evidence was called about Partridge's Trade
Union activities and the prosecution case was
closed).

DEFENCE

The accused in his defence says:-

I was dismissed from my employment owing to a
trade dispute in the Melinore Works. Having a wife
and family to keep I had to get employment and I
was able to get it in the Insurance Branch of the
Transport Workers Union. I was then transferred
to the Trades Union Section of this society as
Secretary Melinore Branch. In 1914 I toured England
on behalf of my society and at the end of that
year the Irish Citizen Army was formed. Mr Larkin
was the chief and Captain White the instructor.
I joined as a private but did not attend drills
owing to my age. The Citizen Army was formed as an
antidote to the Ulster Volunteers, the Government
allowed us equally to carry arms. Mr. Connolly
succeeded Mr Larkin and he appointed me organiser
for the whole Trade Union. As such I had to tour
Ireland, found new branches and keep the others up
to the mark. After this appointment I practically
ceased to take any part in the Citizen Army. Mr.
Mallin took away my armband on big demonstrations,
only after this did I attend, merely to swell
the ranks. I only stood guard at Liberty Hall to
relieve a sentry to get his food etc. This was all
before the Rising. My visits to Kerry were solely
as a Trades Union Organizer, and it was solely
in this capacity I had anything to do with the
leaders of the Rising they being trades unionists
also. When the Rising took place, I was unwell
and in bed and upon hearing the firing I got up
and dressed and went towards Liberty Hall, the
Union's head offices. I went by the South Circular
Road and Stephen's Green so to avoid the fighting.
Then passing the Green, I was recognised by the
rebel guard and ordered into the Green. That is
how I got mixed up with the Rising. There I saw

> Mr Mallin who ordered me to stay there. The injury
> to my head was caused by a blow from a trap door,
> I passed through in retreating from the Green.
> I took no part whatever in the fighting and had
> no arms. I could not get away from the rebels. I
> am a member of the Dublin Corporation and Dublin
> Port and Docks Board and serve on 25 committees
> including the Distress Committee and the Prince of
> Wales Fund Committee. There are over 3,000 members
> of my union serving at the front.'

Partridge was sentenced to fifteen years' imprisonment. Maxwell remitted five years of the sentence.

Partridge's evidence was a mixture of fact and fiction. He was a founder member of the Irish Citizen Army.[2] He had been sent down to Kerry by Connolly to assist with the cargo of arms sent by Germany. Just off the coast of Kerry, the *Aud* had dropped anchor waiting for the rebels to make contact. On board there were 20,000 rifles, a quantity of machine guns and a million rounds of ammunition.

A car carrying a radio operator was sent down to make contact with the *Aud*. The car went off Ballykissane pier in the dark. Three of the four men on board drowned. The captain of the *Aud* failed to make contact with the rebels. The *Aud* was intercepted by a British warship and the arms landing failed. Sir Roger Casement, one of the instigators of the shipment, was captured and the whole affair became a fiasco.

Partridge's instructions had been to land the arms at Fenit. Using union dock labour he was to commandeer a train, load up and drop off arms at Limerick and Cork before going on to Dublin. On Good Friday, Partridge learned about Casement's capture and the failure of the arms landing. He hurried back to Dublin by train. There were other couriers who saw him at Limerick and Mallow but he took care not to acknowledge them.[3] His caution was well founded since it transpired that he was being followed by plain-clothes officers of G Division.

Partridge reported back to Connolly at Liberty Hall before returning home to his family. His health suffered a severe relapse but he turned out on Easter Monday and marched to Saint Stephen's Green. He appears to have served as a private although contemporary accounts hint that he had far more influence than his rank suggests.[4] Contrary to what he told the Court, he played a full part in the fighting.[5]

After the surrender, Partridge was remembered by other prisoners giving encouragement to ICA women as they passed through a hostile mob on the way to captivity,[6] or allowing himself to be used as a pillow by other prisoners who were crammed into Richmond Barracks. Mallin, before being executed, appointed Partridge as godfather to his unborn child. He was recalled by many, even those who outranked him, as 'Mister' Partridge.

Partridge was sent to Dartmoor Prison where his health continued to give cause for concern. The medical treatment he received was of a high standard and his mystery illness was diagnosed as Bright's Disease.[7] He was given an open-air job[8] but his health deteriorated swiftly. In his letters home, he made light of his illness. But he was released in May 1917 because of his failing health. He died some weeks later.

CHAPTER FORTY THREE

Boland's Mills

De Valera commanded the Third Battalion of Volunteers. This battalion occupied a sprawling area in the south-east of Dublin. It included Boland's Mills, a Victorian industrial complex overlooking the docks. The fortified area included the Gas Works, the South Eastern Railway Works, and outposts guarding Northumberland Road and the Grand Canal bridge at Mount Street. The strategic objective of this deployment was to prevent the Army using the train line or road from the port of Kingstown to gain access to the centre of Dublin. All of the outposts were undermanned and some were exposed to flanking attacks.

Apart from the ferocious fighting at the canal bridge, de Valera's unit were involved in sniping, but no significant attacks were made by either side. Again, except for the battle at the canal bridge, casualties on both sides were relatively light.

De Valera's men surrendered on the Sunday. They were marched out to Grattan Street where arms were laid down. Unlike the surrender of most other units, no lists were made of those who were armed and those who were not.[1] No list of officers and NCOs was taken. This may explain why de Valera was tried but not his officers or NCOs. The men were not moved to Richmond Barracks but marched south to the Royal Dublin Showground in Ballsbridge. This introduced a delay, which may have saved de Valera's life.

Many have questioned why de Valera was spared and one historian has doubted that he was ever tried at all. A number of theories have been advanced as to why he was not executed; that he was saved by his American citizenship, or that he became a British spy.[2] There is no evidence to support any of these theories although the debate about whether he was tried probably originated with William Wylie. The two men met in their twilight years in the foyer of Stephen's Green Club. De Valera quizzed Wylie about his trial. Wylie responded bluntly 'You were never tried.'[3] That was Wylie's memory but his recollection has proved unreliable on many key issues.

In his memoir written many years after the event, Wylie insisted that he advised Maxwell that de Valera was 'not one of the leaders' and therefore unlikely to make trouble in the future. On Wylie's account, Maxwell decided to stop the trials and move straight onto 'the public trials' meaning trial by General Court Martial. Again, Wylie's account is unreliable. The Trial Register shows that de Valera was tried on 8 May and the trials by FGCM in camera continued for a further two weeks before trials in public commenced.

Wylie prosecuted many trials but there were two standing courts at Richmond Barracks, not one, and de Valera was probably tried in the other court. Furthermore, after the first rush of trials, Wylie was detailed to interview the 82 women in custody with a view to determining how they might be dealt with. He may have been occupied with that task when de Valera was tried.

John Turi has suggested that 'there is no trace in the British Public Record office at Kew of any trial, sentence or commutation of sentence involving de Valera'.[4] This is plainly incorrect. There is a record in the Trial Register for 8 May which shows the trial of de Valera, Thomas Ashe, the Lawless brothers and Dr Hayes. This can be cross referenced with De Valera's personal diary which shows the following entry for 8 May; 'Trial with Ash, two Lawlesses and Dr Hayes.'[5]

A few words need to be said here about the way in which the Trial Register was compiled. After the trials the case papers went to the office of the JAG in London where the details were logged. It was, therefore, a contemporaneous document compiled by a disinterested party. The Trial Register has proved to be correct in all other respects and there is no reason to doubt the reliability of this entry.

John Turi argues that because the trial transcript no longer exists, it can be inferred that de Valera was not tried. In fact, only the trial transcripts of executed prisoners were preserved by the Public Record Office in London.

De Valera was taken to Richmond Barracks, arriving on foot with his men on Tuesday 2 May.[6] There is evidence from a number of prisoners that they shared a cell with him on the evening of 7 May. According to some of the prisoners they were passing the time by carrying out a mock trial of de Valera while he awaited court martial. In this mock trial, he was tried by Count Plunkett on a charge of being a pretender to the ownership of a small island off the coast of Dublin. Sean T. O'Kelly prosecuted and Larry O'Neill defended.[7] The prisoners were living out the game played by the Young Irelanders while they awaited trial in 1848. After this macabre game, some of the prisoners took or were given keepsakes by de Valera; a pen and some tunic buttons before he was taken off for trial.

In de Valera's biography it is recounted that evidence was given by Captain Hitzen of the Sherwood Foresters who had taken de Valera's surrender. Proof that de Valera commanded the garrison was provided by Cadet McKay who had been a prisoner there for most of the week.

According to Lieutenant Bucknill, a captured document naming de Valera as a commandant was also relied upon as evidence.[8]

A question arises as to why de Valera was not executed. He held the rank of Battalion Commandant, the only officer of his rank to survive Easter Week. Turi's theory that de Valera was spared because he agreed to become an informer, is not supported by any evidence.

It has also been suggested that friends of de Valera made representations to the American Consulate and that President Wilson intervened directly with Asquith.[9] Representations may well have been made to the American Consulate but there is no evidence of this. It has also been suggested in Caulfield's account of the Rebellion that Maxwell was swayed by de Valera's American citizenship.[10] But he cites no evidence for this proposition.

The truth of the matter is probably far more prosaic. De Valera's men surrendered on the Sunday afternoon when Richmond Barracks and Arbour Hill were overflowing with prisoners. De Valera's men were moved to the RDS at Ballsbridge, in the south of the city. De Valera remained there until the afternoon of Tuesday 2 May, when he and his men were marched to Richmond Barracks.[11] By this time all prisoners likely to be tried had been assigned a number and there was a long queue of prisoners awaiting trial.

An examination of the Trial Register and other relevant documents suggests that the prisoners were channelled through two courts in the following order: Pearse, Clarke and MacDonagh were tried on 2 May. The junior officers, NCOs and first aider at Jacob's were also in the first batch to be tried on 2 May. Nearly all the officers in the Four Courts area were tried on 2 and 3 May. All the prisoners from the Mendicity were tried on 4 May. The South Dublin Union prisoners were tried between 3 and 5 May The prisoners from Saint Stephen's Green were tried on 4, 5 and 6 May. No trials took place on Sunday, 7 May. Trials were resumed on Monday 8 May with de Valera and Ashe and others from Ashbourne.

If the usual pattern had been followed, de Valera's case would have gone before Maxwell for confirmation in the next day or two. But it was at this point de Valera's fate became tied up with political considerations at Westminster.

The major issue at Westminster related to Sheehy-Skeffington's death.[12] Sir Francis Vane arrived in London on 10 May and related the full story of the shootings to Kitchener. The same morning Kitchener despatched a wire to Maxwell demanding full details about the execution of Sheehy-Skeffington.[13] This information was passed at once to Asquith. The papers show that some hours later Asquith sent a 'wire' to Maxwell suspending all further executions.

The following day, 11 May, Asquith publicly signalled that barring the execution of the two remaining signatories to the proclamation, there would be no more executions. [14] This analysis is supported by Alfred Bucknill's memoir. [15] Bucknill discounted the idea that de Valera relied or tried to rely on his American citizenship. Bucknill suggests that Asquith faced mounting pressure about the Sheehy-Skeffington affair and that he found Maxwell's responses unsatisfactory and ordered that there be no more executions pending a personal discussion. [16]

Maxwell may have felt politically isolated. The resignation of the Lord Lieutenant had been announced and Maxwell knew the reason why. He may have been willing to ignore the Lord Lieutenant but he was also sensitive to wider political considerations. Kitchener's support was suddenly in question and there was also a cold wind blowing from Westminster. Maxwell's agenda appears to have shifted from how many executions he might permit, to whether the executions of the remaining signatories to the proclamation might still proceed. [17] In this way de Valera and some other notable prisoners were spared the death penalty.

CHAPTER FORTY FOUR

Ashbourne

One of the few Volunteer units to mobilise outside Dublin was the Fingal Battalion, although they were badly depleted by the countermand order. On the Tuesday of Easter Week their numbers were reduced again, when 20 men were sent to reinforce the GPO. The total number of Volunteers remaining was just over 50. In the next few days the battalion began, quite ineptly, to blow up bridges and rail lines. Performance quickly improved, capturing RIC barracks at Swords and Donabate, seizing arms and destroying telegraph wires. The campaign culminated in a shootout near Ashbourne on Friday 28 April.

The RIC barracks were at the Rath crossroad, about half a mile north of the village of Ashbourne. On the morning of Friday 28 April, Thomas Ashe and just under 40 men arrived on bicycles and captured two stray RIC officers. Ashe demanded the surrender of the barracks. This was met with gunfire from the barracks and the Volunteers laid siege.[1] Soon after, a convoy of 24 large touring cars filled with 80 armed police arrived on the scene. The RIC reinforcements were engaged as they pulled up near the crossroads. In the hours that followed, Richard Mulcahy, who was a junior officer under the command of Ashe, manoeuvred the Volunteers so that they surrounded the police and inflicted heavy casualties, forcing another 70 to surrender.[2] In this encounter six RIC men were killed.[3] Fifteen officers were wounded and many captured. Two travelling salesmen and a chauffeur who acted as a driver for the police, were also killed.[4] There were two fatalities in the Volunteer ranks and five wounded.[5]

Two days later, on Sunday morning, news was brought of the general surrender but Ashe insisted on getting verification. Richard Mulcahy was given a police escort to Arbour Hill where he had a short meeting with Pearse. The surrender was confirmed and later that day Thomas Ashe ordered his men to surrender. They were driven in lorries to Richmond Barracks where they joined the other prisoners undergoing the sift.

Of these prisoners, most of the officers were selected for trial, Doctor Richard Hayes, Frank Lawless, James Lawless and Ashe. Oddly, the RIC man who had driven Mulcahy to Arbour Hill to see Pearse, failed to pick him out. It seems that when Mulcahy was driven to Arbour Hill he wore a civilian coat but when the line up took place the following day, he wore his Volunteer uniform and this appears to have thrown the witness.

Ashe, Hayes, Frank and James Lawless were tried and convicted on 8 May. Ashe, Frank and James Lawless were sentenced to death. Doctor Hayes was sentenced to twenty years' penal servitude. The transcripts of their trial cannot be traced.

The cases went for confirmation by Maxwell. Ashe had his sentence commuted by Maxwell to twenty years' penal servitude. The sentences of death on Frank and James Lawless and Doctor Hayes were commuted to ten years. During the course of the encounter at Ashbourne, a significant proportion of the police force in the county were killed, captured or wounded. The dead included the County Inspector Alexander Gray and the popular District Inspector Harry Smyth. By the standards that had been set by General Maxwell this was an extraordinary step back.

There is no obvious explanation for this, save that Ashe and his men did not arrive at Richmond Barracks until the evening of Sunday 30 April. They were not put on identification parades until late the next day, by which time many prisoners had already been selected for trial.[6] Ashe and his men took their place in the list of those to be tried but were not reached until 8 May.

Maxwell reported his decision to commute sentences on Ashe and de Valera on 11 May. It is likely that he made his decision to commute the day before for the reasons set out in the previous chapter.

CHAPTER FORTY FIVE

The Trials in the Provinces

After the general surrender, came the roundups in the provinces. It seems Maxwell was sensitive to the danger of arresting significant numbers of people who presented no danger. Maxwell's instructions permitted the arrest of those who had 'actually supported the movement' but not those who were simply 'strong nationalists'. In cases where there was doubt this was to be exercised 'generously in favour of the nationalists'.[1]

Mobile columns were despatched to all parts of Ireland to take prisoners. On the west coast, the Navy were already active. *HMS Gloucester* had landed a force of 100 marines at Galway to hunt down the rebels. Liam Mellows and a group of about 500 men were pursued across country. Outnumbered and outgunned, Mellows was forced to disband his men even before the general surrender in Dublin. A large number of prisoners were quickly taken. The following week the prisoners were sent to Dublin.[2]

The largest force was sent to relieve Enniscorthy: 1,000 infantry, 60 cavalry and artillery.[3] The rebel forces agreed to surrender once the order given by Pearse had been confirmed.

In general terms, Maxwell's orders to winnow out those who posed no danger were ignored and many hundreds of men who had no connection with the Rebellion were arrested and interned. Many were soon weeded out and sent home, although the whole process seems utterly haphazard.[4] One of the senior Wexford Volunteers had let it be known that there were many in prison that had nothing to do with the Rebellion. He was asked to supply a list and told 'Their cases will be specially considered.'[5]

Simultaneously with the roundups, Maxwell issued a proclamation requiring the surrender of arms by 6 May. In some districts this process had been underway for some days. In Cork Archbishop Cohalan negotiated with the Army to secure the surrender of arms and large quantities of arms were surrendered.[6]

Backed by Maxwell's proclamation, the RIC hunted down the guns: surrender arms or face internment was the message and in some districts the tactic worked. In towns as far apart as Ballynoe,[7] Cahirciveen and Listowel guns were handed into RIC barracks.[8]

In some areas, like Killarney, the clergy played a major part in securing the handover of weapons. In Limerick guns were surrendered to the Mayor and passed on to the authorities.[9]

In County Clare, only one company of Volunteers succumbed to pressure to hand guns over to the military. In the rest of the county, stolen guns were returned to their owners or simply hidden away.[10] In west Cork threats of internment were ignored and guns remained hidden.[11]

While the arms issue was being played out, mobile army columns carried out joint raids with the RIC to arrest and intern suspects. Most did not hide. A small number of men went on the run and only a few offered resistance.

Very few prisoners were court martialled in the provinces. It is difficult to be sure of the exact number, partly because in the subsequent accounts of some prisoners, they confused formal interrogation with trial by court martial.[12] The Trial Register suggests that in the two weeks following the general surrender there were only four trials by court martial in the provinces.[13] Thomas and William Kent were tried after a siege near Fermoy. Richard Donoghue and Thomas Doyle were tried in Wexford. The cause of their trial is not recorded.[14] The fact that these trials took place at all is attributable to an order given by General Maxwell to the officers carrying out roundups: 'any Sinn Féiner who actually resists arrest may be dealt with on the spot by a court martial'.[15]

There was at least one unauthorised trial. Robert Brennan, who had taken an officer's role in Enniscorthy, vividly described such a trial in the barracks at Wexford. Brennan, Seán Etchingham and Seamus Doyle were resting; sleeping on hay in the blockhouse, when they were awoken:

> 'Suddenly the door opened and there entered two orderlies carrying a small table, a chair, some candles, pens, ink and paper. When they had lighted the candles and placed the pens etc., in the correct positions, they made way for a procession consisting of the Resident Magistrate, the District Inspector of the Constabulary and a couple of military officers.'[16]

The charge of rebellion was put but the trial, such as it was, descended into farce when Etchingham claimed the protection of the First Offenders Act. 'You swine', intoned the officer in charge. 'I'd like to take you all outside right now and finish you off.'

Wiser counsel prevailed. No verdicts were returned and the prisoners were taken to Waterford Gaol and later allowed into the exercise yard where they were confronted with an unexpected sight: 'We saw filing out into the exercise yard practically every able bodied man in Enniscorthy and many who were not able bodied.' The men were soon loaded onto a train and despatched to Dublin. It was a scene being played out in different parts of the country. In this process nearly 2,000 men were rounded up and sent to Dublin for trial or deportation.

Of the prisoners tried in the provinces only Thomas Kent was executed. On the night of 2 May RIC officers under head Constable Rowe toured the Fermoy area picking up known Volunteers. The convoy consisted of two army lorries fitted with the old solid rubber 'boneshaker tyres' travelling on unlit, unmade side roads. With two local men already under arrest they drove on to Bawnard House at Coole Lower, near Fermoy. This raid was one of hundreds all over the country and was remarkable only because it led to fatal shootings.

The house and two hundred acres of land were owned by Mrs Kent, who was then about 75 years old. She shared the house with her four middle-aged sons. Richard had been a hurler of note but had developed mental health difficulties and had spent some time in an asylum. David and Thomas were senior Volunteers. Thomas was a member of the Gaelic League. He had joined the Volunteers in 1913. When the split came he sided against the Redmondites. He campaigned against recruitment to the British army and was in and out of prison in the run up to the Easter rebellion. By May 1916, he was still a single man in his late forties, not in the best of health.[17]

After the Rebellion began in Dublin the Kent brothers stayed away from home to avoid arrest and to wait orders They had returned home on the night of the 1 May and were half expecting a raid.[18]

The RIC raid on Bawnard House led to a shootout which has given rise to many lurid accounts. It is now very hard to separate fact from myth. What is certain is that Head Constable William Rowe was shot dead from the farmhouse. Rowe was 49 years old and left a widow and five children of school age. He had 28 years' service and was close to retirement. David Kent was severely wounded in the side and lost two fingers. A rifle was later recovered with blood on the stock.

Many years later William Kent related that the RIC men were incensed over the killing of Head Constable Rowe and made ready to shoot the prisoners. Richard Kent jumped a hedge and ran. He was shot and wounded. The shooting of the other men was prevented by an army officer who placed himself between the police and the prisoners.

William Kent wrote that all four brothers had joined in the attack on the RIC and their elderly mother had played a part re-loading weapons.[19] This account has become the accepted version. One of the RIC men gave a less heroic account: the Kents offered to surrender at an early stage and passed three shotguns out of the window. These three shotguns were of poor quality and the ammunition had jammed. A blood-stained rifle was also passed out.[20]

The brothers were taken to Fermoy the same night. Richard Kent died in hospital two days later. David Kent was too badly wounded to face trial immediately and this delay probably saved his life.[21] William Kent was tried and acquitted the same week. Thomas Kent was tried less than 48 hours after capture. He was convicted and his trial record is now set next.

CHAPTER FORTY SIX

Thomas Kent

Thomas Kent[1] was tried by Field General Court Martial on 4 May 1916 at Cork Detention Barracks, Cork. Major R.G.B. Jeffreys of the Royal Dublin Fusiliers presided.

> 'The Charge
> The accused, Thomas Kent of Fermoy, in the County of Cork, is charged with the following contravention of the Defence of the Realm Regulations Consolidated (1914), that is to say, in that he at Banard, (sic) Kent's house near Fermoy, Co. Cork, on the 2nd day of May, 1916, took part in an armed rebellion and in waging war against His Majesty the King, such act being of such a nature as to be prejudicial to the Defence of the Realm and being done with the intention of and for the purpose of assisting the enemy.
> The prisoner entered a not guilty plea.
> Sergeant Caldbeck R.I.C. having been duly sworn is examined by the prosecutor & states:-
> On 2nd May 1916 between 3.45am and 4am I proceeded with Head Constable Rowe to the house of Mrs Kent with instructions to arrest Thomas Kent and his brother David Kent. Five other police accompanied us. The Head Constable knocked on the door and, when challenged, said he was a policeman and ordered the occupants to come down and open the door. A reply from the lobby window to the effect "We will never surrender. We will leave some of you dead." One shot was fired from the lobby window on the north side, a second shot was fired from a bedroom window facing east. A third shot was fired from the lobby window which blew the face off Head

Constable Rowe. This happened about five minutes after they were told to come down.

About 4.50am someone from within called out that one of the occupants was dying & asked for the priest. I answered "If you throw out all your arms I may send for the Priest."

At about ten minutes after this three firearms were thrown out but the occupants did not come out themselves. All these arms, on my examining them, had recently been fired out of.

On the arrival of the military, four men, including the prisoner, who came out second, and his brothers, came out and surrendered to the officer in charge. Constable Dolan brought me another firearm which he found in a bedroom on searching the house. I examined it. It had quite recently been fired.

Cross examined

Q. Did not Constable Dolan let this firearm off by mistake?

A. Yes.

Q. After the firearms had been thrown out of the house, did not the police continue to fire into the house?

A. Yes, occasionally.

Q. Was there any firing from the house after the arms had been thrown out?

A. No.

Q. Why did you continue to fire after we threw out our arms?

A. Having reason to believe that all the arms were not surrendered.

2nd Witness Constable F. King R.I.C. having duly sworn is examined by the prosecution and states:-
On 2nd May 1916, I accompanied Head Constable Rowe and other RIC to Mrs Kent's house to carry out an arrest. I (indecipherable) on the west side of the house. Almost immediately I heard some shots fired. On the 3rd shot being fired, I saw it hit Head Constable Rowe and he dropped dead. The shot came from the house.

3rd Witness. Constable James Norris RIC being duly sworn is examined by the prosecutor & states:-
On 2nd May 1916 at about 4am I arrived at Mrs Kent's house in company with Head Constable Rowe and other RIC. I accompanied Head Constable Rowe to the back door. The Head Constable knocked at the door. A voice from the window asked who was there and head Constable Rowe answered "Police" and to come down and let him in. Shortly after a shot was fired from the lobby window, where the voice came from. Shortly after two more shots were fired in succession. Previous to this when the occupants were told to come down and open the door, a voice from inside called out: "We will die before we surrender." Later, after the firing had taken place, and the Head Constable had been killed, a man inside the house called out, that one of them had been wounded and asked for a priest. About 4.55am three firearms were thrown out of the windows, and they offered to surrender but they were told by Sergeant Caldbeck to hold back until military assistance arrived. On the military arriving the occupants came out and surrendered. On searching the house later I saw 6 cartridges, 12 bore, number 6 shot lying on the floor. The accused was the second man to come out of the house. We went to Mrs Kent's home originally to arrest Thomas (the prisoner) & David his brother as being prominent Sinn Feiners.
Cross examined
Q. Had you previously come to my house with the intention of arresting me?
A. Yes
Q. Did I resist?
A. No.
Q. Was I acquitted for this offence?
A. Yes.
Q. Was not my brother Richard in an asylum?
A. Yes but is now released.
4th Witness 2nd Lieutenant Q.F.M. Chesney 15th R.

Fusiliers being duly sworn is examined by the prosecutor and states:-

On 2nd May 1916 at some time between 6am and 8am I proceeded with some other officers to the house of the Kents, with arms, to prevent anyone escaping from the house. On my arrival I found a police sergeant & a constable, also the body of the dead Head Constable. I heard the Sergeant RIC ask the occupants to "surrender" to that officer. Someone inside asked if there was an officer present. I said that I was one, and called upon them to surrender. They did so coming down one by one through a window on the ground floor. The prisoner now before the court was the second to come out. Four men and one woman came out altogether. One of the men tried to escape and was severely wounded, when he had gone about 25 yards. An old service rifle was lying outside the house. Also, another firearm. I handed these over to the Sergeant RIC. I then searched the house. There were two shot guns leaning against the wall of the house outside. One had an empty cartridge case in it. There was also a bandolier with ammunition with these guns. The Head Constable's revolver was also with these arms.

Cross examined

Q. Did I try to escape?

A. No.

5th witness 2nd Lieutenant R.S. Page Green 14th Royal Fusiliers being duly sworn is examined by the prosecutor & states:-

On 2nd May 1916 about 6am I proceeded with four other officers to the home occupied by the Kent's, close to Fermoy with instructions to prevent anyone from escaping from the house. The occupants of the house were called upon to surrender by the police sergeant and they said they would surrender to an officer. On being informed that an officer was present, they came out and surrendered. There were four men and one woman came out of the house.

The Prisoner Kent states:-
On 2nd of May 1916, during the night, I was awakened
by the sound of firearms, and immediately went into
my mother's room where my brother William was.
They were standing on the bed in the corner of
the room. I immediately went into the corner where
they were, where the three of us remained until
the military officers arrived, when we immediately
surrendered. I never fired and never had arms in
my hand.'

Kent was found guilty and sentenced to death. The findings of the court
were confirmed by Maxwell on 6 May. On 9 May Kent was shot by firing
squad.

As to the trial process, there was no Judge Advocate at this trial and
therefore no summing up and it is difficult to know the basis of conviction.
There was no evidence as to who fired the fatal shot and no direct evidence
who had fired the other shots. Nor is there any evidence to show why
Thomas Kent was convicted and his brother William was acquitted the same
day. An RIC officer who took part in the raid later wrote that he had given
William a good character reference at his trial.[2] There appears to be no
other point of distinction.

An officer convening a court martial for a capital offence was obliged to
convene a General Court Martial unless that was 'impracticable'. In which
case a FGCM would be convened.[3] In this case the officer convening the
court made a finding that a GCM was 'impracticable' although it is hard
to see what circumstances existed in Cork which made that a necessity. The
effect of trying the prisoner by FGCM in these circumstances was to deprive
him of any entitlement to representation.

CHAPTER FORTY SEVEN

Postscript

Sarah Rowe, widow of the late Head Constable Rowe received a generous pension but it must have been a small consolation for her five children growing up without a father. Old Mrs Kent from Bawnard House suffered her share of grief also: one son shot dead, one executed and one severely wounded in prison awaiting trial. In the days that followed the Rebellion, the Army attempted to try David Kent but the garrison's medical officer, Dr Brody, refused to certify him fit to be moved for two vital weeks.[1]

David Kent was tried a few weeks later and convicted of murder and aiding and abetting the Rebellion. The Court made a 'strong recommendation' for mercy on account of the prior good character of the accused. A sentence of five years' penal servitude was confirmed by General Maxwell.[2] In the wider context, this trial shows how quickly the political landscape was changing. The policy of repression had backfired and was being replaced by conciliation. By any terms of reference, a five-year sentence for rebellion and murder of a senior police officer was derisory. General Maxwell was struggling to appear humane and statesmanlike.

While these events were being played out, Captain Bowen-Colthurst was court martialled for the murders of Sheehy-Skeffington, MacIntyre and Dickson. He was convicted but found to be insane. There is little doubt that he was unhinged during the Rebellion but it is unlikely that he could ever meet the legal test of insanity.[3] Bowen-Colthurst spent five years in Broadmoor although he was free to roam the hospital grounds and he was frequently seen in local villages. He even fathered a child whilst he was there. He was released in 1921 and immediately emigrated to Canada. Bowen-Colthurst never returned to Ireland[4] but his crimes were not forgotten in Cork where his upright and generous-hearted mother was ostracised and driven from the family estates.[5]

There were other more significant events in the summer of 1916. The redoubtable Hannah Sheehy-Skeffington secured a Royal Commission into the death of her husband[6] although there was no Royal Commission for the victims of the North King Street Massacre and many others.

The Government appointed Lord Sankey to decide what should be done with the prisoners who had been deported but not tried. The Sankey Advisory

Committee convened and started to interview the internees with a view to release. Some had already been released and this committee accelerated the process.[7] All were released by Christmas.

Conciliation did not extend to those who had broken ranks with their own kind. Sir Francis Vane was frozen out of the Army for his part in blowing the whistle on the Sheehy-Skeffington murder. In August, Sir Roger Casement was tried and executed.

The direction of events began to become clear the following year. The agitation to secure the release of the prisoners culminated in a series of by-elections. Prisoners were elected to Westminster at South Longford and in Kilkenny on Sinn Féin tickets. In an effort to forestall further by-election victories, Lloyd George ordered the release of all prisoners in June 1917.

Coincidentally an election at east Clare had been triggered by the death of the sitting MP, Major Willie Redmond who had held the seat for 25 years. Many had followed his lead and gone into the British army in the hope of winning Home Rule. But Redmond was one of hundreds of Irishmen killed at Messines Ridge in June 1917, causing the election. He was respected, even by his opponents, and Ireland was momentarily united in regret before the race was on to elect his successor. The Irish Party fielded a very strong local candidate – Patrick Lynch, Kings Counsel.

Many of the erstwhile prisoners joined de Valera's campaign at east Clare. De Valera, campaigning in a Volunteer uniform, won an emphatic victory. His telegram to his wife said it all 'De Valera 5020 – Lynch 2035.'[8] The moderate Irish Party never recovered. The momentum towards the War of Independence became unstoppable. The legacies of 1916 are many and complex and war, partition and civil war are but three. Perhaps the most unfortunate legacy which still persists is politically inspired violence.

There were mixed fortunes for those concerned in the suppression of the Rebellion. A few weeks after the Rebellion, Lord Kitchener was aboard HMS Hampshire on a diplomatic mission to Russia when the ship hit a mine. Kitchener drowned and the influence of his protégé, General Maxwell, began to wane. Maxwell became known in Ireland as 'Bloody Maxwell' and in the autumn of 1916, he was relieved of his command and posted General Officer Commanding (GOC) the North of England. His last remaining years in the Army were dominated by arguments about his rank, pay and pension.

General Blackader returned to the Western Front where he served with distinction. In 1918 he caught rabies from his pet dog and made a slow and painful recovery. He was appointed GOC Southern Ireland in 1919 but succumbed to cancer and died in 1921, leaving his wife and two daughters close to penury.

Colonel Douglas Sapte married the very young widow of a private soldier, presumed killed in action. But unfortunately for Sapte, the husband reappeared. In a very public court case Sapte sued his new wife for divorce.[9] Afterwards, he quickly disappeared from polite society without even leaving the War Office a forwarding address for his campaign medals.

Captain Lea Wilson, who had been responsible for the mistreatment of prisoners at the Rotunda, left the Army and joined the RIC as a District Inspector. He was shot dead at Gorey, Wexford in 1920. Michael Collins readily admitted that Wilson was shot because of the events at the Rotunda and for no other reason.

Brigadier Maconchy was posted to the Western Front, eventually retiring in 1917. He and his wife moved to Hampshire, where he wrote his memoirs and farmed chickens for very many years.

Alfred Bucknill was promoted and awarded an OBE. He was later made Deputy Judge Advocate General in Ireland. After the war he resumed his career at the Admiralty Bar and later became a Lord Justice of Appeal.

William Wylie was mentioned in despatches and spent the rest of the war on home service. He became the government Law Adviser in Ireland in 1920, a position he used to argue against the excesses carried out by the Black and Tans and the Auxiliaries. He became a Judge of the Irish High Court in 1920. Although it was well known that he had prosecuted many of the leaders in 1916, he was not harassed or attacked. The explanation for this must lie in the manner in which he had conducted the prosecutions. After the Treaty, Wylie was kept on by the new administration and served for many years on the High Court Bench. Chief Justice Kennedy complained bitterly in his diary that Wylie sat only once a week and spent 'the rest of the week at horse shows, hunts and races'.[10]

The officers of G Division of the DMP fared worst. During the War of Independence they were in the front line. The men of the G Division were particularly at risk, although oddly not because of their involvement in the 1916 trials but because they were the persistent and determined opponents of the emerging insurgent movement. Sergeant Patrick Smyth was the first to be killed in April 1919. He was shot down on his way home late one night. His children, hearing the shots ran out into the street and found their father grievously wounded. They carried him inside but he died a few days later.[11]

Detective Sergeant Daniel Hoey was targeted after narrowly failing to capture Michael Collins in a raid on Sinn Fein headquarters at Harcourt Street in Dublin. Hoey had much in common with the men he tracked: he was Irish, devoutly Catholic and loyal to his cause. In September 1919, he was killed at the gates of his barracks at Brunswick Street.

A few weeks later Detective John Barton was followed up Grafton Street and shot dead in the street.[12] Sergeant Bruton retreated into Dublin Castle and remained there until the Truce, before disappearing to England. It does not seem that other witnesses were pursued because they gave evidence at these trials. Henry de Courcy Wheeler had accepted the surrender of Pearse. At the time he was criticised by General Lowe for returning the prisoner's salute. De Courcy Wheeler gave evidence against a number of the prisoners, including Pearse, MacDiarmada and Markievicz.

De Courcy Wheeler ran a farm in Kildare for many years.[13] Although his part in the suppression of the Rising was well known, he continued to live peacefully in Kildare through many troubled years. He appears to have come to terms with the new order. In 1949 he presented Sean T. O'Kelly, President of Ireland, with the arms and equipment seized from Pearse.[14]

These are the personal stories of those who were involved in the Rising although there is another dimension to be considered. The 1916 trials have a significant place in history. The trials may be viewed as an aspect of the War of Independence or the first of a series of colonial conflicts that unravelled the British Empire. These trials also provide revealing insights into the circumstances in which the rule of law may be abrogated in times of crisis.

During the War of Independence that followed the Rising, Westminster relied heavily on statutory courts martial to try civilians. This power was used extensively in conjunction with internment. There were 13 executions. Martial law was once again briefly deployed in south-west Ireland in December 1920 and remained in force until after the Truce. Under this regime, prisoners were tried by military courts established by the Army, but not sanctioned by common law or statute. In total 2,450 people were tried and 37 death sentences were passed of which 11 were carried out.[15]

After the War of Independence, Westminster leaned against invoking martial law in the colonies in favour of special powers granted by Parliament, although in distant and obscure colonies breathtaking excesses still took place.

One must step back at this point and observe that the practice of reverting to military courts in times of crisis has never been restricted to the British Empire. In the Irish civil war that followed the Truce and the Treaty, 77 men were executed after trial by military commissions. One of these was Erskine Childers who was famously executed while habeas corpus proceedings were still unresolved by the High Court.[16] The Irish Free State, brought about by revolution, found itself dogged by politically-inspired violence. Like many states formed through revolution, it was sometimes all too ready to abandon or abrogate the rule of law. In the 1930s there was a resurgence of IRA and Blueshirt Fascist violence, accompanied by intimidation of witnesses and jurors. The response, when it came, was draconian. Emergency legislation was passed and Military Courts were created again.

Some counsel and at least one Kings Counsel declined to appear before the Military Court[17] but it functioned well enough. In 1940, two IRA men, Patrick Harte and Thomas McGrath were tried in Dublin by Military Court for the murder of a police officer. A few days before the men were due to be shot there was a last-ditch challenge to the legality of the Military Court. A writ of habeas corpus was applied for and a conditional writ was granted while the judge studied the papers.

By a curious irony, the case was heard by Justice Gavan Duffy. Many years before, Duffy had been the solicitor in *ex parte Doyle:* the habeas corpus action challenging the legality of the 1916 trials. Duffy, now a judge of the Irish High Court found himself faced with a similar challenge. The facts and legal framework were quite different but the central dilemma was much the same: to what extent can the rule of law be abrogated to protect the state from those bent on its destruction by force of arms?

Duffy dismissed the application for habeas corpus. His ruling was upheld by the Supreme Court and the men were shot by firing squad.[18] A few years later, another IRA man, Charlie Kerins was tried and convicted by Military Court for murdering a police detective.[19] He was sentenced to death. This time, the British government loaned Ireland the services of Albert Pierrepoint to carry out the hanging. The irony was lost on no one.

The military court phenomenon has been used much further afield. It is the first recourse of every dictator but it also appears occasionally in times of crisis in democracies, almost as a reflex action. In the American civil war, President Lincoln suspended habeas corpus and permitted the trial of civilians by military court.[20]

Much more recently, the Guantanamo trials raise the same vexed questions about the jurisdiction of military courts. The American Supreme Court has wrestled with this question in many cases. In a series of landmark decisions, the Court has ruled that detainees are entitled to challenge the legality of detention and should be afforded counsel for that purpose.[21] In a later judgment the Court ruled that the Army cannot try prisoners without applying accepted standards of due process.[22] Subsequently in *Boumediene v Bush*[23] the Supreme Court struck down the Military Commissions Act[24] and ruled that prisoners at Guantanamo still had a right to test the legality of their detention by applying to the courts for a writ of habeas corpus.

The 1916 trials took place in the context of a nationalist war of independence but that perspective is too narrow. There are conflicts in every age and the trigger points may be ethnic tensions, religious differences or a desire for self-determination. The enduring issues are always the same: due process and the legality of detention, trial and punishment. The nature of the relationship between the State and those it seeks to govern is fundamental in a country that subscribes to the rule of law. The great dilemma is always the same: the extent to which due process may be departed from in times of crisis. It is submitted that the greater the crisis, the more important it is to remember that adherence to the rule of law is what underpins democracy.

Select Bibliography and Note on Sources

Abbott, R., *Police Casualties in Ireland 1919–1922* (Dublin: Mercier, 2000).

Babington, A., *For the Sake of Example* (London: Leo Cooper, 1983).

Barton, B., *Behind a Closed Door: Secret Court Martial Records of the 1916 Rising* (Belfast: Blackstaff Press, 2002).

Barton, B., *Secret Court Martial Records of the Easter Rising* (Stroud: The History Press, 2010).

Bradbridge, E.U., (ed.), *59th Division 1915–1918* (Chesterfield: Wilfred Edmonds, 1928).

Brennan, R., *Allegiance* (Dublin: The Richview Press, 1950).

Brennan-Whitmore, W.J., *Dublin Burning* (Dublin: Gill & MacMillan, 1996).

Campbell, C., *Emergency Law in Ireland 1918–25* (Oxford: Clarendon Press, 1994).

Caulfield, M., *The Easter Rebellion* (London: Frederick Muller, 1964).

De Groot, G., *Douglas Haig* (London: Unwin Hyman, 1998).

Ferguson, K., *King's Inns Barristers, 1868–2004* (Dublin: The Honourable Society of King's Inns, in association with the Irish Legal History Society, Irish Academic Press, 2005).

Ferguson, S., *GPO Staff in 1916* (Cork: Mercier, 2012).

FitzGerald, D., *Desmond's Rising – Memoirs 1913 to Easter 1916* (Dublin: Liberties Press, 2006).

Fitzpatrick, D., *Harry Boland's Irish Revolution* (Cork: Cork University Press, 2003).

Fox, R.M., *History of the Irish Citizen Army* (Dublin: James Duffy & Co, 1944).

Foxton, D., *Revolutionary Lawyers: Sinn Fein and Crown Courts* (Dublin: Four Courts Press, 2008).

Foy, M., *Michael Collins's Intelligence War* (United Kingdom: Sutton Publishing, 2006).

Geoghegan, S., *The Campaigns and History of the Royal Irish Regiment* (Cork: Schull Books, 1997).

Geraghty, Hugh, *William Patrick Partridge and His Times* 1874–1917 (Dublin: Curlew Books, 2003).

Gibbon, M., *Inglorious Soldier* (London: Hutchinson and Company Limited, 1968).

Griffith, K. and O'Grady, T.E., (eds), *Curious Journey* (London: Hutchinson, 1982).

Heuston, John M., *Headquarters Battalion: Army of the Irish Republic – Easter Week 1916* (Dublin: Nationalist, 1966).

Hopkinson, M., (ed.) *Frank Henderson's Easter Rising* (Cork: Cork University Press, 1998).

Jeffery, K., (ed.) *The Sinn Fein Rebellion As they Saw It* (Dublin: Irish Academic Press, 1999).

Jenkins, R., *Asquith* (London: Collins, 1969).

Jordan, J., (ed.) *Boer War to Easter Rising* (Dublin: Westport Books, 2006).

Kiberd, D., (ed.) *1916 Rebellion Handbook* (Dublin: Mourne River Press, 1998).

Lieberson, G., *The Irish Uprising 1916–1922* (New York: MacMillan, 1966).

Longford, Earl, and O'Neill, T.P., *Eamon de Valera* (London: Hutchinson & Company, 1970).

Lyons, F.S., *John Dillon: A Biography* (London: Routledge and Kegan Paul, 1968).

Macardle, D., *The Irish Republic* (London: Corgi, 1969).

MacCarthy, C., *Cumann na mBan and the Irish Revolution* (Cork: The Collins Press, 2007).

MacLochlainn, P., *Last words letters and statements of the leaders executed after the Rising at Easter 1916* (Dublin: Kilmainham Jail Restoration Society, 1971).

Meakin, W., *History of the 5th North Staffords 1914–1919* (London: Hughes and Harper, 1920).

Montgomery Hyde, H, (ed.) *Trial of Sir Roger Casement* (Edinburgh: William Hodge and Company Limited, 1960).

Oates, W.C., Lt-Colonel, *History of the 2/8th Sherwood Foresters 1914 –18* (Nottingham: J.H. Bell, 1920).

O'Brien, P., *Uncommon Valour: 1916 and the battle for the South Dublin Union* (Cork: Mercier Press, 2010).

Ó Broin, L., *W.E. Wylie and the Irish Revolution* (Dublin: Gill & Macmillan,1989).

O'Callaghan, J., *Revolutionary Limerick* (Dublin: Irish Academic Press, 2010).

O'Casey, S., *The Story of the Irish Citizen Army* (London: Journeyman Press, 1980).

O'Donoghue, F., *No Other Law* (Dublin: Irish Press Limited, 1954).

O'Duibhir, L., *The Donegal Awakening: Donegal and the War of Independence* (Dublin: Mercier Press, 2009).

O'Malley, E., *On Another Man's Wound* (Dublin: Anvil, 2002).

Officers of the Battalions: *The Robin Hoods* (Uckfield: The Naval and Military Press, 2010).

Oram, G., *Death Sentences Passed by Military Courts of the British Army 1914–24* (London: Francis Boutle Publishers, 1998).

Robbins, F., *Under the Starry Plough: Recollections of the Irish Citizen Army* (Dublin: The Academy Press, 1977).

Toomey, T., *The War of Independence in Limerick* (Limerick: privately published, 2010).

Townshend, C., *Easter 1916: The Irish Rebellion* (London: Penguin 2005).

Turi, J., *England's Greatest Spy: Eamon de Valera* (London: Stacey International, 2010).

Yeates, P., *A City in Wartime, Dublin 1914–18.* (Dublin: Gill & MacMillan, 2011).

1/7th,2/7th,3/7th Battalion Sherwood Foresters 1914–1918 (London: N & M Press, 2009).

Memoirs

Quinton, W.A., War Memoirs, IWM.
Dickson, A.A., Captain, Sherwood Foresters, IWM.
Orchard, Captain John, Leicestershire Regimental Archive, County Record Office.
Maconchy Memoir, NAM,
Memoir of L/Ç B.C. Webster, Foresters Museum,
Memoir of Private Archie Bennett, Foresters Museum.
Wylie Memoir, PRO.

Regimental Archives

Lincolnshire Regiment, Lincolnshire County Archives, Rumbold Street, Lincoln.
Museum of the Sherwood Foresters, Chilwell, Nottinghamshire.
Leicestershire Regiment, Leicestershire County Archive, Wigston, Leicestershire.
Lancers Archive, Grantham, Lincolnshire.

Public Record Office Kew

Trial Records WO 71 344 – et seq.
Trial Register WO 213/8
Chief Secretary's List CO 903/19

National Library of Ireland

Gavan Duffy Papers
Irish National Aid Association and Voluntary Dependants Fund Papers

UCDA

De Valera Papers

Bodleian Library

Asquith Papers

British Library

Miscellaneous Letters and Papers ff.55-60

Irish Military Archives

Contemporary Documents 45
BMH Witness Statements

Army Publications

Kings Regulations and Orders for the Army 1914
Manual of Military Law, 1907 (6th Edition)

Essays

Hardiman, A., 'Shot in Cold Blood: Military law and Irish Perceptions of the 1916 Rebellion in 1916', in Doherty, G. and Keogh D., (eds), *The Long Revolution,* (Dublin and Cork: Mercier 2007).
Jenkins, R., 'Old Black: The Life of Major General C.G. Blackader, 1869–1921', Leicestershire Archaeological and Historical Society, 80 (2006).

Royal Commissions and Government Reports

The Royal Commission on the Arrest and Subsequent Treatment of Mr Francis Sheehy-Skeffington, Mr Thomas Dickson, and Mr Patrick James MacIntyre upon and after their arrest on the twenty-fifth day of April last. Cd. 8376.
The Royal Commission on the Rebellion in Ireland 1916 Cmnd. 8279.
Statistical Tables of the Dublin Metropolitan Police for the Year 1916, Cmd. 30, 1919.

Statutes and Cases

Ex parte Milligan 71 US 2 (1866).
R v Governor of Lewis Prison ex parte Doyle [1917] 2 KB 254.
R (Childers) v Adjutant General of the Provisional Forces [1923] 1 IR 5.
In the matter of the application of Patrick McGrath and Thomas Harte. [1941] IR 68.
Rasul v Bush 542 US 446 (2004).
Hamdan v Rumsfeld 548 US 577.
Boumediene v Bush 553 US 723 (2008).
Defence of the Realm Act 4 & 5 Geo V c.29.
Defence of the Realm (Consolidation) Act 5 Geo V.
Defence of the Realm (Amendment) Act 5 & 6 Geo V.

Notes

ABBREVIATIONS, EXPLANATIONS
AND BIOGRAPHIES

1. *The Royal Commission into the causes of the recent outbreak of rebellion in Ireland, and into the conduct and the degree of responsibility of the civil and military executive in Ireland in connection therewith. (1916).* Cd 8279. Evidence of the Chief Commissioner, Lt Colonel Edgeworth-Johnstone, p.52.
2. Fox, R.M. *The History of the Irish Citizen Army* (Dublin: James Duffy Limited, 1944), p.227.

CHAPTER 1

1. The government made ex gratia payments of over £1m to compensate for loss. A further £742,926 was paid out in rebuilding grants. See: *Statistical Tables of the Dublin Metropolitan Police for the Year 1916*, Cmd. 30, 1919.
2. See *Statistical Tables of the Dublin Metropolitan Police for the year 1916*, Cmd. 30, 1919. These show 429 killed and 2,592 wounded. These statistics were compiled in 1917 and appear to be reliable but they only refer to casualties in the Dublin Metropolitan Police District, which extended in an eight-mile radius of Dublin Castle. To these figures should be added the execution of Thomas Kent in Cork, the death of Richard Kent and Head Constable Rowe, killed at Coole Lower, near Fermoy. Sergeant O'Rourke and Constable Hurley killed in Moanour. Constables Clery and McLoughlin wounded at Firies, in County Kerry. Constable Whelan, who was killed in Galway. Also, the three men drowned at Ballykissane Pier, Kerry, in connection with the arms landing. Eleven dead at Ashbourne, County Meath, including six police, two rebels and three civilians (who acted as drivers for the police) and 20 wounded in that encounter. In addition, Constable Charles McGee killed at Castlebellingham, County Louth and Casement who was executed at Pentonville prison in August. It is submitted that the figures issued by GHQ Parkgate 11 May 1916, immediately after the Rebellion and included in PRO WO 32/4307 were compiled too hastily and must be regarded as significantly understating the casualties.
3. Kiberd, D., (ed.), *1916 Rebellion Handbook* (Dublin: Mourne River Press, 1998), p.57.
4. This was a common theme in talks given by MacDonagh. See BMH Witness Statement, No. 328, Holohan, p.52.
5. PRO WO 32/4307.
6. *Hansard* HC Debates 11 May 1916 col. 958–9.
7. In his private correspondence Asquith expressed no reservations about the legality of the trials. British Library Miscellaneous Letters and Papers ff.56–60.
8. JAG Advice 15 January 1917. PRO WO 141/27.
9. *Hansard* HC Debates 24 October 1916 vol. 86 cols. 917–19.
10. *Hansard* oral answers 19 July 1915; 26 January 1916; 5 April 1916.
11. Babington, A., *For the Sake of Example* (London, Leo Cooper, 1983), p.xii. This seminal study of the cover up of trials on the Western Front was written by Judge Babington and I acknowledge the influential nature of his work.

12. On the issue of representation, see for instance HC Debates 1 March 1917, vol. 90 cols. 2178. And; 20 February 1918 vol. 103 cols. 767–882. On the issue of confirmation of sentence: HC Debates 15 March 1917 vol. 91 col. 1274.
13. Sir Reginald Brade was Permanent Under-Secretary for War, 1914–1919. He had been Secretary to the Army Council between 1902 and 1914. He spent his entire career at the War Office.
14. HC Debates 20 February 1918, vol. 103 cols. 767–882.
15. WO 35/69.
16. The reasons and the process by which the decision to withhold publication were drawn to my attention by David Foxton's excellent study, *Revolutionary Lawyers: Sinn Fein and Crown Courts* (Dublin: Four Courts Press, 2008) at p.115 et seq. I acknowledge that debt. See also Townshend, C., *Easter 1916: The Irish Rebellion* (London: Penguin, 2006).
17. *R v Governor of Lewes Prison ex parte Doyle* [1917] 2 KB 254.
18. *Hansard* HC Debates 5 March 1917 vol. 91 cols. 24–6.
19. See Babington, *For the Sake of Example* (London: Leo Cooper, 1983).
20. BMH Witness Statement, No. 268, Cosgrave, Annexe B.
21. In the aftermath of the Rebellion a number of men applied under the Army Act for their trial records. These were passed to George Gavan Duffy who selected two for use in a legal action brought to challenge the legality of the trials. These records went to the National Library of Ireland where they surfaced a few years ago. Duffy also donated trials records relating to 16 other men to the Bureau of Military History.
22. Foxton, D., *Revolutionary Lawyers*, p.64.
23. The last death sentence passed following trial by FCCM was imposed on Jeremiah Lynch on 17 May. Sentence was commuted to penal servitude within a few days. PRO WO 213/8.
24. PRO WO 213/8.
25. MacLochlainn, P., *Last Words: letters and statements of the leaders executed after the Rising at Easter 1916* (Dublin: Kilmainham Jail Restoration Society, 1971). And see Barton, B., *Secret Court Martial Records of the Easter Rising* (Stroud: The History Press, 2010). Brian Barton was the first historian to examine the trials of the executed prisoners.

CHAPTER 2

1. Lord Wimborne in evidence to *The Royal Commission on the Rebellion in Ireland 1916*, Para. 802.
2. Ibid, Para. 804.
3. Robbins, F., *Under the Starry Plough*, p.97.
4. BMH Witness Statement, No. 1758, Burke, p.8. This is a recurring theme among those who made statements to the BMH.
5. BMH Witness Statement, No. 923, Callender, p.2.
6. BMH Witness Statement, No.1768, McDonnell, p.2. Also BMH Witness Statement, No. 413, McCrea, p.2 and BMH Witness Statement, No. 488, Plunkett, p.10.
7. PRO WO 32/4307.
8. BMH Witness Statement, No.1750, O'Donovan, p.5. O'Donovan was charged with mobilising men on Easter Monday and found that many had gone to Fairyhouse Races. See also BMH Witness Statement, No. 208, Kavanagh, p.7.
9. BMH Witness Statement, No. 264, Ceannt, p.23.
10. BMH Witness Statement, No. 293, Heron, p.3.
11. BMH Witness Statement, No. 1758, Burke, p.3.
12. BMH Witness Statement, No. 638, Caldwell, p.5.
13. Jeffery, K., (ed.), *The Sinn Fein Rebellion As They Saw It* (Dublin: Irish Academic Press, 1999), p.38.
14. *The Irish Times*, 9 April 2012 An Irishwoman's Diary.
15. Townshend, C., *Easter 1916* (London: Penguin 2005), p.165.
16. BMH Witness Statement, No. 687, Curran, p.44.

17. BMH Witness Statement, No. 189, Soughley, p.1.

18. BMH Witness Statement, No. 358, Dillon, p.18.

19. BMH Witness Statement, No. 497, Bulfin, p.8.

20. BMH Witness Statement, No. 391, Molony, p.36. Halpin survived the Rebellion. He was seen by Dr Lynn after the surrender. He was covered in soot, having tried to hide up a chimney at City Hall. BMH Witness Statement, No. 357, Lynn, Part II, p.1. He was taken from a chimney 'in an exhausted condition'. His main concern was his wife who had been in a poor state of health when he left home.

21. BMH Witness Statement, No. 348, Gerrard, p.4.

22. BMH Witness Statement, No. 579, Byrne, p.2.

23. Jeffery, *The Sinn Fein Rebellion as They Saw It,* p.65.

24. O'Duibhir, L., *The Donegal Awakening: Donegal and the War of Independence* (Dublin: Mercier, 2009) p.40.

25. In Galway, an RIC man was shot and killed. Near Galbally, two RIC men were shot dead pursuing a suspect. In Kerry, Constables McClery and McLoughlin were shot while nailing up a proclamation. In Louth, Constable McGee was shot and killed.

26. See *The Irish Law Times and Solicitors Journal,*17 February,1917, p.15.

27. BMH Witness Statement, No. 687, Curran, p.56.

28. *1916 Rebellion Handbook*, p.16: the source is contemporary and usually reliable. It suggests 26 fatalities but the names of the dead do not appear in any record that charts the casualties. See BMH Witness Statement, No.1686 Henderson, that shows that the fatalities among the Volunteers and ICA numbered 63 but none are attributed to the storming of the newspaper offices. Henderson suggests that the men holding the newspaper offices withdrew before the final assault. It is suggested that Henderson's account is likely to be reliable. Another account suggests that only five men held the newspaper offices and no fatalities were sustained. Fox, R.M., *History of the Irish Citizen Army* (Dublin: James Duffy & Co, 1944), p.150. It is likely that the newspaper offices were evacuated before the final assault and that during the decisive charge the Dublin Fusiliers were fired on from a number of rebel positions situated around Dublin Castle.

29. BMH Witness Statement, No. 497, Bulfin, p.8.

30. Jeffery, *The Sinn Fein Rebellion as They Saw It,* p.42.

31. Oates, C., *The History of the 2/8 Battalion Sherwood Foresters 1914–18*, p.38.

32. See *Irish Law Times and Solicitors Journal* 17 February 1917.

33. The following year the retrospective effect of the proclamation was challenged in *R v Governor of Lewes Prison ex parte Doyle* [1917] 2 KB 254: Doyle had been captured on 24 April, the first day of the Rebellion. This appeal was rejected by the High Court on the ground that the effect of the proclamation was procedural only: it simply prescribed the method by which offenders might be tried after 26 April 1916.

34. Yeates, P., *A City in Wartime* (Dublin: Gill and Macmillan, 2011), p.113.

35. *Royal Commission*, Cd. 8376, Para. 25.

36. Gibbon, M., *Inglorious Soldier* (London: Hutchinson & Co., 1968), p. 43.

37. BMH Witness Statement, No. 707, Noyk.

38. Evidence to *the Royal Commission on the Arrest and Subsequent Treatment of Mr Francis Sheehy-Skeffington, Mr Thomas Dickson and Mr Patrick James MacIntyre, upon and after their arrest on the twenty-fifth day of April last.* Cd. 8376.

39. BMH Witness Statement, No. 348, Gerrard.

40. BMH Witness Statement, No. 251, Balfe, p.7.

41. BMH Witness Statement, No.1035, Cody, p.11.See also BMH Witness Statement, No. 1760, Coughlan, p.2.

42. Orders for O.C. Troops Disembarking from England PRO W0 35/67, 25 April.

43. BMH Witness Statement, No. 348, Gerrard, p.6.

44. Brigadier Maconchy Memoir. National Army Museum, p.450.

45. Oates, C., *The History of the 2/8 Battalion Sherwood Foresters 1914–18*, p.41.

46. Brigadier Maconchy Memoir, National Army Museum, p.451.

47. Maconchy Memoir, National Army Museum, p.451.

48. BMH Witness Statement, No. 422, Byrne, p.12.

49. Jeffery, *The Sinn Fein Rebellion as They Saw It*, p.43.
50. BMH Witness Statement, 687, Curran, p.58.
51. Jeffery, *The Sinn Fein Rebellion As They Saw It*, p.53
52. BMH Witness Statement, No. 687, Curran, p.65.
53. Jeffery, *The Sinn Fein Rebellion as They Saw It*, p.55.
54. Memoir of Private Archie Bennett, Sherwood Foresters. Museum of the Sherwood Foresters.
55. Wylie Memoir PRO 30/89/2 and see Jeffery, *The Sinn Fein Rebellion As They Saw it*.
56. Meakin, W., *History of the North Staffords 1914–1919* (London, Hughes & Harper, 1920), p.72.
57. *Curious Journey*, Griffiths, K. & O'Grady, T., (eds), (London: Hutchinson, 1982) p.65.
58. Jeffery, *The Sinn Fein Rebellion As They Saw It*, p.52
59. Geoghegan, S., *The Campaigns and History of the Royal Irish Regiment* (Cork, Schull Books, 1997), p.103.
60. BMH Witness Statement, No. 1431, Dr Ridgeway, p.3.
61. BMH Witness Statement, No. 694, De Burca, p.15.
62. BMH Witness Statement, No. 694, De Burca, p.15.
63. BMH Witness Statement, No. 687, Curran, p.64.
64. Private Henry Wyatt was later tried for the murder of William Glaister a naval officer and the attempted murder of William Gray, a hotelier. A charge of manslaughter was proved. Five-years' penal servitude was ordered. See *1916 Rebellion Handbook*, p.127.
65. *1916 Rebellion Handbook* (Dublin: Mourne River Press, 1998) p.276.
66. Towers, Sir George, *General Sir John Maxwell* (London: John Murray, 1932), p.211 et seq.
67. See for instance, Foxton, D., *Revolutionary Lawyers* (Dublin: Four Courts Press, 2008), p.67.
68. *Hansard* H.C. Debates 10 May 1916 cols. 674–5.
69. Maxwell to Lady Maxwell, 28 April 1916, cited in Arthur, G, *General Sir John Maxwell*, p.248
70. BMH Witness Statement, No.1019, Bucknill, p.1
71. Ibid. p.2.
72. PRO WO 32/4307.
73. De Valera Papers UCDA P150/512, Advice of the Law Officers.
74. Townshend, C., *Easter 1916* (London: Penguin, 2005), p.290.
75. Sir Joseph Byrne. See Abbreviations, Explanations and Biographies.
76. Barton, B., *The Secret Court Martial Records of the Easter Rising* (Stroud: The History Press, 2010) p.75. Brian Barton describes General Byrne as the 'Deputy Advocate General'. No such post existed. Byrne was Deputy Adjutant General (DAG) which was an administrative post which is easily confused with the post of Deputy Judge Advocate General (DJAG) which was a legal post.
77. Maxwell brought with him a new Chief of Staff, General Hutchinson, who in fact took no active part in the suppression of the Rebellion because of the decisive steps already taken by Brigadier William Lowe. Also with him was Deputy Adjutant General Byrne. Maxwell's aide de camp was Prince Alexander of Battenberg, a grandson of Queen Victoria. Alfred Bucknill was the final member of the group. He came from a distinguished and well-known legal family, the son of Sir Thomas Bucknill. The service record of his son, Alfred Bucknill shows that he joined up in 1914 and served in France in 1915 and briefly in Egypt. He was a barrister at the Admiralty Bar, with no experience of criminal or court martial work. He was promoted in June 1916 and became Deputy Judge Advocate General in September 1917. See PRO WO 374/10588. He returned to private practice after the war and took silk in 1931. He became a High Court Judge of the Admiralty and Probate Division. He conducted the inquiry into the loss of the submarine Thetis and another inquiry in the circumstances in which the German warships Scharnhorst and Gneisenau broke out of Brest and forced their way into the channel in 1942. Bucknill later wrote *The Law of Tug and Tow*. He became a Lord Justice of Appeal and died in 1963.

78. This system of government is as described and accepted by the *Royal Commission 1916* Cd. 8279.
79. Telegram to Asquith, 29 April 1916, Asquith Papers, Bodleian Library.
80. Maxwell to Lady Maxwell, 28 April 1916. Cited in Arthur, G, *General Sir John Maxwell*, p.248.
81. BMH Witness Statement, No. 687, Curran.
82. Maconchy Memoir National Army Museum, p.454.
83. NLI, Michael Kent, Ms 15, 292.
84. PRO WO 32/4307.
85. BMH Witness Statement No. 687, Curran, p.64.
86. *Curious Journey*, p.72. Griffiths, K. & O'Grady, T., (eds), (London: Hutchinson, 1982).
87. BMH Witness Statement No. 694, De Burca, p.20.
88. Memoir of Private Archie Bennett, p.11. Museum of the Sherwood Foresters: 'Our Battn. were all ready for the final assault.'
89. UCDA de Valera Papers P150/512.
90. BMH Witness Statement, No. 638, Caldwell, p.13.
91. BMH Witness Statement, No. 244, McGallogly, p.12.
92. BMH Witness Statement, No. 370, Addendum by Desmond Ryan.
93. Brennan Whitmore, W., *Dublin Burning* (Dublin: Gill and MacMillan 1997). See also BMH Witness Statement No.1511, Doyle, p.9. BMH Witness Statement, No. 510, Thornton, p.23. BMH Witness Statement, No. 920, Augustine, p.7. In fact, this view, though strongly and widely held, did not translate into summary executions, with the notable exception of events at North King Street.
94. Walton, *Curious Journey*, Griffiths, K. and O'Grady, T., (eds),(London: Hutchinson, 1982), p.76.
95. Memoir of Private Archie Bennett, p.12. Museum of the Foresters.
96. BMH Witness Statement, No. 842, p.17. See also BMH Witness Statement, No. 370, Murphy and Addendum by Desmond Ryan.
97. Hopkinson, M., (ed.), *Frank Henderson's Easter Rising* (Cork: Cork University Press, 1998) p.67. Described by Henderson, an otherwise restrained observer, as 'a night of horror'.
98. Conditions for prisoners held at the Customs House were very similar. See BMH Witness Statement, No. 510, Thornton, p.25.
99. Sean Etchingham and Seamus Doyle.
100. See BMH Witness Statement, No. 1758, Burke, p.8. This was a common theme in the recollections of prisoners.
101. BMH Witness Statement, No. 264, Ceannt, p.40.
102. BMH Witness Statement, No. 207, Aloysius, p.10.
103. Wylie Memoir PRO 30/89/3.
104. BMH Witness Statement, No. 268, Cosgrave, p.14.
105. BMH Witness Statement, No. 399, Mulcahy, p.22.
106. BMH Witness Statement, No. 422, Byrne, p.16.
107. See PRO WO 32/4307.
108. Kiberd, D., (ed.), *1916 Rebellion Handbook*, p.41.

CHAPTER 3

1. The first historians to attempt an analysis of the legal implications of Maxwell's orders were Charles Townshend and David Foxton. See Townshend, *Easter 1916* (London: Penguin, 2005) p.275. Also Foxton D., *Revolutionary Lawyers* (Dublin: Four Courts Press, 2008). I acknowledge the influence of those works.
2. This was because the proclamation issued under the Defence of the Realm Act 1915 applied only to Ireland. A prisoner in England could still elect jury trial.
3. 1,867 prisoners were deported in what was the largest operation of its kind since the Boer War, where the Army had judged the tactic a success.

4. For an analysis of the legality of the internment orders see: Foxton, D., *Revolutionary Lawyers*.

5. Sean McEntee was brought back after only a few weeks. He was tried in June 1916 with three others for the murder of Constable McGee and the attempted murder of Lieutenant Dunville. There is evidence that RIC detectives travelled over to England to the camps at Stafford and Frongoch where the prisoners were paraded for identification. There is no evidence that they were successful in picking out suspects. Some prisoners, like Garry Holohan, wanted for the shooting of a young man at Islandbridge, took steps to disguise themselves. See for instance BMH Witness Statement No. 328, Holohan, p.71.

6. Asquith Papers, Bodleian Library Oxford. Situation Report 11am, 30 April 1916. Major General Shaw to Lord French.

7. PRO WO 32/4307. 1 May. Major General Shaw.

8. PRO WO 32/4307. Telegram 29 April 1916.

9. Caulfield, M., *The Easter Rebellion* (London: Frederick Muller Ltd., 1964) p.357.

10. See for instance WO 32/4307 correspondence between Horse Guards and Maxwell in the weeks following the surrender.

11. BMH Witness Statement, No. 153, Dore, p.6.

12. BMH Witness Statement, No. 359, Lynn, Part I, p.1.

13. BMH Witness Statement, No.186, Doyle, p.14.

14. BMH Witness Statement, No. 926, McCabe, p.11.

15. BMH Witness Statement, No. 304 Coughlan, p.27.

16. See BMH Witness Statement, No. 200, Aloysius, p.10. See also *1916 Rebellion Handbook*, p.67.

17. Brennan-Whitmore, W., *Dublin Burning* (Dublin: Gill & McMillan, 1996) p.125.

18. BMH Witness Statement, No. 694, De Burca, p.26.

19. Robbins, F., *Under the Starry Plough*, (Dublin: The Academy Press, 1977), p.133.

20. *The Times* 2 May 1916.

21. See Abbreviations, Explanations and Biographies. See *'Old Black': The Life of Major General C.G. Blackader, 1869–1921*, Robin Jenkins, Leicestershire Archaeological and Historical Society, 80 (2006).

22. Wylie memoir.

23. Brigadier Blackader sat with two other officers, Lieutenant-Colonel German, Fifth Leicester Regiment and Lieutenant Colonel Kent, RFA.

24. It appears that Maconchy stepped down from courts martial duty on or about 5 May and returned to finish a few part-heard trials on 6 May only. He was replaced by Colonel Sapte. The officers who sat on this court with Maconchy were Lieutenant-Colonel Bent of the Royal Munster Regiment and Major Woodward C.M.G. of the North Lancashire Regiment.

25. Longworth had previously edited the *Daily Express*. In 1916, Longworth was 36 years old. Longworth stayed in Ireland and prosecuted many notable trials for sedition under the emergency legislation, including the trials of J.J. Walsh (TD for Cork) and Piaras Beaslai (TD for East Kerry). He later became Deputy Judge Advocate General in Ireland and acted as Judge Advocate in some of the trials under martial law in 1921 and the Restoration of Order in Ireland Act. See obituary of Lieutenant Colonel Longworth KC. *The Times* 25 January 1935. See also PRO WO 339/23701.

26. De Valera Papers UCDA P150/512.

27. Defence of the Realm Act 1915, s1. (7).

28. Defence of the Realm Act 1914, section 1(4).

29. See Brennan-Whitmore, W., *Dublin Burning* (Dublin: Gill & MacMillan, 1996)

30. De Valera Papers P150/512 Maxwell to Kitchener 2 May 1916. And WO 32/4307 Maxwell to Army Council, telegram 3 May which spoke about 'unavoidable delay' and hinted at legal difficulties.

31. De Valera Papers UCDA P150/512.

32. PRO WO 32/4307. Byrne was almost certainly influenced by Bucknill who had been sent to Ireland to keep the army within the law. See BMH Witness Statement No. 1019, Annexe.

33. For an account of this aspect of the Rebellion, see Yeates, P., *A City in War Time, Dublin 1914–18* (Dublin: Gill & McMillan, 2011), p.118–121.
34. BMH Witness Statement, No. 189, Soughley, p.1.
35. For a description of this process, see Memoir of Captain Orchard. Leicestershire County Archive.
36. See Spender and Asquith, *The Life of Lord Oxford and Asquith*, vol. ii, p.176. Birrell's resignation was announced two days later: HC Debates 3 May 1916 vol. 82 cc 30–9. The Under Secretary Nathan left Dublin on 2 May for England. His resignation was accepted on 3 May.
37. See for instance de Valera Papers P150/512 – letters 1 May, 2 May and 6 May. See also British Library Miscellaneous Letters and Papers ff. 56–60.
38. Redmond Papers. John Dillon to John Redmond 30 April 1916.
39. De Valera Papers P150/512.
40. The Trial Register, WO 213/8. In respect of some trials, the dates are at variance with those suggested in the *1916 Rebellion Handbook*. It is submitted that the *1916 Rebellion Handbook* is to be preferred. The errors such as they are, may arise because the compiler of the Trial Register has confused the date of trial with the date that Maxwell gave the order convening the trial of the prisoner.
41. Kiberd, D., *1916 Rebellion Handbook* (Dublin: Mourne River Press, 1998) p.71
42. Ibid. p.44.
43. Jeffery, K, (ed.), *The Sinn Fein Rebellion As They Saw It* (Dublin: Irish Academic Press, 1999) p.68
44. BMH Witness Statement, No. 923, Callender, p.25.
45. Leicestershire County Record Office, Regimental Archive, *Memoir of Captain Orchard*.
46. Jury trial at the Four Courts resumed on 19 May.
47. *Statistical Tables of the Dublin Metropolitan Police for the year 1916*. 431 were arrested. 30 were acquitted. 134 were imprisoned and the rest were fined.
48. BMH Witness Statement, No. 1052, McEntee, p.118.
49. BMH Witness Statement, No. 979 Barton, p.2.
50. The officer provided the information to Bucknill within hours of the execution. See BMH Witness Statement No. 1019, Bucknill p.5.
51. BMH Witness Statement, No. 189, Soughley, p.1.
52. BMH Witness Statement, No. 687, Curran, p.7.
53. Asquith was the son of a prosperous wool merchant. He went to Balliol College and then to the Chancery Bar. He appeared as counsel for the defendant in *Carlill v Carbolic Smoke Ball Company* [1892] QB 484. He was Prime Minister from 1908 to 1916. On the question of drink, see Jenkins, R., *Asquith* (London: Collins, 1969) p. 412.
54. Jenkins, R., *Asquith* (London: Collins, 1969) p.396. Jenkins suggests that this conversation took place on 2 May. However, a reliable contemporary source shows that Birrell was still in Dublin on 2 May and made his resignation speech at Westminster on 3 May. See Kiberd, D., (ed.), *1916 Rebellion Handbook* p.274. Therefore the author suggests that this conversation took place on 3 May immediately before Birrell's resignation speech.
55. De Valera Papers UCDA P150/512, 3 May 1916.
56. John Denton Pinkstone French. First Earl of Ypres. When the Great War came he was appointed to command the British Expeditionary Force. This much-decorated cavalry veteran found that tactics had changed beyond recognition. His deployment of the BEF led to disaster and the retreat from Mons. In 1916, French was close to retirement, although not quite a spent force. In 1918 he was appointed Lord Lieutenant and Governor General of Ireland.
57. *Death Sentences passed by military courts of the British Army 1914–1924*, Oram, G., (London: Francis Boutle, 1998).
58. De Groot, G., *Douglas Haig 1861–1928* (London: Unwin Hyman, 1998), p.239.
59. *Hansard* HC Debates 3 May 1916 cols. 30–39.
60. *Hansard* HC Debates 4 May 1916 vol. 82 col. 125.
61. PRO WO/32/4307.

62. Tried in Fermoy by FGCM for the killing of Head Constable Rowe.
63. PRO WO 32/4307. The name 'Costrave' is used in the original. It is submitted this must be Cosgrave.
64. BMH Witness Statement, No. 687, Curran, p.78.
65. BMH Witness Statement, No. 286, Connolly-O'Brien, p.49.
66. BMH Witness Statement, No. 687, Curran, p.79.
67. Kiberd, D., (ed.), *1916 Rebellion Handbook* (Dublin: Mourne River Press, 1998) p.74.
68. Memoir of L/Cpl B.C. Webster. Museum of the Sherwood Foresters.
69. PRO CAB 41 37/19 6 May 1916. Quoted in Townshend, C., *Easter 1916* (London: Penguin, 2005).
70. De Valera Papers, UCDA, P150/512, Wimborne to Maxwell, 6 May.
71. Lyons, F.S., *John Dillon: A Biography* (London: Routledge and Kegan Paul, 1968).
72. Ibid. p.379.
73. 'After our conversation last night I was, I admit, dismayed to learn that three comparatively unknown insurgents were executed this morning.' Lord Lieutenant's letter to Maxwell written some hours later, after the executions had taken place. British Library, Miscellaneous Letters and Papers ff.53–4. There were in fact four men executed that morning. The fourth was Ceannt, who was a signatory to the proclamation of Independence. It may be inferred that Wimborne did not dissent from the decision to execute Ceannt.
74. BMH Witness Statement, No. 348, Gerrard, p.7.
75. Kiberd, D., (ed.), *1916 Rebellion Handbook* (Dublin: Mourne River Press, 1998), p.78.
76. 8 May 1916 Wimborne to Maxwell, The British Library Miscellaneous Papers and Letters ff. 53–4. The same day Wimborne also wrote letters of thanks to Colonel Edgeworth-Johnstone, Commissioner of the DMP and Sir Neville Chamberlain, Inspector General of the RIC. See Kiberd, D., *1916 Rebellion Handbook* (Dublin: Mourne River Press, 1998), p.105. These are the last known letters he wrote while in office and the inference is that he wrote these letters as he was clearing his desk. His resignation was made public the following day.
77. PRO WO 32/4307.
78. *Hansard* HC Deb. 10 May 1916 vol. 82 cols. 673.
79. *The Royal Commission to inquire into and report upon the facts and circumstances connected with the treatment of Mr. Francis Sheehy-Skeffington, Mr Thomas Dickson and Mr Patrick J. MacIntyre upon and after their arrest on the Twenty-fifth day of April last.* (Cd 8376) para.55.
80. PRO WO/4307, Telegram 10 May 1916.
81. PRO WO 32/4307.
82. It was later suggested that Maxwell had threatened to resign if the executions of these two men were not permitted to go ahead. See BMH Witness Statement No. 1,431, Ridgeway, p.4. The surviving paperwork set out in PRO WO 32/4307 contradicts this suggestion emphatically. Maxwell was still an ambitious officer and it is unlikely that he would jeopardise his career in this way.
83. BMH Witness Statement, No. 729, Browne, p.7
84. Ibid.
85. This is supported by BMH Witness Statement, No. 1019 Bucknill. Addendum signed by F. H. Boland.
86. PRO WO 32/4307.
87. PRO WO 32/4307 – Kitchener to Maxwell 14.45pm: 'Unless you hear to the contrary from Mr Asquith you may carry out tomorrow the extreme sentence of death on McDermott and Connolly.'
88. BMH Witness Statement, No. 200, Aloysius, p.13.
89. *Hansard* HC Deb. 11 May 1916 vol. 82 cols. 935–970.
90. *The Times* 12 May 1916.
91. *Hansard* 11 May 1916 cols. 935–970.
92. Related by Eoin MacNeill. MacNeill Papers NLI 11437.

93. BMH Witness Statement, No. 398, Martin, p.13.
94. For an analysis of events at North King Street, see Foxton, D., *Revolutionary Lawyers* (Dublin: Four Courts, 2008) at p.75–8. See also Townshend, *Easter 1916*, (London: Penguin, 2005) at p.293–94.
95. Sergeant Robert Flood of the Royal Dublin Fusiliers was later prosecuted before a General Court Martial for the murder of William Rice, a Guinness employee and Lieutenant Lucas of the King Edward Royal Horse. Flood was acquitted.
96. Private Wyatt was later tried by court martial for murder and attempted murder. He was acquitted of murder and found guilty of manslaughter. Five years' penal servitude was ordered. Private M. Hand, Royal Dublin Fusiliers was also tried for murder before a General Court Martial. The result of his trial is not recorded.
97. *Hansard* HC Debates 12 July 1916, vol. 84 col. 321 and see *Hansard* HC Debates 17 July 1916 col. 661.
98. BMH Witness Statement, No. 200, Aloysius, p.17.
99. BMH Witness Statement, No. 979, Barton. There is a discrepancy between Barton's account and that given by Nora Connolly, who saw her father that night and recalled he was conscious and coherent only hours before his execution. It is probable that Connolly was given painkillers to withstand the journey by horse-drawn ambulance from Dublin Castle to Kilmainham and this affected his level of consciousness.
100. BMH Witness Statement, No. 200, Aloysius, p.14.
101. BMH Witness Statement, No.242, Tannam, p.47.
102. British Library Miscellaneous Letters and Papers ff.55–60.
103. A situation as described to and accepted by *The Royal Commission into the causes of the recent outbreak of rebellion in Ireland, and into the conduct and the degree of responsibility of the civil and military executive in Ireland in connection therewith. (1916).* Cd. 8, 279. See pp.5 and 7.
104. *The Times* 12 May 1916.

CHAPTER 4

1. In the colonies the proclamation of martial law was governed by Guidance issued by the Foreign and Colonial Office. PRO CO/323/287. The Guidance was issued in the aftermath of the Jamaica Rebellion and still had force of law in the early twentieth century. *See Tilonko v Governor General of Natal AC* [1907] 93.
2. See for instance Finlason, W.F., *Report of the case of the Queen v Governor Edward John Eyre* (London: Chapman and Hall, 1868).
3. Dicey, A.V., *The Law of the Constitution*, Eighth Edition (London: MacMillan, 1915) p.283.
4. *Coke Third Inst.* Chapter 7. Petition of Right 3. Chas. C.1.
5. *Report of the Jamaica Royal Commission* 1866.
6. Cd. 981 of 1902.
7. *The Royal Commission into the arrest and subsequent treatment of Mr Francis Sheehy-Skeffington, Mr Thomas Dickson and Mr James McIntyre.* Cd. 8376.
8. *The Royal Commission* Cd. 8376.
9. See *The Irish Law Times and Solicitors Journal*, 17 February 1917, p.15.
10. 4 & 5 Geo. 5 c.29.
11. The Act was soon amended to allow any British citizen who was not subject to military law to elect trial by jury rather than trial by courts martial. Defence of the Realm (Amendment) Act *1915* 5 Geo 5. c.34.
12. The Defence of the Realm (Amendment) Act 1915.
13. The following year the retrospective nature of the proclamation was challenged in *R v Governor of Lewes Prison ex parte Doyle* [1917] 2 KB 254: the prisoner had been captured on 24 April, the first day of the Rebellion and tried for acts done that day. This appeal was rejected by the High Court on the ground that the effect of the proclamation was procedural only: it simply prescribed the method by which offenders might be tried after 26 April 1916.

14. Proclamation of 26 April 1916. This analysis of the law owes something to Professor Campbell who carried out the seminal work in this field. See Campbell, C., *Emergency Law In Ireland 1918–1925* (Oxford: Clarendon Press, 1994). See also *The Royal Commission into the causes of the recent outbreak of rebellion in Ireland, and into the conduct and the degree of responsibility of the civil and military executive in Ireland in connection therewith. (1916),* Cd. 8,279, p.5.

15. *Rules of Procedure 1907,* Reg. 4. Under this procedure the witnesses gave their evidence to an officer in the presence of the accused. The officer wrote out the evidence contemporaneously. The accused was permitted to cross-examine and make a statement if he wished. This procedure was recognised as a safeguard against prosecution malpractice. It also allowed the accused to know the exact case he had to meet.

16. *Rules of Procedure 1907,* Reg. 13.

17. *Rules of Procedure 1907,* Reg.78.

18. *Rules of Procedure 1907,* Reg. 87.

19. *Rules of Procedure 1907,* Notes to Regulation 105.

20. *Rules of Procedure 1907,* Reg. 68.

21. *Rules of Procedure 1907,* Reg 105. In fact, the DORA (Amendment Act) 1915 gave the Army a wide discretion on whether to convene a FGCM or a GCM. But in deciding whether to convene a GCM or a FGCM, the Army appear to have adhered to the test of practicality set out in the rules of procedure. The DORA (Amendment Act) 1915 gave the Army wide powers unregulated by Parliament.

22. This may explain why Asquith was so surprised at the rapidity with which the early trials and executions took place. (See Chapter 3 this volume). Asquith may have been unaware of Maxwell's decision to order trials by FGCM or the implications of that step.

23. *Manual of Military Law,* Sixth Edition, Regulations 104 and 13 and 14.

24. Babington, A., *For the Sake of Example* (London: Leo Cooper, 1983) p.121. The use of Judge Advocates on the Western Front did not become common until September 1916. It cannot be said, therefore, that the Dublin prisoners were treated less favourably than others on this account. At this juncture in the Great War the Army started to utilise significant numbers of officers with legal training to act as Judge Advocates in France. Most of these officers were unfit for front-line service by reason of wounds received or poor health.

25. *Rules of Procedure 1907,* Reg. 119(c) required the trial to be in 'open court' meaning a court to which the public had access.

26. *R v Governor of Lewes Prison ex parte* Doyle [1917] 2 KB 254. Affidavit of General Maxwell. It is curious to say the least that a copy of this order does not survive and is not endorsed on any of the case papers that are kept at the Public Record Office. At that time, it was usual for officers conducting these trials to note any deviation from usual procedures in the file.

27. Defence of the Realm (Amendment) Act 1915. S.2. The origin of not permitting a prisoner to give evidence on his own behalf was historic. It was a legacy of an age where proof was established by the swearing of oaths, rather than the giving of evidence. The notion that two people might swear conflicting oaths was unpalatable and undermined the logic of establishing facts by the swearing of oaths. Therefore the rule emerged that the prisoner was not permitted to give sworn evidence. The quid pro quo for the prisoner was the requirement that the prosecution prove their case beyond doubt. The rule that a prisoner could not give evidence on his own behalf was abolished in England in 1898. But in Ireland the rule remained. It was regarded as a protection for prisoners who were thought to make poor witnesses in their own defence

CHAPTER 5

1. BMH Witness Statement, No. 422, Byrne, p.19.

2. BMH Witness Statement, No.1511, Doyle, p.15.

3. BMH Witness Statement, No.1758, Burke, p.6. BMH Witness Statement, No. 923, Callender, p.25. And see BMH Witness Statement, No. 833, Knightly, p.11.

4. Brennan-Whitmore, W., *Dublin Burning* (Dublin: Gill & McMillan, 1996), p.114.
5. BMH Witness Statement, No.1052 McEntee, p.118 and see BMH Witness Statement, No. 162, Shouldice, p.10.
6. BMH Witness Statement, No. 148, Crenigan, p.4
7. BMH Witness Statement, No. 268, Cosgrave, p.10
8. NLI, Jack Plunkett, Ms. 11,397.
9. BMH Witness Statement, No. 1766, O'Brien, p.20.
10. BMH Witness Statement, No. 268, Cosgrave, p.10.
11. Brennan-Whitmore, W., *Dublin Burning* (Dublin: Gill & McMillan, 1996), p.114.
12. For a contemporaneous account by a prisoner, James Sullivan, an American citizen, see PRO WO 35/69.
13. BMH Witness Statement, No. 833, p.13
14. BMH Witness Statement, No. 94, Leahy, p.5.
15. BMH Witness Statement, No. 132, Spillane, p.10.
16. BMH Witness Statement, No. 398, Martin, p.14.
17. NLI, Jack Plunkett, Ms.11, 397.
18. The Dublin Metropolitan Police was split into seven Divisions, A-G. The 'G Men' were the Detective Division based at Brunswick Street. They were responsible for combating politically-inspired crime.
19. BMH Witness Statement, No. 280, Holland, p.48.
20. BMH Witness Statement, No. 167, Byrne, p.9. See also BMH Witness Statement No. 63, Caldwell, p.11.
21. BMH Witness Statement, No. 804, O'Connell, p.28
22. Frank Thornton was a London émigré who had come over to avoid conscription. He had been using the alias Frank Drennan and was tried in that name.
23. BMH Witness Statement, No. 367, Gleeson, p.11.
24. BMH Witness Statement, No. 328, Holohan, p.67.
25. Brennan-Whitmore, W., *Dublin Burning* (Dublin, Gill & McMillan, 1996) p.114.
26. BMH Witness Statement, No. 618, O'Duffy, p.4.
27. BMH Witness Statement, No. 370, Murphy, addendum by Desmond Ryan.
28. BMH Witness Statement, No. 800, O'Flanagan, p.30.
29. BMH Witness Statement, No. 1019, Bucknill, p.3.
30. BMH Witness Statement, No. 370, Murphy, addendum by Desmond Ryan.
31. BMH Witness Statement, No. 1753, Tobin, p.10.
32. BMH Witness Statement, No. 244, McGallogly, p.12.
33. NLI, Plunkett, Ms.11,397.
34. BMH Witness Statement, No. 697, Bermingham, p.4.
35. Stockholm syndrome.
36. BMH Witness Statement, No. 550, Collins, p.4.
37. BMH Witness Statement, No. 800, O'Flanagan, p.18.
38. NLI, Jack Plunkett, Ms 11,397.
39. BMH Witness Statement, No. 865, Plunkett, p.3.
40. Wylie Memoir, PRO WO 30/89/2.
41. BMH Witness Statement, No. 268 Cosgrave, p.13.
42. Mulcahy had travelled down from Swords on Saturday 29 April to get confirmation of the surrender from Pearse. The officer who travelled to Arbour Hill with him failed to pick him out on parade. BMH Witness Statement, No. 1043, Lawless, p.126.
43. BMH Witness Statement, No. 1019, Bucknill, Annex.
44. PRO WO 71/350.
45. BMH Witness Statement, No.1019, Bucknill, p.7.
46. BMH Witness Statement, No. 1758, Byrne, p.6.
47. BMH Witness Statement, No. 1511, Doyle and No.1758, Burke, p.6.
48. BMH Witness Statement, No. 1511 Doyle, p.23.
49. BMH Witness Statement, No. 327 Egan, p.32.
50. BMH Witness Statement, No. 833, Knightly, p.10.
51. BMH Witness Statement, No. 310, Grace, p.13.

52. Brennan-Whitmore, W., *Dublin Burning* (Dublin: Gill & McMillan, 1996) p.113.
53. BMH Witness Statement, No. 1052, McEntee, p.118.
54. NLI, Lynch, Ms. 11,128.
55. BMH Witness Statement, No. 865, p.1.
56. BMH Witness Statement, No. 1768, McDonnell, p.21.
57. BMH Witness Statement, No. 687, Curran, p.89.
58. An exception might be Desmond FitzGerald who made a very full and voluntary confession to the Head Constable at Bray and to the Assistant Provost Marshal before he arrived at Richmond Barracks. See trial of Desmond FitzGerald, this volume. For a full transcript, see Irish Military Archives. See also the trial of William Partridge, this volume: Irish Military Archives. BMH CD 45/3/3.
59. BMH Witness Statement, No. 1,511 Doyle, p.11.
60. BMH Witness Statement, No. 264, Ceannt, p.33.
61. BMH Witness Statement, No. 270, O'Reilly, p.10.
62. BMH Witness Statement, No.1758, Burke, p.6.
63. BMH Witness Statement, No. 201, Laffan, p.10.
64. BMH Witness Statement, No. 463, Sister of Mercy, p.3.
65. Also, Manus McMenamin, Liam Clarke, Joe Beggs and Harry Shiels. See BMH Witness Statement No. 568, UiChonnaill, p.13.
66. James Connolly and Willie Corrigan were wounded. Joseph Plunkett was gravely ill.
67. BMH Witness Statement, No. 251, Balfe, p.7
68. BMH Witness Statement, No. 1687, Colley, p.26.
69. BMH Witness Statement, No. 188, O'Keefe, p.8.
70. BMH Witness Statement, No.220, Daly, p.12. Also hospitalised at Dublin Castle was Daniel McCarthy. See BMH Witness Statement No. 722, McCarthy. This prisoner avoided trial but was deported.
71. BMH Witness Statement, No. 268 Cosgrave, p.10. See also BMH Witness Statement, No. 304, Coughlan, p.26. See NLI Plunkett, Ms. 11,397. Plunkett also obliquely refers to this process of weeding out young prisoners. Also, NLI Ms. 10,915 Seosamh MacSuibhen, Major General. Also, BMH Witness Statement, No.280, Holland, p.48 and by way of example, BMH Witness Statement, No. 252, O'Brian, p.8 and BMH Witness Statement, No. 314, O'Carroll, p.16.
72. BMH Witness Statement, No.1, 768, McDonnell, p.21.
73. BMH Witness Statement, No. 421, Oman, p.13.
74. A handful of young men were tried despite their youth. James Crenigan was 16. John McGallogly and James Wilson were 17.
75. BMH Witness Statement, No. 398, Martin, p.10.
76. See BMH Witness Statement, CD 117 Father Aloysius. For the role of women generally, see MacCarthy, C., *Cumann na mBan and the Irish Revolution*, p.68.
77. BMH Witness Statement, No. 391, p.33, Molony. See BMH Witness Statement, No. 280, Holland, p.23 and 34.
78. BMH Witness Statement, No. 546, Hackett, p.8.
79. BMH Witness Statement, No. 348 Gerrard.
80. Constance Markievicz.
81. Wylie Memoir PRO 30/89/2.
82. *Manual of Military Law. Sixth Edition.*
83. See for instance trial papers of John MacBride PRO WO 71/350 and the affidavit of Gerald Doyle, *R v Governor of Lewes Prison ex parte Doyle* 2 KB [1917] 254.
84. BMH Witness Statement, No. 268 Cosgrave, Appendix 1.
85. BMH Witness Statement, No. 1019, Bucknill, p.3.
86. BMH Witness Statement, No. 1511, Doyle. All of the men captured on the first day of the Rising at the South Dublin Union were tried by courts martial, saving one who was wounded and escaped from hospital.
87. Heuston, J.M., *Headquarters Battalion Easter Week 1916* (Dublin: Nationalist Printers, 1966) p.72.

88. In the trials that took place under GCM later that spring, there is direct evidence that the charges were framed by Lord Campbell. See PRO WO 35/67. It is highly likely having regard to the complexities of the law, that he drafted the template for the trial of Pearse. This charge was adopted for all the trials by FGCM that followed.
89. See Chapter 3 as to how this charge came to be preferred.
90. The charge is marked in some of the surviving case papers as 'alternative'. See, for instance, Connolly PRO WO 71/354.
91. Townshend, C., *Easter 1916* (London: Penguin, 2006) p.289.
92. Barton, B., *The Secret Court Martial Records of the Easter Rising* (Stroud: The History Press, 2010), p.318
93. BMH Witness Statement, No. 366 McGarry, p.25
94. BMH Witness Statement, No. 1758 Burke, p.7.
95. NLI, John Plunkett, Ms. 11,397.

CHAPTER 6

1. BMH Witness Statement, No. 162, Shouldice, p.10.
2. NLI, John Plunkett, Ms. 11397.
3. Brennan, R., *Allegiance* (Dublin: The Richview Press, 1950), p.85.
4. Ibid.
5. BMH Witness Statement, No. 268 Cosgrave, Appendix 1.
6. BMH Witness Statement, No. 244, McGallogly, p.12.
7. Rules of Procedure, *Manual of Military Law, Sixth Edition,* r19(v).
8. Brigadier Maconchy was commanding officer of the 178 Brigade, which included the Sherwood Foresters who had suffered heavy casualties.
9. BMH Witness Statement, No. 268 Cosgrave, Appendix 1.
10. Rules of Procedure, rules 87 and 88 *Manual of Military Law Sixth Edition.*
11. BMH Witness Statement, No. 268, Cosgrave, p.14. It seems that Ronayne, the barrister, was himself a Volunteer, p.3. He was a National Volunteer and a Lieutenant in the Royal Navy Reserve.
12. So far as can be ascertained, no prisoner was represented by a lawyer in these trials. Most prisoners simply did not raise the issue. See for instance BMH Witness Statement, Plunkett No. 865, p.4.
13. PRO WO 32/4307.
14. 50 *ILT and SJ* 1916 128. A complaint was made to General Sandbach by the Law Society. The complaint, made in the most craven terms, pointed out that the practice of not permitting legal representation was depriving lawyers of work and income.
15. *ILT and SJ* 1916, p.128. See Foxton, D., *Revolutionary Lawyers* p.74. Hugh O'Brien Moran, a busy Limerick solicitor, complained he was able to see clients only in the presence of an army officer.
16. BMH Witness Statement, No. 1758 Burke, p.7.
17. BMH Witness Statement, No. 1511 Doyle, p.26
18. O'Brion, L., *W.E. Wylie and the Irish Revolution* (London: Gill and MacMillan, 1989) p.24 – see also PRO 30/89/2.
19. *Hansard* HC Debates, 4 July 1916 vol. 83 col. 1372.
20. Captain Bowen Colthurst, Private Henry Wyatt, Sergeant Flood and Private Hand.
21. BMH Witness Statement, No. 865, Plunkett, p.4.
22. BMH Witness Statement, No. 268, Cosgrave, p.16. See also BMH Witness Statement No. 244, McGallogly.
23. BMH Witness Statement, No. 244, McGallogly, p.10.
24. BMH Witness Statement, No. 865, Plunkett, p.4
25. Cosgrave BMH Witness Statement, No. 268, Appendix A.
26. BMH Witness Statement, No. 1753, Tobin, p.9.
27. NLI, Ms. 11,128, Lynch.
28. BMH Witness Statement, No. 97, Hayes, p.5.
29. NLI, Plunkett, Ms. 11397.

30. Defence of the Realm (Amendment) Act 1915. S2
31. See for instance BMH Witness Statement, No. 1,399, Peppard, p.5.
32. Irish Military Archives, BMH CD 45 for the trial of Marks, Wilson and Crenigan and see Mendicity, Chapter 24 of this volume.
33. Irish Military Archive, BMH records CD 45.
34. Ibid.
35. Crofts was released from prison early, owing to his skin condition. So there may have been some substance in what he said although his later involvement in the War of Independence suggests that he also was a willing participant in the Rebellion.
36. PRO WO 71/348.
37. BMH Witness Statement, No. 268, Cosgrave.
38. BMH Witness Statement, No. 244, McGallogly, p.12.
39. William Kent (Bawnard House, Castle Lyons) J.R. Reynolds and Joseph Callaghan.
40. John Kennedy of Athenry. PRO WO 213/8.
41. This finding was a necessary precondition to convening a court martial: See *FORM FOR ASSEMBLY AND PROCEEDINGS OF FIELD GENERAL COURT MARTIAL ON ACTIVE SERVICE*; Rules of Procedure 1907.
42. See Babington, A., *For the Sake of Example* (London, Leo Cooper, 1983), p.119.
43. NLI, Plunkett, Ms 11397.
44. This point is reinforced by trial records of servicemen tried on the Western Front. Also by other trial records relating to the 1921 martial law period in Ireland. See for instance PRO WO 71/380.
45. *Maconchy Memoir*, National Army Museum, p.456.

CHAPTER 7

1. William Corrigan. See BMH Witness Statement, No. 268, Cosgrave, p.12.
2. Babington, A., *For the Sake of Example*, p.15.
3. Arthur, G., *General Sir John Maxwell* (London: John Murray, 1932).
4. WO 32/4307. Communiqué, Major General Shaw, 1 May 1916.
5. PRO WO 32/4307.
6. Wylie Memoir.
7. By way of example Gerald Doyle's death sentence was commuted to three years' penal servitude. Francis Fahey was sentenced to ten years' penal servitude at first instance, but his sentence was not disturbed by Maxwell. PRO WO 213/8.
8. *Short History of rebels upon who it has been necessary to inflict the supreme penalty.*11 May 1916. Asquith Papers, 43 Bodleian Library.
9. PRO WO 32/ 4307.
10. Ibid.
11. PRO WO 32 4307. Telegram – Asquith's orders communicated to Maxwell via Lord French, C in C – 4 May 'no sentence of death on any woman, including Countess Markievicz, should be confirmed and carried out without reference to the Field Marshal, commanding in chief and himself'.
12. Montgomery Hyde, H., *Trial of Sir Roger Casement.*
13. See for instance Babington, A., *For the Sake of Example,* p.16, where this process is described.
14. See BMH Witness Statement, No. 1019, Bucknill front sheet. In the front sheet of this statement, Bucknill is described as Deputy Judge Advocate General but in the body of his statement, he does not assert that he held this position. A review of his service record shows that in April 1916, he was still a second Lieutenant. He was promoted Lieutenant in June 1916 and he did not become Deputy Judge Advocate General until September 1917. See PRO WO 374/10588.
15. By way of example, Bucknill took summaries of evidence in the case of Markievicz and those captured on the first day of the Rebellion at the South Dublin Union.
16. BMH Witness Statement No.1019, p.3.
17. PRO WO 32/4307. It is also submitted that Maxwell's *'Short History of rebels'* justifying the executions was drafted by Bucknill. The style is very different from Maxwell's known

work and the analysis is that of a lawyer. The annexe to Bucknill's own witness statement refers to him drafting memos of this description; see BMH Witness Statement No.1019.

18. He was concerned in the preparation of the prosecution of David Kent. See WO 35/67.
19. Bucknill was appointed OBE in 1917.
20. An examination of the Minute Book of the Judge Advocate General suggests that the office of the JAG sent no lawyers to Ireland until 17 May, when Major Kimber DSO was assigned to prosecute court martials in Dublin. Acting Deputy Judge Advocate Kenneth Marshall followed to act as Judge Advocate. By this date nearly all the trials by FGCM had been completed. See PRO WO 81/149. In Brigadier Maconchy's Memoir, he suggests that he was relieved from court martial duty by Colonel Sapte who was from the Judge Advocate General's department. The records of the Judge Advocate General do not support the suggestion that Colonel Sapte was on the staff of the JAG.
21. Milvain had enjoyed an unexceptional parliamentary career as a Tory MP. He was appointed JAG in 1905 and held the post until his death in September 1916. He was the first JAG to draw a salary and undertake the job as a full-time post but he seems to have been ill-prepared to deal with the huge caseload generated by the Great War. The records of the JAG suggest that he did little work in the spring and summer of 1916. PRO WO 81/149.
22. Cassel was a Tory MP. He served in the trenches until 1915, when he was transferred to the office JAG with a view to appointment to JAG on Milvain's retirement. Cassel was in fact born in Germany. His parents were German, although there was a strong rumour that he was the illegitimate son of the late King. This rumour gathered strength in 1915, when he was plucked from the trenches and sent to the safety of the office of the JAG. After the death of Thomas Milvain, Cassel was appointed JAG in October 1916 (See *London Gazette*, October 1916). He served with distinction in that capacity until 1934.
23. See Enright, S. *The Trial of Civilians by Military Courts*, p.48. (Dublin, Irish Academic Press, 2012). See also PRO141/48.
24. *De Freitas v Benny* [1976] AC 239. It is submitted that this modern statement of the state of the law was equally valid in 1916.
25. See for instance BMH Witness Statement, No. 707, p.68 Michael Noyk. See also Enright, S. *The Trial of Civilians by Military Courts* (Dublin, Irish Academic Press, 2012).
26. See Lyons, F.S., *John Dillon, A Biography* (London, Routledge and Kegan Paul, 1968) p.379.
27. 8 May 1916 Wimborne to Maxwell the British Library Misc. Letters and Papers ff.54–60. Brought to my attention by a passage in Townsend, C., *Easter 1916*.
28. PRO WO 142/25.
29. See BMH Witness Statement, No. 1511, Doyle, p.32.
30. BMH Witness Statement, No. 1758, Burke, p.8; BMH Witness Statement, No. 865, p.4. BMH Witness Statement, No. 162, Shouldice, p.11. BMH Witness Statement, No. 268, Cosgrave, p.20. Also, Brennan, R., *Allegiance* (Dublin: The Richview Press, 1950), p.92.
31. BMH Witness Statement, No. 1753, Tobin, p.10.
32. BMH Witness Statement, No. 923, Callender p.12.
33. BMH Witness Statement, No. 1019, Bucknill, p.6.
34. Sniping continued in Dublin at least until 10 May. See Lincolnshire Regimental Archive, Diary of Quay Patrol, Box 7, No.175.
35. For an excellent account of the executions see Barton, B., *Secret Court Martial Records of the Easter Rising* (Stroud: The History Press, 2010). Also MacLochlainn, P., *Last Words*.
36. MacLochlainn, P., *Last Words*, p.157.
37. BMH Witness Statement, No. 979, Barton.
38. Memoir of A.A. Dickson, IWM.
39. PRO WO/35/67.
40. PRO WO 71/344.
41. PRO WO 35/67. Orders were issued by Brigadier Young that expressly required that a separate firing squad be assembled for each prisoner.
42. BMH witness statement, CD 117, Transcript p.14 Father Aloysius.

43. He returned to Kingstown immediately after the execution of Pearse, MacDonagh and Clarke and wrote up his report of the executions. There is evidence he remained at Kingstown and assisted with the sift of prisoners. There is evidence for instance that whilst at Kingstown he took a summary of evidence from Desmond FitzGerald on 10 May. See Irish Military Archives CD 45.

44. PRO WO 339/8377. He relinquished his commission in December 1916 and is shown arriving at Ellis Island, New York in January 1917. His wife was American and therefore this is not remarkable.

45. Commissioned in the Sherwood Foresters in 1897, he remained in the regular army until 1907. He then returned to civilian life where his area of expertise was the design and construction of factories. He remained part of the territorial reserve and returned to full-time service in August 1914. He remained in the army until 1920. In the Second World War he served as an ARP Divisional Commissioner. PRO WO 374/32349.

46. See Memoir of A.A. Dickson, IWM.

47. BMH Witness Statement, No. 189, Soughley.

48. Arthur, M., *Forgotten Voices of the Great War* (London: Ebury Press, 2003) p.89, p.203.

49. Babington, A., *For the Sake of Example*, p.52.

50. *War Memoirs*. Diary of W.A. Quinton, IWM.

51. 'I had the satisfaction of knowing this; that no bullet from my rifle hit the target, for as soon as I fired, I knew by the absence of any recoil from my rifle, that I had merely fired a blank cartridge.' *War Memoirs*, Diary of W. A. Quinton, IWM.

52. See Babington, A., *For the Sake of Example*, p.45 et seq. (London: Leo Cooper, 1983).

53. The organisation of the RAMC was regulated by *The Manual of Military Law, (sixth edition), The Kings Regulations and Orders to the Army, 1914* and *Standing Orders for RAMC*; IWM WO/ 2925 and *Regulations for the Army Medical Service* IWM, 00/143T. It is submitted that the uniform approach of RAMC officers to the process of execution must have been the result of careful regulation. The Army had a process for all eventualities but the procedure cannot be found in any of the above publications.

54. Babington, A., *For the Sake of Example,* p.47 (London: Leo Cooper, 1983).

55. PRO WO 71/347.

56. BMH Witness Statement, No. 304, Ceannt, p.41. One would be inclined to treat evidence from a source close to the prisoner with caution but Áine Ceannt's statement to the Bureau of Military History is detailed, balanced and entirely free from rancour. Her evidence is credible but hearsay. And it should be said that her account was not corroborated by Father Augustine, who attended Éamonn Ceannt's execution. His account written soon after the executions is framed in terms of spiritual deliverance. Oddly when he came to make a statement to the BMH, many years later, Father Augustine's statement stops abruptly exactly at the point he turns to deal with the executions on 8 May.

57. See PRO CO 904/209/297.

58. Memoir A.A. Dickson, IWM, Catalogue Reference 01/4/1. Second Lieutenant A.A. Dickson was promoted Acting Captain in September 1917, while commanding a Trench Mortar Battery in Nieuport. Quoted by kind permission of Mr Hugh Dickson.

59. BMH Witness Statement, No. 482, McNamara, p.10.

60. BMH Witness Statement, No. 348, Gerrard, p.7.

61. BMH Witness Statement, No. 348, Gerrard, p.7.

62. Examples of trial records from the Western Front in the spring of 1916 include: WO 71/452 Corporal Lewis, WO 71/455 Private Martin, WO 71/459 Private Bolton, WO 71/462.

63. See for instance the execution of Thomas Keane, in 1921. PRO WO/71/384 Certificate of Death reads 'Death in my opinion was practically instantaneous and was caused by shock and haemorrhage due to rifle fire. (signed) Captain A.J. Ireland RAMC.' See also by way of example, the execution of Cornelius Murphy, PRO WO 71/ 376. 'I found death to be instantaneous. Captain Alan Wise Clark.'

64. PRO WO 71/350.

65. PRO WO 35/67.

66. PRO WO 32/4307.
67. See de Valera Papers UCDA p.150/512, cipher 9 May: 'please report on Connolly's condition'. See also reply Maxwell to Asquith PRO WO 32/4307 Cipher 10 May 'Message for Prime Minister.'
68. From an account given by an Assistant Provost Marshal to Robert Barton, who was then an army officer. He was later a cabinet member in the Dáil and a signatory to the Treaty in 1921. See BMH Witness Statement No. 979, Barton, p.5. Barton relates Connolly 'was almost dead'. It is highly unlikely that Connolly was dying. His daughter's account of their last meeting earlier that night shows that Connolly was ill but lucid. It is more likely that Connolly was heavily drugged to withstand the journey by horse-drawn cart to Kilmainham.
69. *Hansard* 24 October 1916 Vol. 86 col. 917–19.
70. The circumstances in which publication was successfully resisted have been charted in detail by Foxton, D., *Revolutionary Lawyers* (Dublin: Four Courts Press, 2008), p.115.
71. *Hansard* 5 March 1917 vol. 91 cols. 24–6. Bonar Law.
72. See for example Edward Daly PRO WO 71/344 and Éamonn Ceannt PRO WO 71/348.

CHAPTER 8

1. There were a number of arguments canvassed but the 'in camera' order was the central matter in issue and the only one with merit. See *R v Governor of Lewis Prison ex parte Doyle* [1917] 2 KB 254.
2. See also Papers of Gavan Duffy, NLI.
3. It is remarkable that this order, which was without precedent, is nowhere recorded in the surviving case papers or other records of the Rebellion held by the National Archives in England or Ireland. Context of course is important. The Army was an organisation in which every order of significance was reduced to writing and was noted and acknowledged by written endorsement. This was particularly so in the sphere of capital trials of this period. It does raise the question as to whether Maxwell ever directly applied his mind to whether the trials should be in camera and what consequences that might have on the trial process.
4. Ferdinand Philip Maximilian Schiller, 1868–1946. A second-generation German. Appointed Kings Counsel in 1913, he was a highly successful silk. A Bencher and Treasurer of Inner Temple. Later Recorder of Bristol 1935–1946.
5. PRO WO 141/27. In October 1916, the AG wrote in an opinion that: 'The law officers of the Crown have been consulted and they are of the opinion that there was no legal justification for holding these cases in camera.' Cassel, the new Judge Advocate General broadly agreed but suggested that this course of conduct might be justified as a measure taken under martial law.
6. See Foxton, D., *Revolutionary Lawyers*, p.81 where David Foxton skilfully draws back the veil, to show the close relations between Lord Chief Justice Reading and the Cabinet.
7. [1917] 2 KB 254 at p.262.
8. Foxton, D., *Revolutionary Lawyers*.
9. Daniel Hoey, John Barton and Patrick Smyth. For an account of these killings, see Abbott, R., *Police Casualties in Ireland 1919–22* (Dublin: Mercier Press, 2000). See also Postscript, this volume.
10. Captain Henry de Courcy Wheeler was a reserve officer with a house and land in Kildare. He gave evidence against a number of prisoners but continued to live and farm in Kildare for many years.
11. Enright, S., *The Trial of Civilians by Military Courts – Ireland 1921*. (Dublin: Irish Academic Press, 2012). It should be noted that in these trials only a handful of civilian witnesses gave evidence for the Crown.
12. [1917] 2 KB 254 at p273.
13. *R v Sussex Justices, ex parte McCarthy* [1924] 1 KB 256.

14. The Army Act 1881, s.124.
15. De Valera Papers UCDA P150/512, Advice of the Law Officers.
16. *Manual of Military Law,* Sixth Edition. Regulation 104 and 13 and 14.

CHAPTER 9

1. BMH Witness Statement, No. 1686, Henderson. Tabulated Summary, p.1.
2. It is difficult to establish the precise number of GPO prisoners tried. The primary source is the Trial Register at Kew. However, a few prisoners were tried under names which were taken down wrongly and others later rejected the anglicised version of their names in whole or in part. Finally, some prisoners fought at more than one location and there is a need to avoid double counting.
3. Pearse, MacDonagh, Clarke, Plunkett, MacDiarmada, and William Pearse
4. Death commuted to 10 years: Jack Plunkett; George Plunkett; J.J. Walsh; John Dougherty; Jeremiah Lynch. Commuted to eight years: John McGarry; Commuted to five years: Vincent Poole. Commuted to three years: Michael Brady and Sean T.O'Kelly commuted to three years.
5. Frank Thornton (tried in the name of Drennan) – 20 years reduced to ten years; Thomas FitzGerald (tried in his given name but more commonly known as Desmond FitzGerald) 20 years reduced to ten years. Gerald Crofts and Harry Boland – ten years reduced to five; Conor McGinley – ten years – seven remitted; Patrick Weafer two years – 18 months remitted; Joseph Ledwich two years –18 months remitted.
6. NLI Ms. 24,363 Irish National Aid Association and Voluntary Dependants Fund Papers.
7. BMH Witness Statement, No. 195 Reynolds, p.9.
8. PRO WO/213/8.

CHAPTER 10

1. The account of this trial is taken from PRO WO 71/345.
2. The prisoner's desire to face the firing squad has been well documented by Barton, B., *The Secret Court Martial Records of the Easter Rising* (Stroud: The History Press, 2010), p.111.
3. Defence of the Realm Act 1915, section 1 (7).
4. Defence of the Realm Act 1914, section 1(4).
5. BMH Witness Statement, No. 1019, Bucknill.
6. BMH Witness Statement, No.1019, Bucknill, Annex, letter, Boland to Nunan, 5 February 1953.
7. Seamus Doyle and Sean Etchingham.
8. BMH Witness Statement, No. 1041, Doyle, p.14.
9. See MacLochlainn, P., *Last Words*, p.28

CHAPTER 11

1. The account of this trial is taken from PRO WO 71/347.
2. Wylie memoir. PRO 30/89/2.
3. BMH Witness Statement, No. 366, McGarry, p.25.

CHAPTER 12

1. The account of this trial is taken from PRO WO 71/349.
2. Regimental Museum of the Sherwood Foresters, Chilwell, Nottingham.

3. Bradbridge, E.U., (ed.), *59th Division 1915–1918* (Chesterfield: Wilfred Edmonds, 1928)
4. NLI, John (Jack) Plunkett, Ms 11397.
5. Abbott, R., *Police Casualties in Ireland* (Dublin and Cork: Mercier Press, 2000).

CHAPTER 13

1. The trial record is reproduced with the consent of the Irish Military Archives, CD 45.
2. BMH Witness Statement, Good, No. 388, p.6.
3. BMH Witness Statement, McGallogly, No. 244, p.7.
4. BMH Witness Statement, No. 488, p.10.
5. BMH Witness Statement, No. 1,744, p.4.

CHAPTER 14

1. The evidence in this trial is reproduced with the permission of the Irish Military Archives, BMH CD 45.
2. BMH Witness Statement, No. 488, Plunkett.
3. BMH Witness Statement, No. 865, Plunkett p.3. Plunkett appears to have thought that the police officers were probably being untruthful. A careful review of the evidence in both cases, suggests an identification error.

CHAPTER 15

1. PRO WO 71/358.
2. The trial record does not stipulate where cross examination commences but the tenor of the evidence suggests it starts at this point.
3. BMH Witness Statement, No. 244, McGallogly, p.12.
4. BMH Witness Statement, No. 244, McGallogly p.12.
5. BMH Witness Statement, No. 366, McGarry, p.25.
6. BMH Witness Statement, No. 91, Walsh.
7. BMH Witness Statement No. 244, McGallogly, p.14.
8. NLI John Plunkett, Ms 11397.
9. James Joseph Walsh was a member of Dáil Éireann from 1918 until 1927.
10. BMH Witness Statement, No. 244, McGallogly.

CHAPTER 16

1. The evidence in this trial is reproduced with the kind permission of the Irish Military Archives. BMH CD 45/3/3/(o).
2. Fitzpatrick, D., *Harry Boland's Irish Revolution* (Cork: Cork University Press, 2003), p.23.
3. *Sinn Fein Rebellion Handbook*, p.13.
4. BMH Witness Statement, No. 586, O'Donovan, p.6. This detail was drawn to my attention by David Fitzpatrick's definitive biography of Harry Boland.
5. *New York Times*, 2 August 1922.

CHAPTER 17

1. The account of this trial is taken from PRO WO 71/355.
2. See for instance BMH Witness Statement, No. 1,666, O'Donoghue, p.29. See BMH Witness Statement, No. 804, McConnell, p.28 and No. 1052, McEntee, p.119, BMH Witness Statement, No. 318, Scollen. See also Hopkinson, M. (ed.), *Frank Henderson's Easter Rising*, (Cork: Cork University Press, 1998), p.69.
3. See in particular, BMH Witness Statement, No. 550, Collins, p.4.
4. BMH Witness Statement, No. 196, Reynolds, p.9.
5. The incident was remembered by a number of prisoners. See BMH Witness Statement, No. 1,041, Doyle, p.35. This witness maintains that MacDiarmada was removed from

the line of men awaiting deportation on 8 May. This account derives some support from a reliable contemporaneous report: an entry in the *1916 Sinn Fein Rebellion Handbook*, p.78, which shows that T. Doyle from Enniscorthy was deported on 8 May. See also Brennan, R., *Allegiance* (Dublin: The Richview Press, 1950), p.82.

6. This document was an order requiring Volunteers to attend at Liberty Hall on Easter Monday.
7. Asquith Papers 43. Bodleian Library. *Short History of rebels on whom it has been necessary to inflict the supreme penalty.* 11 May 1916.
8. *Hansard* 11 May 1916, vol. 82, cc. 935–79.

CHAPTER 18

1. The account of this trial is taken from PRO WO 71/354.
2. NLI Ms 11,128, Lynch.
3. NLI Ms 13,947.
4. Commandant Gideon J. Sheepers. See Cd 981 of 1902.
5. Connolly-O'Brien, N., *Portrait of a Rebel Father* (Dublin: The Talbot Press, 1935). For a powerful account of the last meeting see pp. 320–23.
6. For an account of his execution, see Chapters 3 and 7 of this volume.

CHAPTER 19

1. This account is reproduced with the consent of the Irish Military Archives. BMH CD/45/3/(e).
2. The account given at his trial is consistent with his vivid memoir: FitzGerald, D., *Desmond's Rising – Memoirs 1913 to Easter 1916* (Dublin: Liberties Press, 2006).

CHAPTER 20

1. Not including the Mendicity which was not regarded as part of the Four Courts command and which is dealt with separately in this work. See BMH Witness Statement, No. 1686, Henderson, Tabulated Summary, p.14.
2. Army casualties were mainly from the South Staffords, but are nowhere recorded. Volunteer fatalities numbered at least 7: John Dwan, Patrick Farrell, Sean Hurley, Sean Howard, Peter Manning, Patrick O'Flanagan and Philip Walsh. After the Rebellion a Military Court of Inquiry was convened in private under Brigadier Maconchy to deal with allegations that soldiers had massacred 13 civilians. The troops were exonerated and the detail of the inquiry was suppressed. For an analysis see: Townshend, C., *Easter 1916* (London: Penguin, 2005), p.293. For a devastating analysis of this episode, see Foxton, D., *Revolutionary Lawyers* (Dublin: Four Courts Press, 2008), p.75. A review of contemporary sources and BMH statements makes it clear that none of the 13 men who were killed were later acknowledged in the casualty lists of the Volunteers or Citizen Army. These casualty lists were compiled with considerable care by those who had fought. This raises a compelling inference that the men were not combatants. The origins of this massacre probably lies in an order issued to the South Staffs on disembarking at Kingstown earlier that week. PRO WO 35/67. The substance of the order was that no house held by the rebels could be bypassed and that 'Every man found in any such house whether bearing arms or not, may be considered a rebel'. The ambiguity in this order was heightened by a perception that rebels did not enjoy the protection of the laws of war.
3. BMH Witness Statement, No. 800, O'Flanagan.
4. Nicholas Laffan commanded the North Brunswick sector. He sustained a serious head wound and was not tried for that reason. See BMH Witness Statement No. 1868, Henderson, Tabulated Summary, p.15.
5. BMH Witness Statement, No. 800, O'Flanagan, p.29.
6. A small number of the men guarding Cabra Bridge and the North Circular Road, which was part of the Four Courts garrison, were also tried and sentenced to death. These

included John O'Brien, Maurice Brennan, James Dempsey, John Faulkner, John McArdle, P. Fogarty. Their sentences were commuted to imprisonment.
7. Ned Daly.
8. The following men were sentenced to death but had their sentence commuted to ten years' penal servitude: Patrick McNestry, Peter Clancy, Denis O'Callaghan, Liam Tobin, Thomas Bevan, John Williams and Finian Lynch (later Circuit Judge). One prisoner, James O'Sullivan, had his death sentence commuted to eight years' penal servitude. The following prisoners had their death sentence commuted to five years: Cornelius O'Donovan and John Shouldice. The following prisoners had their death sentence commuted to three years: Edward Duggan, Pierce Beasley and Joseph McGuinness.
9. Francis Fahey, 10 years. Charles Bevan and Michael Scully: ten years – seven remitted.

CHAPTER 21

1. The account of this trial is taken from PRO WO71/344.
2. Brennan-Whitmore, W., *Dublin Burning* (Dublin: Gill & McMillan,1996), p.113.

CHAPTER 22

1. Each prisoner later made an application for a copy of their trial record under the Army Act. Each of the two prisoners later received a copy only of that part which pertained to the applicant. O'Donovan's record was used by George Gavan Duffy for a test case on the legality of the trials. It later went to the NLI as part of the Gavan Duffy papers. It is reproduced with the consent of the NLI. The parts of the record which pertain to Shouldice are reproduced with the permission of the Irish Military Archives. BMH CD 45/3/3/l.
2. BMH Witness Statement, No. 195, Reynolds, p.9.
3. BMH Witness Statement, No. 1,750, O'Donovan, p.5.
4. BMH Witness Statement, No. 162, Shouldice.

CHAPTER 23

1. The evidence in the trial of this prisoner is reproduced with the permission of the Irish Military Archives CD 45/3/3.
2. In the trial transcript the word Camera appears which must be a misspelling of Cabra.
3. Heuston, P., *Headquarters Battalion* (Dublin: Nationalist Press, 1966). Little further is known about the identity of the prisoner. An address, given by him, shows St Michael's Hill, Dublin, aged 31 and a labourer.

CHAPTER 24

1. PRO WO 71/351.
2. Stephenson, P.J., *Heuston's Fort* (Privately Published, 1966).
3. BMH Witness Statement, No. 290, McLoughlin, p.7.
4. BMH Witness Statement, No.251, p.5, Balfe.
5. BMH Witness Statement, No. 148, p.4, Crenigan.
6. Ibid.
7. BMH Witness Statement, No. 251, p.8, Balfe.
8. See for instance BMH Witness Statement, No. 1,758, p.7, Burke
9. NLI Ms 24,363. Irish National Aid Association and Volunteer Dependants Fund.
10. Irish Military Archives, BMH CD 45/3/3.
11. Ibid.
12. BMH Witness Statement, No.148,p.4, Crenigan. James Crenigan confirms his age was a decisive factor in sentence although he wrongly recalls the sentence as three years and does not state the basis of his defence.
13. BMH Witness Statement, No. 1399, Peppard.

14. PRO WO/213/8 – the full list of those dealt with by courts martial is as follows. Heuston, sentenced to death and executed. The following were sentenced to death and had their sentences commuted to three years' penal servitude: James Brennan; Fred Brooks; Jon Jo Byrne; John Clarke; Dick Coleman; John F. Cullen; John Derrington; William O'Dea; Richard Kelly; George Levins; James Marks; William Meehan; Joseph Norton; Patrick O'Kelly; Thomas O'Kelly; Thomas Peppard; Peter Wilson; William Wilson. Sentenced to short terms of imprisonment: James Crenigan; William Derrington; Edward Roach; James Wilson.

CHAPTER 25

1. The account of this trial is taken from PRO WO 71/351.

CHAPTER 26

1. BMH Witness Statement, No.1686, Henderson, Tabulated Summary p.15 and BMH Witness Statement, No. 312, p.19, de Brun. p.19.
2. BMH Witness Statement, No. 1686, Henderson, Tabulated Summary, p.14.
3. BMH Witness Statement, No. 204, Murphy, p.4.
4. BMH Witness Statement, No.139, Walker, p.4.
5. The Volunteers suffered one fatality, John O'Grady. Army casualties are not recorded.
6. Caulfield, M., *The Easter Rebellion* (London: Frederick Muller, 1964), p.341.
7. The colonel referred to by Wylie in his memoir as 'Colonel H', was almost certainly Lieutenant Colonel H. Taylor of the South Staffordshires – see Wylie Memoir PRO 30/89/2.
8. This incident was described by Meakin,W., *History of the 5th North Staffords, 1914–1919* (London: Hughes and Harper, 1920), p.72. Also by O'Ceallaigh, *Cappuchin Annual,*1966. It is suggested that Wylie exaggerated the scale of the casualties.
9. BMH Witness statement, No. 697, Bermingham, p.4.
10. Executed: MacDonagh, MacBride and Michael O'Hanrahan. Sentenced to death and commuted to ten years' penal servitude: Thomas Hunter, Patrick Sweeney; Henry O'Hanrahan. Sentenced to ten years' penal servitude; Richard Davys (sic-Davis). James Melinn and James Hughes were sentenced to twenty years' penal servitude, reduced to ten.
11. BMH Witness Statement, No. 532, MacDonagh, p.15.

CHAPTER 27

1. The account of this trial is taken from PRO WO 71/346.
2. Caulfield, M., *The Easter Rebellion* (London: Frederick Muller Ltd, 1964), p.360. See also BMH Witness Statement No. 532, MacDonagh, p.15.

CHAPTER 28

1. The account of this trial is taken from PRO WO 71/357.
2. See Wylie Memoir PRO 30/89/2.

CHAPTER 29

1. The account of this trial is taken from PRO WO 71/350.
2. Jenkins, R.,'Old Black':The Life of Major General C.G.Blackader,1869–1921 (Leicestershire Archaeological and Historical Society, 80, 2006).
3. Census 1911.
4. See Jordan, J. (ed.), *Boer War to Easter Rising* (Dublin: Westport Books, 2006). The appointment to any post with Dublin Corporation seems to have occasioned political intrigue. In this instance the Corporation voted 59–32, in favour of MacBride. The nationalists voting for MacBride, not out of personal sympathy one suspects but because

he was the last visible manifestation of the physical force tradition. It was in their interests that he be rescued from poverty and ridicule.

5. BMH Witness Statement, No. 268, Cosgrave, p.14.
6. The evidence was probably disallowed on the application of Wylie, who prosecuted. It is likely that the inspector sought to adduce in evidence the Irish Brigade Flag, which was kept at MacBride's lodgings.
7. BMH Witness Statement, No. 268, Cosgrave, p.14.
8. Ibid.
9. See for instance BMH Witness Statement, No. 312, de Brun, p.18.
10. McCracken, D.P., *MacBride's Brigade* (Dublin: Four Courts Press, 1997), p.163.
11. BMH Witness Statement, No. 1511, Doyle, p.24.This remark or something like it has been attributed to MacBride by a number of witnesses in different circumstances. See for instance BMH Witness Statement, No. 920, Augustine.
12. Allen Library. Some doubt was later expressed about the identity of the prisoner shown in this photo. But see BMH Witness Statement, No. 1511, Doyle, p.24. Doyle was one of the men in this photo. He later recalled the incident: 'MacBride came out of the court carrying a dust coat on his arm...'. Doyle later viewed this photo and positively identified MacBride. He asserted that the officer who took the photo recognised MacBride from the Boer campaign. This officer asked two soldiers to stand back to allow the photo to be taken and they did so. *The Daily Mirror* 10 May 1916, showed this photo and identified MacBride by name. Private Archie Bennett of the Sherwood Foresters also referred to this photo. Although he was not present when it was taken, he asserted that others who were, said that the man in the photo had just come down from his court martial but he was named Cosgrave and he had been sentenced to ten years' penal servitude. This could only be Liam or Philip Cosgrave. However, the Trial Register shows that the Cosgrave brothers were sentenced to death on 4 May. Sentence on Liam was commuted to 25 years. Sentence on Philip was commuted to three years' penal servitude, which tends to suggest that Bennett was wrong. Doyle was able to identify most of the prisoners in the photo including himself, Willie Corrigan, Éamonn Ceannt, George and Sean Plunkett, James Downey, John O'Brien and Major MacBride. He does not identify Liam or Philip Cosgrave. Doyle and the Cosgrave brothers would have been well known to each other. They both served in the Fourth Battalion Volunteers. Consent to copy photo declined.
13. Barton, *The Secret Court Martial Records*, p.216.
14. Jordan cites *Devoy's Postbag* 5 June 1919. Whether this was anything more than an emotional attachment cannot be said. Clara Allen was the wife of Fred Allen, an officer of the Dublin Corporation whose post involved long hours. MacBride had lodged with them for years and until 1911 was without employment. He would have seen a great deal of Clara Allen.

CHAPTER 30

1. The trial is reproduced with the permission of the Irish Military Archives. BMH CD 45. The date given for the trial in that record is 1 May. It is submitted that although the trial may have been convened on 1 May, no trials took place until 2 May, owing to legal difficulties. See PRO WO 32 4307: Maxwell to Lord French. See also Chapter 5 in this volume.
2. 'Clean' must mean unloaded, it is suggested.

CHAPTER 31

1. BMH Witness Statement, No. 268, Cosgrave, p.7.
2. BMH Witness Statement, No. 531, Young, p.5.
3. BMH Witness Statement, No. 186, Doyle, p.9.
4. BMH Witness Statement, No. 264, Ceannt, p.17.
5. BMH Witness Statement, No. 1604, Desborough, p.2.

6. Probably Major Riggs of the Third Royal Irish Regiment. He is referred to in the trial of James Morrissey. Irish Military Archives BMH CD 45.

7. See trial of James Burke. Irish Military Archives, BMH CD 45.

8. BMH Witness Statement, No. 1511, Doyle, p.9.

9. Geoghegan, S., *The Campaigns and History of the Royal Irish Regiment*, (Cork: Schull Books, 1997), vol. II, p.103.

10. Maconchy Memoir, p.453. National Army Museum.

11. For an account of the fighting see BMH Witness Statement, No. 199, Doolan.

12. Oates, W.C., *History of the 2/8th Battalion Sherwood Foresters 1914–1918.*

13. John Adams, William Burke, Brendan Donellan, Nurse Keogh, William McDowell, Richard O'Reilly, John Owens, James Quinn, Sean Traynor. See BMH Witness Statement No. 1686, Summary, p.23.

14. In addition to the casualties suffered earlier in the week, the Foresters lost five men: L/C T.H. Chapman, Privates G.W. Barrett, J.R. Forth, H. Rodgers and A. Warner. Also killed was an RIC man, Christopher Miller.

15. PRO WO 32/4307. Maxwell to French 30 April.

16. A few men left Dublin and camped out in the hills until the police raids slackened. BMH Witness Statement, No. 327, Egan, p.40.

17. Colbert and Ceannt.

18. PRO WO 213/8. George Irvine, William Corrigan, Gerald Doyle, James Burke, James Morrissey and John Downey. Patrick Morrissey escaped from hospital.

19. This can be seen in the trial of Philip Cosgrave (who was at the SDU) BMH CD 45/3/3/. Also the trial of Con Colbert PRO WO 71/ 352 (Colbert had been at Marrowbone Lane) and see the trial of P. Doyle, CD 45/3/3/ and BMH Witness Statement No. 155, Doyle, p.19.

20. BMH Witness Statement, No. 199, Doolan, Appendix, p.5.

21. Doyle was later a member of the Dublin Corporation, a Lord Mayor and served for 33 years in the Dáil.

22. The identity of this prisoner is uncertain. There is a record of a very young prisoner by the name of O'Neill who served in the South Dublin Union. Aged 19, a printer from Merchant's Quay, Dublin. See Chief Secretary's List.

CHAPTER 32

1. The trial record does not survive. This account has been compiled from a number of sources: BMH Witness Statement, No. 268, Cosgrave; the Wylie Memoir PRO 30/89/2 and PRO WO 213/8. Cosgrave wrote or contributed to a note on the trial process in 1917, which was smuggled out of prison and was later attached as an appendix to his statement to the BMH. Cosgrave's statement to the BMH does not acknowledge Wylie's assistance but is otherwise broadly consistent with Wylie's account, which is also detailed.

2. BMH Witness Statement, No. 268, Appendix A. Cosgrave.

3. BMH Witness Statement, No. 268, Cosgrave, p.15.

4. BMH Witness Statement, No. 268, Appendix 1, p.6.

5. BMH Witness Statement, No. 268, Cosgrave, p.18.

6. PRO WO 32/4307.

CHAPTER 33

1. The account of this trial is taken from PRO WO 71/348.

2. MacLochlainn, *Last Words.*

3. Wylie Memoir. PRO 30/89/2.

4. Barton, B., *Behind a Closed Door* (Belfast: Blackstaff Press, 2002)

5. After the trials of the leaders on 2 May, they were moved to Kilmainham Gaol. A number of prisoners awaiting trial were also moved with them. One of these men was Gerald Doyle who passed some hours with Tom Clarke before his execution. Doyle and the other prisoners heard the volleys signalling the execution of the leaders. Later the same morning Doyle and

the others were brought back to Richmond Barracks where they joined Ceannt and others who were awaiting trial. See for instance BMH Witness Statement No. 1511, Doyle, p.24.

6. See the Wylie memoir.
7. BMH Witness Statement, No. 268, Cosgrave, p.17. Cosgrave's statement was written in 1949 without the aid of notes. Although he exhibits a detailed account smuggled out of Lewes Prison in 1917, to which he contributed.
8. The Trial Register shows the spelling as Davys. In other records such as BMH statements the name is spelled Davis. In respect of Davys the Trial Register shows the date of trial as 1 May. This must be an error. It was certainly intended that the trials should start on that date but they were put back a day. See PRO WO 213/8. The clerk compiling this record has plainly taken the date on which the trial was ordered as the date of trial.
9. BMH Witness Statement, No. 312, de Brun, p.13.
10. BMH Witness Statement, No. 268, p.13.
11. BMH Witness Statement, No. 397, Pugh, p.9.
12. Hopkinson, (ed.), *Frank Henderson's Easter Rising* (Cork: Cork University Press, 1998), p.31.
13. Sweeney's death sentence was considered and commuted by General Maxwell on 4 May. Asquith Papers, Maxwell to the War Office, 4 May 1916. In the usual course of events Sweeney would have been informed a day or two after Maxwell had completed the process of confirmation.
14. Wylie Memoir PRO 30/89/2
15. BMH Witness Statement, No. 264, Ceannt, p.32
16. BMH Witness Statement, No. 264, Ceannt, p.33
17. Mervyn Richard Wingfield, 8th Viscount Powerscourt, attached to the special reserve of Irish Guards and later a senator of the Irish Free State.
18. BMH Witness Statement, No. 264, Ceannt, p.34
19. Letter to Asquith 9 May 1916, PRO WO 32/4307.

CHAPTER 34

1. The account of these proceedings is taken from PRO W0 71/352.
2. BMH Witness Statement, No. 268, Cosgrave, Appendix 1.
3. BMH Witness Statement, No. 328, Uallachain, p.34, in which the witness suggested that when the prisoners got to Richmond Barracks, Colbert volunteered to act as officer in charge instead of Seamus Murphy who was the senior officer. In fact, it is submitted, it is self evident from the trial record that the Provost Marshal (wrongly) believed Colbert had come from the vicinity of Jacob's factory and knew nothing more than that.
4. BMH Witness Statement, No. 264, p.41–2.
5. Townshend, C., *Easter 1916: The Irish Rebellion* (London: Penguin, 2005), p.280.
6. See the BMH Witness Statement No. 300, Murray.
7. BMH Witness Statement, No. 280, Holland, p.40
8. BMH Witness Statement, No. 167, Byrne, p.8. The recollection of this witness is confirmed in an account by Seamus Murphy, *Last Words*, MacLochlainn, P., p.131. See also BMH Witness Statement, No. 186, Doyle, p.8. and BMH Witness Statement, No. 386, Gaskin, p.3. See also BMH Witness Statement, No. 158, Kenny, p.9. BMH Witness Statement, No. 1686, Henderson, Summary of Events, p.10. And BMH Witness Statement, No. 300, Murray. BMH Witness Statement, No. 482, McNamara. BMH Witness Statement, No. 805, O'Brien, p.8.
9. Asquith Papers, 43. Bodleian Library. *Short History of rebels on whom it has been necessary to inflict the supreme penalty.*
10. BMH No. 167, Byrne, p.8.
11. BMH Witness Statement, No. 856, Appendix A. Colbert, and see BMH Witness Statement, 264, p.42, Ceannt.

CHAPTER 35

1. The evidence in this case is reproduced with the kind permission of the Irish Military Archives CD 45/3/3/. Philip Cosgrave was Liam Cosgrave's brother.

CHAPTER 36

1. This account is taken from the papers of George Gavan Duffy at the National Library of Ireland and the permission of the NLI is hereby acknowledged.
2. PRO WO 213/8.
3. BMH Witness Statement, No.1511, Doyle, p.26.
4. *R v Governor of Lewes Prison ex parte Doyle* [1917] 2 K B 254.

CHAPTER 37

1. BMH Witness Statement, No. 1,511, Doyle.
2. Census of 1911.
3. Yeates, P., *A City in Wartime*, p.125.
4. BMH Witness Statement, No. 268, Cosgrave, p.12. This was a reference to J.B. Powell KC, who later acted for the Army in the Royal Commission into the death of Sheehy Skeffington and two others, see Cd. 8376.
5. BMH Witness Statement, No. 250, Corrigan, p.2.
6. NLI Ms. 24,363.
7. PRO WO 213/8.
8. BMH Witness Statement, No. 268, Cosgrave, p.4.
9. BMH Witness Statement, No. 250, Corrigan, p.1.
10. BMH Witness Statement, No. 250, Corrigan, p.2.
11. Corrigan fixes the date by reference to the killing of Councillor John Lynch at the Exchequer Hotel in Dublin. O'Donoghue records that the killing took place at the Exchange Hotel on 22 September 1920: see O'Donoghue, F., *No Other Law* (Dublin: Irish Press Ltd, 1954), p.93.

CHAPTER 38

1. The evidence in this case is reproduced with the kind permission of the Irish Military Archives CD45/3/3/.
2. BMH Witness Statement, No. 1758, Burke.

CHAPTER 39

1. BMH Witness Statement, No. 1686, Henderson, Summary of Events, p.11.
2. Robbins, F., *Under the Starry Plough* (Dublin: The Academy Press, 1977), p.103.
3. BMH Witness Statement, No. 546, Hackett, p.8.
4. Robbins, *Under the Starry Plough*, p.114.
5. BMH Witness Statement, No. 546, Hackett, p.8.
6. Philip Clarke, James Corcoran, James Fox, Daniel Murray and Fred Ryan. See BMH Witness Statement, No. 1686, Henderson, p.22. Also John Adams according to Fox, R.M., *History of the Irish Citizen Army* (Dublin: James Duffy & Co, 1944).
7. Ibid., p.229.
8. PRO WO 213/8.
9. BMH Witness Statement No. 421, Oman, p.10. See also Caulfield, M., *The Easter Rebellion* (London: Frederick Muller Ltd, 1964), p.94.

CHAPTER 40

1. The account of this trial is taken from PRO HO/144/1580/316818.
2. PRO WO 32/4307.
3. See Chapter 7 in this volume.
4. Diary entry for Mahaffy, 6 May 1916, TCD MS. 2074. Cited by Townshend, C., *Easter 1916* (London: Penguin, 2005), p.286. The diarist was the daughter of the Provost at Trinity College. Wylie knew the Provost and was living in Trinity in the weeks after the Rebellion.
5. Barton, B., *Behind A Closed Door* (Belfast: Blackstaff Press, 2002), p.80.
6. An example might be Wylie's description of a conversation between himself and General Maxwell which resulted in a decision not to court martial de Valera. There is an abundance of evidence that de Valera was court martialled. There is other evidence that contradicts Wylie on the detail of what discussions took place on de Valera's fate. BMH Witness Statement No. 1019, Bucknill, Annexe. In later life, Wylie and de Valera met and de Valera asked Wylie if he could recall details of his trial. Wylie replied: 'You were not prosecuted at the time. There is nothing to remember.' See O'Brion, L., *W.E. Wylie and the Irish Revolution* (London: Gill & McMillan, 1989), p.34.
7. Industrial Schools Act, 1868.
8. *The Irish Times,* 3 March 1912. The Master, John Kelly, died of a fractured skull. Three of the youths were acquitted and never named in the press.
9. BMH Witness Statement No. 1019, Bucknill, p.4.
10. BMH Witness Statement No. 1019, Bucknill, p.5.
11. Memoir of Captain A.A. Dickson, IWM.
12. Caulfield,M., *The Easter Rebellion* (London: Frederick Muller Ltd, 1964), p.96.
13. BMH Witness Statement No. 1666, O'Donoghue, p.25.
14. Markievicz was gaoled in 1911 for her part in a protest against a visit to Ireland by King George V. She came to political prominence during the Dublin lockout in 1913. Her efforts to relieve poverty and hunger were funded from her own income and eventually by the sale of her jewellery. She became the first woman MP in the Coupon election of 1918. She declined to take up her seat and joined the First Dáil. She was appointed a Cabinet Minister in Dáil Éireann in 1919. She was a founder member of Fianna Fail. She was elected to the Fifth Dáil but died before she could take up her seat.

CHAPTER 41

1. PRO WO 71/353.
2. Robbins, F., *The Starry Plough* (Dublin: The Academy Press, 1977), p.107.

CHAPTER 42

1. O'Casey, S., *The Story of the Irish Citizen Army* (London: Journeyman Press, 1980), p.15. The evidence in the trial is reproduced by permission of the Irish Military Archives.
2. See for instance BMH Witness Statement, No. 1766, O'Brian, p.49.
3. BMH Witness Statement, No. 123, Mullins, p.3.
4. BMH Witness Statement, No. 585, Robbins, p.79. See also BMH Witness Statement, Hackett.
5. BMH Witness Statement, No.1666, O'Donoghue, p.25.
6. BMH Witness Statement, No. 546, Hackett, p.9.
7. Geraghty, H., *William Patrick Partridge and His Times* (Dublin: Curlew Books 2003).
8. BMH Witness Statement, No. 155, Doyle, p.29.

CHAPTER 43

1. See BMH Witness Statement, No. 377, O'Mara; 157, O'Connor.
2. Turi, J., *England's Greatest Spy: Eamon de Valera* (London: Stacey International, 2010).

3. O'Brion, L., *W. E. Wylie and the Irish Revolution* (London: Gill & MacMillan, 1989), p.34.
4. Turi, *England's Greatest Spy*. It is submitted that John Turi's book is strong on conspiracy theories but ignores evidence that contradicts the central theory in his book.
5. Diary entry quoted in *Eamon De Valera*, The Earl of Longford and O'Neill T.P. (London: Hutchinson, 1970), p.46.
6. See for instance BMH Witness Statement, No. 377, O'Mara.
7. Lieberson, G., *The Irish Uprising 1916–22* (New York: MacMillan, 1966).
8. BMH Witness Statement, No. 1019, addendum. The letter was signed by Connolly and dated 28 April 1916. It named all Commandants.
9. BMH Witness Statement, No. 907, Nugent, p.48.
10. Caulfield, M., *The Easter Rebellion* (London: Frederick Muller Ltd, 1964), p.362.
11. De Valera personal diary entry. De Valera's arrival at Richmond Barracks on Tuesday, 2 May was noted by a number of prisoners. See for instance BMH Witness Statement, No. 248, O'Flaherty, p.6.
12. *Hansard* Debates 9 May, col. 454 and again on 11 May col. 82.
13. PRO WO 32/4307.
14. *Hansard* HC Deb. 11 May 1916 vol. 82 cols. 935–70.
15. BMH Witness Statement, No. 1019.
16. BMH Witness Statement, No. 1019, Bucknill, Addendum, p.3.
17. See Chapter 3 this volume.

CHAPTER 44

1. BMH Witness Statement, No. 904, Austin, p.2.
2. For a detailed account of this episode see BMH Witness Statement, No. 1043, Lawless.
3. Killed were Sergeants John Shanagher and John Young. Also Constables James Hickey, James Gormley, Richard McHale and James Cleary. See Kiberd, D., (ed.), *1916 Rebellion Handbook* (Dublin: Mourne River Press, 1998).
4. BMH Witness Statement, No. 1043, Lawless, p.95. See also BMH Witness Statement, No. 904, Austin, p.2.
5. Thomas Rafferty and Crenigan were killed.
6. BMH Witness Statement, No. 1043, Lawless, p.140.

CHAPTER 45

1. PRO WO 35/67.
2. PRO WO 32/4307. Report from Royal Kilmainham Hospital to Horse Guards, 1 May 1916.
3. PRO WO 32/4307. Report from Royal Kilmainham Hospital to Westminster, 1 May 1916.
4. For an account by one of the Kerry prisoners, see BMH Statement, No. 132, Spillane.
5. Brennan, R., *Allegiance* (Dublin: The Richview Press, 1950), p.86.
6. See BMH Witness Statement, No. 1598, Murphy.
7. BMH Witness Statement, No. 39, Ahern, E., p.4.
8. *Killarney Echo and South Kerry Chronicle,* 13 May 1916.
9. Toomey, T., *The War of Independence in Limerick 1912–1921* (Limerick: Privately Published, 2010), p.157.
10. Ó Ruairc, *Blood on the Banner*, p.54.
11. BMH Witness Statement, No.138, Riordan, T., p.4
12. See for instance: Toomey, *The War of Independence in Limerick 1912–1921*, p.158. The men referred to were plainly interrogated with a view to internment or trial but it is clear that they were not court martialled.
13. PRO WO 213/8.
14. PRO WO 213/8. Richard Donoghue and Thomas Doyle were tried on 8 May. Both were convicted and sentenced to 10 years, later reduced by General Maxwell, to seven years penal servitude. It is not clear why these two men were tried in Wexford. BMH Witness

Statement, No. 170, Galligan, p.9 records that a party of Volunteers were required to blow up a bridge near Wexford but were surprised by the RIC. Two men were captured and it is possible that these men were Donoghue and Doyle.
15. PRO WO 35/69 Order by Cypher 3 May 1916.
16. Brennan, *Allegiance*, p.74.
17. See Census 1911 and BMH Witness Statement, No.75, Kent.
18. BMH Witness Statement, No. 75, Kent, p.2.
19. Ibid.
20. BMH Witness Statement, No. 635, King, p.5.
21. BMH Witness Statement, No. 75, Kent, p.2.

CHAPTER 46

1. The account of this trial is taken from PRO WO 71/356. The case papers are very full and include two plans of Bawnard House. The trial record does not show any evidence was called about the plans and it is probable that the plans migrated from William Kent's file, which has not survived.
2. BMH Witness Statement, No. 635, King, p.4.
3. Rules of Procedure 1907, *Manual of Military Law*, Sixth Edition.

CHAPTER 47

1. BMH Witness Statement, No. 75, Kent, p.2.
2. PRO WO 35/68.
3. The standard test of legal insanity at that time was that it must be clearly shown that the accused was labouring under such a defect of reason, from disease of the mind, as not to know the nature and quality of the act he was doing, or, if he did know it, that he did not know what he was doing was wrong. Archbold, J.F., *Criminal Pleading Evidence and Procedure*, 25th Edition.
4. Some years later, John Bowen-Colthurst was recognised by a Cork émigré near Vancouver. When greeted, Bowen-Colthurst reached for his coat pocket, still fearful of an assassin's bullet. He looked back on 1916 as 'the greatest calamity of my life'. There were no words of regret for the men he had killed. Bowen-Colthurst became a prosperous hotel owner and businessman but remained an embittered figure until his death, aged 85.
5. There were wider consequences for the Colthurst family estates in Dripsey. Local men were warned from working at Dripsey Castle. Colthurst's mother Georgina remained dignified and generous in adversity: she gave character evidence for one of the men tried for the Dripsey ambush in 1921. After the trial five men were sentenced to death. The Military declined to meet clergy and local leaders who were urging clemency but Mrs Bowen-Colthurst managed to secure an interview with General Strickland to plead the men's case. She was unsuccessful. Despite all this the Bowen-Colthursts were gradually driven out of Cork. John Bowen-Colthurst had been destined to inherit Oakgrove House, a fine old Georgian mansion in Killinadrish but this was burned to the ground in 1920. See Sheehan, T., *The Lady Hostage* (Cork: Lee Press Ltd., 2008).
6. Royal Commission Cd. 8376.
7. For an analysis of the work of the Sankey Advisory Committee, see Foxton, D., *Revolutionary Lawyers* (Dublin: Four Courts Press, 2008), pp.94–103.
8. Clare County Library.
9. *Auckland Star*, 1 February 1919.
10. Ferguson, K., *King's Inns Barristers, 1868–2004* (Dublin: The Honourable Society of King's Inns, in association with the Irish Legal History Society, Irish Academic Press, 2005), p.321. Wylie served as a judge of the Irish Land Commission and the High Court until 1936. He became involved in many charitable causes. He was President of the Royal Dublin Society and Senior Steward of the Jockey Club. He died in 1965.
11. Abbott, R., *Police Casualties in Ireland*, p.41.

12. Foy, M., *Michael Collins's Intelligence War* (United Kingdom: Sutton Publishing, 2006), p.193.
13. Census 1911. He had served as a Justice of the Peace and High Sheriff of Kildare and with the King's Royal Rifle Corps throughout the Great War.
14. Obituary, *The Irish Times* 14 December 1956.
15. See Enright, S., *The Trial of Civilians by Military Courts: Ireland* 1921 (Dublin: Irish Academic Press, 2012).
16. *R (Childers) v Adjutant General of the Provisional Forces* [1923] 1 IR 5.
17. Albert Wood KC.
18. *In the matter of the application of Patrick McGrath and Thomas Harte.* [1941] IR 68.
19. Kerins was tried and executed for the murder of a police detective, Denis O'Brien, who was gunned down in front of his wife.
20. *Ex parte Milligan* 71 US 2 (1866). And see Goodwin, D.K., *Team of Rivals* (London: Penguin, 2009), p.354. Even after Lincoln's assassination, military courts were permitted to sit in judgment on those alleged to be responsible for his death: the trial and execution of Mary Surratt and her co-defendants remains a blot on American jurisprudence.
21. *Rasul v Bush* 542 US 446 (2004).
22. *Hamdan v Rumsfeld* 548 US 577.
23. *Boumediene v Bush* 553 US 723 (2008).
24. The Military Commissions Act 2006. Since replaced by the Military Commissions Act 2009, which was intended to give effect to the decision in *Boumediene v Bush*.

Index